A Fisherman's Guide to

# LAKES
# OF
# NORTHEAST
# WASHINGTON
# AND
# NORTHERN
# IDAHO

John E. Moore

First published by Dog Ear Publishing
4010 W. 86th Street, Ste H
Indianapolis, IN 46268
www.dogearpublishing.net

ISBN: 978-159858-345-8

This book is printed on acid-free paper.

Printed in the United States of America

This book is dedicated
to the best fishing partner a person ever had,
my son, Jason Moore.

# INTRODUCTION:

This book contains information on some lakes in both Washington and Idaho. In Washington the lakes are in the northeastern corner, and found in Stevens and Pend Oreille Counties. The Idaho lakes are found in the panhandle. They are located in Boundary, Bonner, Kootenai and Shoshone Counties. There are a mix of high mountain trout lakes and lowland warm water lakes.

The information includes:

**Lake name:** The name shown may not be the only name the lake is known by. Often old maps show the lake with another name, and sometimes the locals call it something else. If another name is known to me, I have included it as an "also known as". Many lakes share a common name, sometimes even within the same county.

**Lake photograph:** I take pictures of each lake I visit. All of the photographs included in this book are mine. I have only myself to blame for the ones that didn't turn out so well. The captions indicate the date the picture was taken, the direction the camera was pointed, and whatever else seemed relevant at the time.

**Size:** The size of the lake is based on best available data, either from State sources or by drawing grids on USGS maps and making my own estimates.

**Elevation:** Elevations are from USGS data.

**Maximum Depth:** Depth is either as reported by reliable sources, or sometimes by my own investigation using a "Humminbird" depth finder. When I show it as "unknown", it's unknown to me. I won't use unsubstantiated reports from individuals.

**County:** This is the county the lake is found in. If it spans a county line, I list both. The state is also shown.

**Coordinates:** When I first started building these files in my computer, I included only the Township, Range and Section information. As the use of portable GPS devices and computer mapping programs became more common, I added longitude and latitude references.

The Section information uses the Willamette Meridian for the lakes in Washington, and the Boise Meridian for those in Idaho. A typical township contains 36 sections. The 1/4 subdivision method for sections, which is what you will usually find on the legal description of your property, is very cumbersome. Because of this, in most cases I used the alphabetical subdivision method here. Just personal preference.

**Species:** Those species listed as confirmed I have either caught myself or witnessed caught. Those listed as reported may or may not be present. Sometimes the reports are questionable. Also, the species present in a lake can change due to natural conditions like winterkill, or because of stocking or management changes by the Washington State Department of Wildlife or the Idaho Department of Fish and Game. Some species do well at self-sustaining their population, while others die out at the end of their life cycle without leaving another generation.

**Characteristics:** This is just a description of the lake and the surrounding area. Both the lake and the area can change due to natural or human activity. Storms, avalanches, drought or other natural events can sometimes bring major changes. What I have described here is current as of my last visit.

**Directions:** This is a big one. The directions I have provided are as accurate as I could make them based on the conditions on my last visit. While even major highways and intersections sometimes change, they are much more stable than the gravel roads in logging areas. Gravel roads are added or decommissioned on a regular basis, and even if the road is unchanged access may not be the same. There are a lot more gated roads now than there used to be. With these directions and a good map, you should be able to get there in spite of changes.

Because the odometer on one vehicle may not exactly match that of another, I have referred to mileposts where possible. Odometers won't usually differ by too much in less that a mile. All directions giving just distances are based on my odometer, so yours may differ slightly.

I should also point out that while I provide an alternate route in some instances, the routes you find here may not be the only ones possible. There are some alternates that I didn't include here because I haven't been over them.

Some of the lakes are found in developed areas that have many roads in the area. The possible routes are too numerous to provide them all. I provided what seemed the most practical to me. If you are familiar with the area you may know a better route.

Some of the directions are for mountain lakes that require hiking to reach. Trail information and directions are provided. Some of the hikes are strenuous, and some of the terrain rough. Know your limits.

**Fishing tips:** In some lakes anything will catch fish anywhere. We're not always that lucky. The tips I have provided here are what worked for me, and what I found to be the best areas. Good luck.

**Miscellaneous notes:** This is a 'catch-all" section. I put information here that didn't fit anywhere else, but seemed important to me.

**Map references:** I have provided a list of the maps I have found most useful. USGS maps provide the best detail of any available, and are recommended for the lakes that require hiking.

To get you into the area, the Washington Atlas and Gazetteer, published by DeLorme, has good maps of the entire state in a single easy to use volume. DeLorme also publishes an Idaho Atlas and Gazetteer.

Metsker's maps are good for locating where you are using section markers, if you known how to read the markers when you find them. They can be helpful for negotiating the roads, but have no topographical information. They are available for all counties, so I didn't bother to list them for each lake.

Forest Service maps are good for both road and section information, as well as trail routes, but also lack topographical detail.

# CONTENTS

This book contains information on the following lakes:

# 1  ANDERSON LAKE

June 21, 1997; Anderson Lake, looking southwest.

SIZE: 720 Acres
ELEVATION: 2,129 Feet
MAXIMUM DEPTH: Unknown
COUNTY: Kootenai, Idaho
COORDINATES: T47N R3W Sec5(northwest 1/4)
    T48N R3W Sec28,29,31,32

    Longitude: 116d 43m 53s to 116d 45m 51s West
    Latitude: 47d 27m 24s to 47d 28m 41s North

SPECIES, CONFIRMED:

SPECIES, REPORTED:
 Bullhead Catfish
 Crappie
 Largemouth Bass
 Northern Pike
 Pumpkinseed Sunfish
 Yellow Perch

CHARACTERISTICS:
 There are timbered hills above the south side of the lake. They have some
cleared and developed areas that are up away from the lake. The shoreline

of the south side is quite steep. A grassy area with gentle slopes is found at the southeast corner, but is posted private property.

A narrow strip of land separates the north side of the lake from the Coeur d'Alene River. The strip is brush covered.

A gravel road that provides access to the lake runs along the east side. In most places it is very close to the water, and just a few feet above it.

There is a small bay located at the southwest corner of the lake, where Bell Canyon Creek enters the lake.

The bottom along the road is rock and gravel, and becomes silt covered with aquatic vegetation once you get away from the road.

The northeast corner has a double row of broken piling crossing the lake from north to south, forming a small bay.

The water has a light brown stain.

DIRECTIONS TO:

Take Interstate 90 to exit 34 east of Coeur d'Alene, Idaho. At exit 34, turn south onto Highway 3.

Take Highway 3 south for about 21.6 miles to mile 95.9, where Highway 97 will be reached.

Turn right and go 0.1 mile to a stop sign. This marks the actual intersection with Highway 97, at Highway 97 mile 60.8. A sign indicates "Harrison 7 Miles, Coeur d'Alene 36 Miles".

Take Highway 97 north, through the town of Harrison, for about nine miles to mile 69.6, where Blue Lake Road will be reached on the right.

Turn onto Blue Lake Road and go east for 1.7 miles to a bridge over the Coeur d'Alene River.

Turn right and cross the bridge, which is a wooden deck, steel frame bridge and is a bit rough. As you exit the south side of the bridge you will cross abandoned railroad tracks.

The gravel road has places along its run that offer limited access to the lake, the best of which will be reached at 0.8 miles after the turnoff to the bridge.

An **ALTERNATE ROUTE** to Anderson Lake is to take Highway 97 south from Interstate 90. Highway 97 leaves the interstate at exit 22.

FISHING TIPS:

I'm unable to offer any tips due to a lack of success in this lake. I fished it only once, very briefly, from shore in a high wind.

MISCELLANEOUS NOTES:

A state record Largemouth Bass of 10 pounds 15 ounces was caught in Anderson Lake in an unrecorded year.

MAP REFERENCES:
*Idaho Atlas & Gazetteer, Page 60.
*USGS Topographic Map, Idaho (47116-D6-TF-024-00)
   Black Lake Quadrangle, 7.5 Minute Series.
*USGS Topographic Map, Idaho (47116-D7-TF-024-00)
   Harrison Quadrangle, 7.5 Minute Series.
*USGS Topographic Map, Idaho (47116-A1-TM-100-00)
   St. Maries Quadrangle, 30x60 Minute Series.

## 2  ANTELOPE LAKE

June 7, 2005; Antelope Lake, looking east-northeast.

SIZE: 16 Acres
ELEVATION: 2,754 Feet
MAXIMUM DEPTH: Unknown
COUNTY: Bonner, Idaho
COORDINATES: T55N R2E Sec12D

> Longitude: 116d 9m 6s <u>to</u> 116d 9m 27s West
> Latitude: 48d 8m 3s <u>to</u> 48d 8m 9s North

SPECIES, CONFIRMED:
  Rainbow Trout

SPECIES, REPORTED:
  Arctic Grayling
  Cutthroat Trout
  Eastern Brook Trout

CHARACTERISTICS:
  The lake lies in a timber covered area.
  The northeast corner has cliffs rising a couple of hundred feet above the

lake, with a lot of vertical rock showing. Steep, timber covered slopes lie between the vertical rock and the lake. Behind the vertical rock, timbered slopes rise to the highest point above the lake.

The other sides of the lake are lower, but also heavily timbered. The ground drops away quickly to the west, behind a thin strip of trees, leaving timbered mountains visible in the near distance to the west and southwest.

There is timber and brush to the waters edge all around the lake. The only breaks in the cover are at the southwest corner where the road reaches the lake, a small area at the northwest corner, and an even smaller area at the center of the south side. The spot on the south shore shows much evidence of bank fishing activity.

At the southwest corner, where the "access" is found, are some crude campsites and a dirt parking area. There are no facilities. The boat launch area is just a rough, but low, dirt bank. It isn't suitable for launching of anything large.

Trails run from the southwest corner along part of the south side and across the west end. The west end trail drops to old roads below and to the north of the lake.

Cattails line the shores on almost all of the north shore and much of the east end. There are also small pockets along the south side, and a good-sized bed at the west end.

The lake has a lot of snags. Most are submerged. Many are found along the shores, both lining shore and extending out from it. They are scattered randomly, but found everywhere.

The bottom is silt, with some rock. The shallower areas have a covering of low, bottom hugging aquatic vegetation. Taller aquatic weeds rise from deeper water out from the shores around the lake.

The water is very clear.

DIRECTIONS TO:

Take Highway 200 to mile 57.2, east of the town of Clark Fork, where a gravel road will be found on the north side of the highway.

Turn onto the gravel road and go 0.3 miles to a fork. The left goes to a house. Keep to the right and continue climbing.

At 0.9 miles you will pass an old road, on the right. Keep Left.

At 1.5 miles you will reach the southwest corner of the lake.

**NOTE:** The road is steep, rough and narrow with very few turnouts. It is not suited to large vehicles, and not a good road on which to meet oncoming traffic.

An **ALTERNATE ROUTE** to Antelope Lake is by trail.

Take Highway 200 to mile 55.2, in the middle of the town of Clark Fork. The road on the north side of the highway, on the west side of the school, is signed for "Forest Entrance".

Turn here and go north out of Clark Fork to an intersection at 0.6 miles. Keep right at the intersection, and the pavement will end in another 0.1 mile.

At 1.2 miles, Lower Mosquito Creek Lane will be reached, on the right.

Turn onto Lower Mosquito Creek Lane, and take it 0.2 miles to a fork.

Take the left fork, and just beyond is a sign indicating "Trail" pointing to the right at an old road.

Turn here, and you will see another sign in the trees on your right saying "Antelope Lake" with an arrow pointing up the road.

As of the spring of 2005, the "trail road" was blocked by a downed tree about 50 feet up. Park here and start walking. The road/trail runs about a mile to the lake, climbing about 450 feet.

FISHING TIPS:
Flies worked along shoreline cover are effective.

MISCELLANEOUS NOTES:
Planting records indicate that the lake received:
  Eastern Brook Trout in 1997;
  Arctic Grayling, 175 adult fish in 1999.

MAP REFERENCES:
*Idaho Atlas & Gazetteer, Page 63.
*USGS Topographic Map, Idaho (48116-B2-TF-024-00)
  Clark Fork Quadrangle, 7.5 Minute Series.
*USGS Topographic Map, Idaho (48116-A1-TM-100-00)
  Sandpoint Quadrangle, 30x60 Minute Series.

## 3  BAYLEY LAKE
Also known as: Cliff Lake

May 17, 1997; Bayley Lake, looking southwest.

SIZE: 16.7 Acres (to maximum 72 acres)
ELEVATION: 2,400 Feet
MAXIMUM DEPTH: Unknown
COUNTY: Stevens, Washington
COORDINATES: T34N R41E Sec29BG

Longitude: 117d 39m 32s to 117d 40m 0s West
Latitude: 48d 24m 47s to 48d 25m 29s North

SPECIES, CONFIRMED:
Rainbow Trout

SPECIES, REPORTED:
Eastern Brook Trout

CHARACTERISTICS:
There are wooded hills on the east and west sides of the lake. Those to the
west have a lot of vertical rock with broken rock slopes below. There is a

strip of trees between the rocks and the water. The east slopes also have some vertical and broken rock, but not as much as the west side. On the east side, the broken rock does reach the water near the south end of the lake.

The south end of the lake is nearly closed in by the hills, but has a narrow gap. The north end is open.

The shorelines are mostly steep and brushy. There are a few places on the shores, especially on the east side, where a boat can be beached. The southeast corner at the extreme end of the lake has a place to beach, and the area has been used as a camp in the past.

The lake is mostly shallow. There are isolated dollar pads and other aquatic weeds dotting the lake, but few large beds early in the season. Later in the summer the lake weeds up badly.

There are some snags scattered along the shorelines.

The water is clear.

DIRECTIONS TO:

Take Highway 20 to mile 363.6, east of the town of Colville, where Kitt-Narcisse Road will be reached.

Turn onto Kitt-Narcisse Road and go south for 1.4 miles to Narcisse Creek Road, on the left.

Turn onto Narcisse Creek Road and go southeast for 1.7 miles to the next intersection. You will pass a sign marking the entrance to the Little Pend Oreille Wildlife Refuge 0.4 miles before the intersection.

At the intersection, turn right and go 1.0 mile to the next one.

*At this intersection, turn left. You will pass the refuge headquarters buildings after 0.7 miles, and Cliff Ridge Road, on the right, after 4.1 miles. Stay on the main road, and at 4.5 miles from the last turn you will come to a four way intersection.

Take the road to the right. It will reach the access area for Potters Pond after 0.9 miles, and the end of the road at the Bayley Lake access at 1.2 miles.

The Bayley Lake access is a total of 9.8 miles from Highway 20.

An **ALTERNATE ROUTE** is to take Highway 20 to mile 364.9, where Starvation Lake Road is reached.

Turn onto Starvation Lake Road and go south. At 0.9 miles a gravel road on the right enters the public access area for Starvation Lake. Continue on Starvation Lake Road, and at 1.3 miles you will reach an intersection.

Go to the right. After 0.4 miles you will reach another intersection.

Stay to the right. After 0.7 miles you will reach the next intersection. This one is signed for McDowell Lake to the left.

Turn to the right, and you will come to a large four way intersection after only 0.1 mile.

At this intersection turn to the left. Go 1.0 mile to the next intersection.

From here, follow the directions above from the point marked with an asterisk(*).

Using the alternate route, the Bayley Lake access is a total of 8.8 miles from Highway 20.

FISHING TIPS:

The lake is fly fishing only, with no motors allowed. I fished it only once, during high winds. All of the fish I caught were at the far end of the lake.

MAP REFERENCES:

*USGS Topographic Map, Washington (48117-D6-TF-024-00)
  Cliff Ridge Quadrangle, 7.5 Minute Series.
*USGS Topographic Map, Washington (48117-A1-TM-100-00)
  Chewelah Quadrangle, 30x60 Minute Series.
*Washington Atlas & Gazetteer, Page 104.

# 4  BEAD LAKE

September 16, 2001; Bead Lake, looking northwest from the access area.

SIZE: 719.8 Acres
ELEVATION: 2,850 Feet
MAXIMUM DEPTH: 170 Feet
COUNTY: Pend Oreille, Washington
COORDINATES: T32N R45E Sec3,4,9,10
          T33N R45E Sec33,34

          Longitude: 117d 5m 40s to 117d 7m 44s West
          Latitude: 48d 17m 20s to 48d 19m 2s North

SPECIES, CONFIRMED:

SPECIES, REPORTED:
 Burbot
 Kokanee
 Mackinaw

CHARACTERISTICS:
 The lake lies in an area of steep, timbered hills. The hills have many open areas where the timber cover becomes sparse.
 The shorelines reflect the steep hills in the area, also being steep and rocky. The shores have very little brush in most places.

Homes are located along the west shore of the lake, and their docks line the shores below them. In addition to the ones along shore, many more houses are found in the timber covered area further up from the water.

The lake has a very irregular shape due to the steep hills in which it is found. It sprawls over a large area, with two very large points extending into it, one from the north and one from the east. The points break the lake up into three distinct sections.

The public access is at the south end, identified as Mineral Bay on the maps. This section of the lake has a maximum depth of 80 feet, which is reached quickly, then maintained over a mostly featureless flat bottom.

The neck between the southern section and the center section of the lake shallows up to a depth of 50 feet, before dropping very quickly to a depth of 170 feet as you move north. This deepest water is maintained over much of the northeast and northwest arms of the lake.

The northeast arm has three very large bays extending outward from it. One is at the northernmost point of the lake, where Lodge Creek enters. Another reaches southeast from the mouth of the northern one. The third extends to the northwest at the center of the northwest shore of the arm.

The northwest arm also has bays, but they aren't as defined as those of the northeast arm.

The lake is almost entirely very deep water. The only shallows are of minimal size, and found at the ends of the fingers of the lake.

The water is clear.

DIRECTIONS TO:

From the north, take Highway 20 to the town of Newport, where it will end at mile 436.8 at an intersection with Highway 2.

At the stop sign in Newport, turn left onto Highway 2. Take Highway 2 into Idaho and the bridge over the Pend Oreille River.

*As soon as you cross the river, you will need to be in the left lane to turn onto the first road as you leave the bridge. This is LeClerc Creek Road, and enters from the north at Idaho Highway 2 mile 0.5.

Turn left onto LeClerc Creek Road.

**Take LeClerk Creek Road north for 2.7 miles to Marshall Lake Road, which enters on the right. Some maps show this to be Bead Lake Road.

Follow Marshall Lake Road 6.0 miles to Bead Lake Drive, on the right. The end of the road is signed with a boat launch symbol.

***Turn onto Bead Lake Drive, and about 100 yards up the road you will pass a sign indicating "Public Launch Facilities, Bead Lake". Take Bead Lake Drive 0.25 miles to Road 3200-412, on the right.

The end of this access road is gated, and marked Bead Lake Boat Launch. As of 2001, signs indicate the area is closed on Wednesdays, is a "Day Use Facility", gates are closed from 10 PM to 6 AM, is for boat launching only, has a capacity of six vehicles, and is a one lane road with turnouts. There is a daily use fee of $5.00 per vehicle, and a "host" is posted at the entrance to the parking area to collect. The access road runs 0.2 miles to the fee station and parking area with pit toilets, and then drops another 0.1 mile over a switchback area to reach the concrete strip boat ramp. The ramp area has only a small turnaround spot next to the ramp.

An **ALTERNATE ROUTE** to Bead Lake is from the south on Highway 2.

Take Highway 2 north about 47 miles from Interstate 90 Exit 281 in Spokane to the town of Newport.

Take Highway 2 into Idaho and the bridge over the Pend Oreille River.

From here follow the directions provided above from the point marked with an asterisk(*).

A **SECOND ALTERNATE ROUTE** is from the east on Highway 2.

Take Highway 2 west about 28 miles from Highway 95 in the town of Sandpoint to LeClerc Creek Road, which will be on the right at Highway 2 mile 0.5.

At mile 0.5, just before you reach the bridge over the Pend Oreille River, turn right onto LeClerc Creek Road.

From here follow the directions provided above from the point marked with a double asterisk(**).

**NOTE:** In 1997, the Pend Oreille River reached elevations that flooded LeClerc Creek Road. When LeClerc Creek Road is not available, there is another route that can be used for access.

East of Newport at Idaho Highway 2 mile 2.3 is the Albeni Falls Machine Shop on the north side of the road. Freeman Lake Road, a gravel road, heads north next to the shop.

Take this road to access Marshall Lake Road, which will be reached after 6.2 miles. Freeman Lake Road becomes Bench Road before you reach the end.

Turn right, and take Marshall Lake Road 5.1 miles to Bead Lake Drive, on the right. The end of the road is signed with a boat launch symbol.

From here follow the directions above from the point marked with a triple asterisk(***).

FISHING TIPS:
I did not attempt to fish this lake.

MISCELLANEOUS NOTES:
Bead Lake has produced state record Burbot of:
15 pounds 8 ounces in 1981.
17.17 pounds on January 14, 2004.
17.37 pounds on April 24, 2004.

MAP REFERENCES:
*USGS Topographic Map, Washington (48117-C1-TF-024-00)
Bead Lake Quadrangle, 7.5 Minute Series.
*USGS Topographic Map, Washington (48117-C2-TF-024-00)
Skookum Creek Quadrangle, 7.5 Minute Series.
*USGS Topographic Map, Washington (48117-A1-TM-100-00)
Chewelah Quadrangle, 30x60 Minute Series.
*Washington Atlas & Gazetteer, Page 105.

## 5  BIG FISHER LAKE

August 15, 2006; Big Fisher Lake,
looking northeast from the trail to the lake.

SIZE: 20 Acres (estimated)
ELEVATION: 6,732 Feet
MAXIMUM DEPTH: Unknown
COUNTY: Boundary, Idaho
COORDINATES: T63N R2W Sec2M

Longitude: 116d 33m 55s to 116d 34m 4s West
Latitude: 48d 50m 19s to 48d 50m 28s North

SPECIES, CONFIRMED:
 Cutthroat Trout, West Slope

SPECIES, REPORTED:

CHARACTERISTICS:
 Steep rocky slopes rise over the west and south sides of the lake. The high
vertical rock of the southern skyline dominates the view.
 Slopes of broken rock extend from the vertical rock above to reach the
waters edge at the south end of the lake. The shorelines at the southeast end

of the lake are open and rocky. At the edges of the rock slopes start growths of sparse timber. The trees become larger and the cover more dense on both sides of the lake as you move away from the boulder field.

The other three sides of the lake have timber and brush to the waters edge in all areas. The brush is low enough and open enough that there are many places suitable for bank fishing.

The lake has a lot of rock around the shorelines in all areas, not just at the rock slope south end. There are many boulders on the bottom far out in the lake. Some are visible from shore, and many more can be seen from the trail above the lake.

The trail to the lake comes through the saddle on the ridgeline to the southwest. It reaches the lake near the center of the west side, and continues around the north end. The trail reaches several nice campsites in the trees at the north end of the lake.

The hillside over the west side of the lake, where the trail comes down, is rocky and steep with sparse timber cover.

The hill to the east is lower and densely covered with timber.

The skyline is open to the north.

An outlet creek exits at the north end. The area out from the creek is fairly shallow, and has a rock strewn silt bottom.

Snags are scattered randomly along the shoreline and bottom areas, with no large accumulations in any one area. Some are at the surface, and many are submerged. Very few are found out in the lake away from the shores.

The bottom, in addition to having big rock, has some smaller rock and silt deposits.

The water is extremely clear.

DIRECTIONS TO:

Take Interstate 90 to exit 12, at the town of Coeur d'Alene.

From exit 12, take Highway 95 north for about 77 miles to mile 507.5, at the town of Bonners Ferry, where Riverside Road will be found on the west side of the highway just south of the bridge over the Kootenai River. The end of the road is signed for "Kootenai Wildlife Refuge 6 Miles".

Turn onto Riverside, and head west out of Bonners Ferry, keeping to the right as the road follows the banks of the river.

At 5.0 miles from Highway 95 the road will reach the base of the foothills, and a "Y" intersection. Keep to the right, and the paved road will begin running to the north. About a quarter mile past the "Y", you will pass the Kootenai Wildlife Refuge headquarters. The pavement ends in another 6.5 miles.

At 14.9 miles from Highway 95 you will reach the end of Forest Service Road 634, also shown on some maps as Trout Creek Road. The end of the road is signed "Junction Trail 6 Miles, Trail 12 7 Miles, Trail 13 9 Miles".

*Turn onto Road 634, and follow it 8.8 miles to a parking area, on the left, for the trailhead, which is on the right. The road ends in another 0.2 miles at a horse facility and camp area.

On the 8.8 mile run to the trailhead, you will reach an intersection at 4.5 miles, where you keep to the left.

You will pass the Fisher Peak trailhead, on the right, at 5.2 miles.

You will pass the Russell Peak Trail #12 parking area, on the left, at 6.1 miles. There are signs here for the trailhead that indicate "Russell Peak 2 1/2 Miles", and for the continuation of the road to the right indicating "Junction Trail #92 3 Miles".

The trailhead provides access to several lakes in the area, found off various branches of the trail system. The lakes include Pyramid, Upper Ball, Lower Ball, Trout, Big Fisher, Long Mountain, and Parker.

To reach Trout Lake, take the trail about 0.5 miles (elevation gain approximately 450 feet) to a fork. Take the right fork.

Go about 0.75 miles (gain about 150 feet) to the next fork. This fork is reached at a wooden footbridge, to the right of which is a sign indicating that the trail to the right is to Trout Lake and Big Fisher Lake, and providing distances. The trail to the left is unmarked.

Take the right fork. This fork will run about 1.75 miles to Trout Lake, gaining about 450 feet of elevation, and then dropping about 150 feet to the lake. The drop to the lake is over slab rock and through boulders, and somewhat steep.

From Trout Lake, the trail continues another 2.25 miles to its end at Big Fisher Lake, gaining about 1,100 feet as it climbs to its high point of just over 7,400 feet, then dropping about 700 feet to the lake. The drop to the lake starts out as a long run of moderate grade, and then becomes mostly short and steep switchbacks as you drop the remaining elevation quickly.

The trail reaches the lake near the center of the west side.

An **ALTERNATE ROUTE** to the Trout Creek trail system would be to take Highway 95 to mile 523.0, north of the town of Bonners Ferry, where Highway 1 will be found on the left.

Turn onto Highway 1, and continue north for 1.1 miles to a road on the left at the town of Copeland. The end of the road is signed for "Sportsman's Access" and "National Forest Entrance".

Turn left onto the road, and head west. At 1.6 miles you will reach a bridge over the Kootenai River. At 3.4 miles from Highway 1 you will reach a "T" intersection with West Side Road. There is a sign opposite the end of the road you are on that indicates "Maravia 20 Miles" to the left, and "Smith Creek Road and Boundary Creek Road 9 Miles" to the right.

At West Side Road, turn left and go south for 2.9 miles to a 90-degree corner. The paved road turns to the left, and a gravel road leaves the pavement straight ahead. Contrary to appearances, the gravel road is the continuation of West Side Road.

Take the gravel road, and after 1.8 miles you will reach the end of Forest Service Road 634, also shown on some maps as Trout Creek Road, on the right. The end of the road is signed "Junction Trail 6 Miles, Trail 12 7 Miles, Trail 13 9 Miles".

From here, follow the directions provided above from the point marked with an asterisk(*).

FISHING TIPS:
Flies cast from shore are very effective. Shore access is good all around the lake, with good openings in even the denser shoreline brush and trees.

MISCELLANEOUS NOTES:
Be alert for moose on the trail.

MAP REFERENCES:
*Idaho Atlas & Gazetteer, Page 48 (name not indicated).
*USGS Topographic Map, Idaho (48116-G5-TF-024-00)
  Pyramid Peak Quadrangle, 7.5 Minute Series.
*USGS Topographic Map, Idaho (48116-E1-TM-100-00)
  Bonners Ferry Quadrangle, 30x60 Minute Series.

## 6  BIG MEADOW LAKE
Also known as: Meadow Lake

May 9, 2005; Big Meadow Lake, looking east-southeast.

SIZE: 72 Acres
ELEVATION: 3,450 Feet
MAXIMUM DEPTH: 23 Feet
COUNTY: Pend Oreille, Washington
COORDINATES: T37N R41E Sec1R
           T37N R42E Sec6NPQ,7BCD

        Longitude: 117d 32m 57s <u>to</u> 117d 33m 47s West
        Latitude: 48d 43m 29s <u>to</u> 48d 43m 51s North

SPECIES, CONFIRMED:
Rainbow Trout

SPECIES, REPORTED:
Eastern Brook Trout

<u>CHARACTERISTICS</u>:
  The lake lies in an area of low, timbered hills. The hills to the north have some sparsely covered spots where meadow shows through. There are higher mountains visible in the distance to the east.

The lake is an enlargement of a natural lake of only 4.1 acres, increased in size by a low, earthen dam built in the mid 1970's. The areas inundated are shallow and weedy, and the deepest water is found near the center of the lake, where the original lake was located.

A gravel road runs across the top of the earthen dam, which has a large fishing platform located near its center. The area west of and below the dam is tree dotted meadow area.

The lake is the headwaters of Meadow Creek, which exits at the dam at the west side. There is also a concrete overflow swale that the road passes over at the northwest corner.

A series of three islands east of the main body of the lake create a narrows that forms an almost separate circular body of water to the east. This area has an almost flat bottom of pretty uniform depth, but with a high spot near its center where grass rises through the surface of the water.

The main channel between the two sections of the lake has two islands to the south, and one to the north. The channel is about 75 yards wide.

Of the islands, the one to the north is the only one with a dense cover of trees and brush. It is small, nearly circular, and separated from shore by a very narrow, shallow channel.

From the south shore extends a low point. The two islands to the south form an extension of the point. These islands are long and narrow, and very low. The high spots on the islands are grassy. There are only a couple of trees on the islands, accompanied by a couple of large, standing snags. There are large growths of aquatic weed and cattails along the islands. The channels between the point and the southern islands are too narrow and shallow to be navigable.

The eastern section of the lake has timbered, brushy shores. There is a clear area under the timber at the extreme east end that shows evidence of camping.

A Forest Service campground is located at the lake. There are two camping loops, one at the northwest corner and another at the southwest corner. The road across the dam links the two camp areas. There are pit toilets and parking areas.

A gravel boat launch area is found to the left just before the first campground loop road. It accesses the cove at the northwest corner of the lake.

There is a day-use wildlife viewing area at the center of the north side of the lake. A gravel road runs the length of the north side, but its only close contact with the lake is at the wildlife viewing area.

There is heavy timber and brush to the waters edge almost everywhere around the lake. The exceptions are at the dam at the west end and at the center of the north side where the wildlife viewing area is located.

The bottom is mostly silt, with some rock, and is heavily covered with growths of aquatic vegetation.

Snags along the shores are randomly scattered and mostly submerged. The water is very clear.

## DIRECTIONS TO:

Take Highway 20 about 47 miles north from the town of Newport, to where it makes a 90-degree turn to the left at mile 390.4, and runs west toward the town of Colville. At this corner is the junction with Highway 31, which goes to the north.

Turn north onto Highway 31, and take it about 4 miles to the town of Ione, where at mile 4.1, Houghton Street will be found on the left.

Turn onto Houghton Street, and take it 0.5 miles to a stop sign at 8th Avenue. This intersection is signed "Big Meadow Lake 8 Miles" and "Colville 35 Miles" to the left.

Turn left onto 8th Avenue, and go 0.1 mile to Smackout Road, on the right. The end of the road is signed for Big Meadow Lake and Colville.

Turn right onto Smackout Road, and go 7.8 miles to the entrance to the Big Meadow Lake Campground, on the left.

In this 7.8 mile stretch, the road will become gravel at 0.7 miles, you will pass under power lines at 1.4 miles, you will keep left at an intersection at 2.5 miles, reach a wildlife viewing area at the lake at 7.3 miles, and pass a 0.1 mile long dead end road on the left at 7.5 miles.

Big Meadow Lake is reached a total of 8.4 miles from Highway 31 in Ione.

An **ALTERNATE ROUTE** reaches the lake from the west.

Take Highway 20 east out of the town of Colville, and watch for Aladdin Road, on the north side of the highway at Highway 20 mile 355.5.

Take Aladdin Road north for 18.8 miles to Meadow Creek Road, on the right. The end of the road is signed for Big Meadow Lake.

Turn right onto Meadow Creek Road, and take it east for 5.8 miles to the Big Meadow Lake Campground entrance, on the right.

## FISHING TIPS:

Because of the weedy conditions, late in the season the best water is at the open area at the center of the lake. Even in early spring the center of the lake is the most productive area, with fish taking trolled flies or spinners.

MISCELLANEOUS NOTES:

For an interesting side trip while in the Ione area, visit the Gardiner Cave at Crawford State Park. The park is just north of Metaline. As of 1998, the park opened at 0900, with guided cave tours every even hour. The tour lasts about 30 to 40 minutes, is provided by the park service, and is free of charge.

Another interesting attraction in the immediate area of the lake is the Hess Homestead, located about 0.3 miles west of the entrance to the campground areas. It has a "replica" log cabin and a historical marker. It can be reached by road or by trail from the first campground loop.

MAP REFERENCES:
*USGS Topographic Map, Washington (48117-F5-TF-024-00)
  Aladdin Mountain Quadrangle, 7.5 Minute Series.
*USGS Topographic Map, Washington (48117-E1-TM-100-00)
  Colville Quadrangle, 30x60 Minute Series.
*Washington Atlas & Gazetteer, Page 118.

# 7  BLACK LAKE

September 7, 2003; Black Lake, looking north.

SIZE: 69.6 Acres
ELEVATION: 3,686 Feet
MAXIMUM DEPTH: 45 Feet
COUNTY: Stevens, Washington
COORDINATES: T35N R41E Sec3(west 1/2)

Longitude: 117d 37m 22s to 117d 37m 40s West
Latitude: 48d 33m 18s to 48d 34m 6s North

SPECIES, CONFIRMED:
 Tiger Trout

SPECIES, REPORTED:
 Eastern Brook Trout
 German Brown Trout
 Rainbow Trout

CHARACTERISTICS:
 The lake is 4,800 feet long, and lies in an area of low, timbered hills.
 The shores are wooded all around, but many homes and a resort are scattered along the shores. Some have docks extending into the lake.

The shores have many snags, mostly fairly small, found along them. The largest concentrations are in the undeveloped shoreline areas.

The only public access to the water is found at the south end. The access has a large gravel parking area, concrete strip boat launch and pit toilets, and is signed for no overnight parking or camping.

An outlet stream exits the south end of the lake to the east of the access area.

The bottom is gravel and silt, and beds of weeds are found in the shallows. The shallow weed beds are primarily sparse growths of lilypads.

The water is clear.

## DIRECTIONS TO:

Take Highway 20 to mile 372.5, east of the town of Colville, where Black Lake-Squaw Creek Road is reached on the north side of the highway.

Turn onto Black Lake-Squaw Creek Road, and take it north about 100 yards to a tee intersection, where you will go to the left.

Continue 1.7 miles to a road on the left that is signed for public fishing.

Turn left onto the side road, and the public access will be reached in 0.2 miles.

## FISHING TIPS:

Trolled flies are very effective. The outside edges of the weed beds are good, and the small, undeveloped point about half way up the right side is productive.

Both flies and spinners trolled or cast along the middle section of the western side of the lake are also very effective.

Tiger Trout made up the catch in the springs of 2005 and 2006. Most were in the 8 to 10 inch range, but one measured 14 1/4 inches.

## MAP REFERENCES:

*USGS Topographic Map, Washington (48117-E6-TF-024-00)
    Park Rapids Quadrangle, 7.5 Minute Series.
*USGS Topographic Map, Washington (48117-E1-TM-100-00)
    Colville Quadrangle, 30x60 Minute Series.
*Washington Atlas & Gazetteer, Page 118.

## 8  BLUE LAKE

August 22, 2002; Blue Lake, looking southwest.

SIZE: 100 Acres
ELEVATION: 2,238 Feet
MAXIMUM DEPTH: Unknown
COUNTY: Bonner, Idaho
COORDINATES: T57N R4W Sec21AH, 22DE

Longitude: 116d 49m 20s to 116d 49m 57s West
Latitude: 48d 16m 29s to 48d 16m 48s North

SPECIES, CONFIRMED:
 Black Crappie
 Largemouth Bass
 Pumpkinseed Sunfish
 Yellow Perch

SPECIES, REPORTED:
 Eastern Brook Trout
 Rainbow Trout

## CHARACTERISTICS:

The area around the lake has open, low ground to the east and west, and timbered hills to the north and south.

The hills to the south are steepest and have a lot of exposed rock across their center. Most of the visible rock is broken rock. One very large rocky area over the center of the south side extends clear to the bottom of the hill.

The low area to the east has timbered hills visible in the distance.

The shorelines all around the lake have a thick, dense concentration of aquatic weeds lining them. There are very heavy growths of cattails, with lilypads along the outer edges between the cattails and open water. There are also many beds of dollar pads along the shores.

The south side has two small areas where broken rock reaches to the waters edge. They are two of the few areas without extensive shoreline weeds. A brushy area with several snags is found between the two stretches of rocky shoreline.

There are few snags found around the lake. The majority of those present are found along the south side.

The "public" access is on private property at the center of the north side of the lake, in an area of scrub trees and dense brush. It is not suitable for launching of trailered boats, and barely suitable for launching of anything. The route to open water is very shallow water over a soft, muddy track through a narrow break in the shoreline weeds. The channel runs about 20 yards before opening up into the lake.

Inlet streams enter at the northeast and southeast corners. At the mouth of the inlet at the southeast corner, which is the only one that is very noticeable, is a small delta of sandy soil. The outside edge of the delta drops off quickly to what passes for deep water around the shores of this lake.

Blue Creek exits at the westernmost point of the lake, but the mouth is obscured by the heavy shoreline weed growth.

The bottom is silt, with a heavy covering of aquatic vegetation and some algae growths.

The water is very clear.

## DIRECTIONS TO:

Take Highway 2 to mile 7.0, at the east side of the town of Priest River, where East Side Road will be found on the north side of the highway.

Turn onto East Side Road, and follow it north for 8.5 miles to Blue Lake Road, on the right.

Turn right onto Blue Lake Road, and go east for 0.7 miles to a rough access area, on the right.

The access area has no facilities, and only a rough dirt road / parking area. There is access to the water, but it can't be called a boat launch. There are no areas for shore fishing. The area is signed for day use only, plus "Attention Sportsmen, All Land Surrounding This Lake, Including This Access Is Private. Please Respect Landowners Rights."

FISHING TIPS:

Fishing can be very good for decent sized fish of all of the species I have confirmed. Cast spinners or small jigs along the weedy shorelines and you never know what's going to grab it next.

MISCELLANEOUS NOTES:

Planting records indicate that the lake received Eastern Brook Trout from 1968 to 1976.

MAP REFERENCES:

*Idaho Atlas & Gazetteer, Page 62.
*USGS Topographic Map, Idaho (48116-C7-TF-024-00)
    Prater Mountain Quadrangle, 7.5 Minute Series.
*USGS Topographic Map, Idaho (48116-A1-TM-100-00)
    Sandpoint Quadrangle, 30x60 Minute Series.

## 9  BROWNS LAKE

July 14, 1999; Browns Lake, looking northeast.

SIZE: 88.1 Acres
ELEVATION: 3,411 Feet
MAXIMUM DEPTH: 23 Feet
COUNTY: Pend Oreille, Washington
COORDINATES: T34N R44E Sec24(north 1/2)

Longitude: 117d 10m 59s to 117d 11m 59s West
Latitude: 48d 26m 11s to 48d 26m 29s North

SPECIES, CONFIRMED:
 Cutthroat Trout, West Slope

SPECIES, REPORTED:

CHARACTERISTICS:
 There are low hills around the lake. They are sparsely to moderately timbered in most places. Where there is little or no timber there is low brush and some grassy areas, with small amounts of rock visible close to the water.

The north side has roads that visibly cut the hillside above the lake, one about half way up and another near the top.

A campground provides access to the lake at the southwest corner. The boat launch is gravel.

A narrow neck and small, somewhat separated section of the lake are at the northwest corner. The point that comes out to separate the bay at this corner is rocky and very sparsely treed.

The main body of the lake has a very irregular north shore, with small bays and points.

The shorelines are steep and inaccessible. In some places brush and trees reach to the waters edge. In many places, especially on the north shore, the shorelines are open, but steep, and can't be reached except by boat.

There is a flat area on the east end of the lake, where the surrounding hills are set back a bit making that end much more open. The shorelines in this area are brushy. The hills above the east end are more densely timbered than others in the area.

The west end skyline is also lower than to the north and south. The shorelines at the west end, while lower, are still moderately steep and have heavy timber.

Snags are found around most shore areas, and many of them extend out into the lake.

Most of the lake is fairly deep water. The visible portions of the bottom in the west half of the lake are mostly rocky. The east end has a primarily silt bottom.

The water is clear.

DIRECTIONS TO:

Take Highway 20 to mile 421.0, about 16 miles north of the town of Newport, where Kings Lake Road will be found on the east side of the highway.

Turn onto Kings Lake Road, and go east through the town of Usk. You will cross a bridge over the Pend Oreille River, and at 1.0 miles from Highway 20 reach a sign that indicates "Skookum Lake 8 Miles", "Browns Lake 11 Miles".

At 5.0 miles, the pavement ends.

At 7.2 miles, you will reach an intersection with Road 5030, on the left. Road 5030 goes to Half Moon Lake and Browns Lake. If you continue straight ahead, the road goes to Skookum Lakes and Kings Lake.

Turn left, onto Road 5030, and go north for 4.0 miles to the Browns Lake campground, on the left. The end of the road entering the camp area is signed as number 5030-390.

The campground is a fee area, with several sites, a pit toilet and boat ramp. A sign says the gates are opened at 6:00 A.M. and closed and locked at 10:00 P.M., and the boat launch is day use only.

FISHING TIPS:
 This is a fly fishing only lake. Check the current regulations before fishing.

MAP REFERENCES:
 *USGS Topographic Map, Washington (48117-D2-TF-024-00)
   Browns Lake Quadrangle, 7.5 Minute Series.
 *USGS Topographic Map, Washington (48117-A1-TM-100-00)
   Chewelah Quadrangle, 30x60 Minute Series.
 *Washington Atlas & Gazetteer, Page 105.

## 10  BRUSH LAKE

September 8, 2000; Brush Lake,
looking northeast from the public access.

SIZE: 29 Acres
ELEVATION: 2,998 Feet
MAXIMUM DEPTH: Unknown
COUNTY: Boundary, Idaho
COORDINATES: T64N R1E Sec15N,22D

Longitude: 116d 19m 26s to 116d 19m 47s West
Latitude: 48d 53m 12s to 48d 53m 40s North

SPECIES, CONFIRMED:
 Largemouth Bass
 Rainbow Trout

SPECIES, REPORTED:
 Bluegill
 Cutthroat Trout, West Slope
 Eastern Brook Trout
 Kokanee
 Pumpkinseed Sunfish

CHARACTERISTICS:

The lake is surrounded by timbered hills. Most of the hills visible from the lake are fairly low.

The east and west sides are timbered to the waters edge. A thin strip of smaller trees and low brush are right along the water.

The north end has a large, grass covered marsh area. A beaver lodge is found at the northeast corner, right at the break between the marsh and open water.

Much of the shoreline along the northwest corner, and all along the north end, is lined with heavy growths of aquatic weed. Lilypad beds are found at the north end.

The south end has a long, narrow, weed choked neck that extends about a hundred yards from open water to the camp area on the southwest corner of the lake. The camp area has a nice concrete strip boat ramp, located at the extreme south end of the neck which provides access to a very shallow channel through the dense weeds.

The main public access area is located at the center of the west side. It has a gravel boat ramp and a fishing dock.

Large rocks are found along and above shore on the southern portion of the west side between the main public access and the camp area. A trail runs from the camps to the rocks and to the lake in that area, providing some bank access.

The water has a light brown stain.

This is reported to be both a popular camping site and a moose area, but on my one visit in mid September during high winds and pouring rain I saw neither people nor moose.

DIRECTIONS TO:

Take Interstate 90 to exit 12, at the town of Coeur d'Alene.

From exit 12, take Highway 95 north for about 94 miles to mile 524.3, 1.4 miles north of the junction with Highway 1, and 17 miles north of the town of Bonners Ferry, where Forest Service Road 1004 will be reached, on the right. The end of the road is signed "Camp 9 Road 1/2 Mile, Brush Lake 2 Miles".

Turn onto Forest Service Road 1004, and take it southeast for 1.6 miles to a fork. Road 2493 is on the right, and signed for "Camp Area". The road to the left is marked "Boat Ramp".

Take the left fork 0.7 miles to reach the end of the road, where the public access is located. The access area has a gravel boat launch, pit toilet, picnic table, fishing dock and gravel parking area. The area is signed for no overnight camping.

To reach the camping area take road 2493, mentioned above, 0.4 miles to the south end of the lake. The camp area has a large circular parking area with sites around it, a pit toilet, and a nice but nearly useless concrete strip boat ramp.

## FISHING TIPS:
From the fishing dock, cast spinners will get bass and flies will get trout.

## MISCELLANEOUS NOTES:
Planting records indicate that the lake received 1,000 Eastern Brook Trout on May 16, 1997.

## MAP REFERENCES:
*Idaho Atlas & Gazetteer, Page 48.
*USGS Topographic Map, Idaho (48116-H3-TF-024-00)
  Hall Mountain Quadrangle, 7.5 Minute Series.
*USGS Topographic Map, Idaho (48116-E1-TM-100-00)
  Bonners Ferry Quadrangle, 30x60 Minute Series.

## 11   BULL RUN LAKE

June 29, 1996; Bull Run Lake, looking southwest.

SIZE: 100 Acres
ELEVATION: 2,150 Feet
MAXIMUM DEPTH: Unknown
COUNTY: Kootenai, Idaho
COORDINATES: T48N R1W Sec4(southwest 1/4),9(northwest 1/4)

      Longitude: 116d 28m 13s to 116d 28m 46s West
      Latitude: 47d 31m 23s to 47d 32m 2s North

SPECIES, CONFIRMED:
 Black Bullhead Catfish
 Black Crappie
 Bluegill
 Largemouth Bass
 Northern Pike
 Pumpkinseed Sunfish
 Tench
 Yellow Perch

SPECIES, REPORTED:
 Rainbow Trout

CHARACTERISTICS:

The area around the lake is open at the north end and northeast corner, with wooded hills on the other sides.

There are some homes along the east shore, and many on the hill above the lake. The east half of the south shore has a home with pastureland.

An old railroad grade, now a paved bicycle trail, runs along the north side of the lake, but is well away from the water. A trailhead for the trail system is located at the northeast corner, and has a pit toilet.

An old dirt road runs parallel to the bicycle trail, between it and the lake. It provides access to the boat launch area at the center of the west shore. The road is usually muddy, and can be pretty bad in the spring.

A gravel road runs the length of the east shore. It offers limited bank fishing access.

The north end of the lake is heavily weeded for a considerable distance out from shore with thick beds of dollar pads and smaller beds of lilypads. The same is true of the entire southern portion of the lake and the west side. A small area found at the east half of the center of the lake has the only truly open water areas, but these open areas are small. Some weeds are found in almost all areas.

The weeds make shore access difficult, with open water reaching shore at only a small area on the northeast corner.

The lake is shallow with a bottom of heavy silt.

The water is clear, but occasionally has bits of suspended vegetation.

DIRECTIONS TO:

Take Interstate 90 to exit 34 east of Coeur d'Alene, Idaho. At exit 34, turn south onto Highway 3.

Take Highway 3 south for 3.1 miles to mile 116.4, where Bull Run Road #216 enters on the left. The end of the road is signed for Bull Run Lake.

Turn onto Bull Run Road, and cross the single lane bridge over the Coeur d'Alene River to a tee intersection at 0.1 miles.

Turn right at the intersection, and go 0.3 miles, to where the lake becomes visible. Continue on the left to reach an open water fishing area at 0.4 miles from Highway 3.

To reach the boat launch area at the center of the west shore, turn right onto the rough, muddy dirt road on the right just after crossing the old railroad grade trail.

The road runs 0.6 miles to the boat launch area. If you take this road, the first road you come to on the left is a dead end that reaches a grassy area used for camping. Take the second left, just past the slough, to reach the boat launch.

The boat launch is crude. It is gravel, very weeded, and not suitable for large boats. Old roads branch out from the launch area.

FISHING TIPS:

Spinnerbaits and jigs cast along the weed beds will get fish. The best spots are where heavy pockets of dollar pads border a section of open water.

Best lure color for me has been yellow, but crappie jigs in red and white have also been very productive. Crappie are abundant, with perch also very plentiful. Bass and tench are also found in the weed areas, with the tench at the bottom.

The crappie fishing along the weeds will also attract an occasional pike. If they take a jig without a steel leader it's usually gone, but they can sometimes be landed. They are also sometimes attracted to a hooked fish, and I have had them attack it at the boat.

Most of the pike fishing done at the lake is by bobber fishermen with fish suspended for bait. My catches have been incidentals on jigs and spinnerbaits while fishing for crappie. The pond on the right side of the road to the boat launch area receives flow from the lake, and also holds pike at times.

The bluegill and pumpkinseed are most plentiful along the weedy shorelines, but are occasionally picked up in the areas fished for crappie. As of 2003, the population of bluegill has increased, and their size is becoming more impressive. I caught a ten inch, 1.0 pound bluegill on June 1, 2003.

The Black Bullhead Catfish are seldom seen, mainly because I don't fish bait, but can sometimes be caught in the outlet area where the culvert passes under the road near the boat launch area.

June 20, 1998; My daughter, Vicki, with a 27.25 inch,
5.3 pound Northern Pike.

MISCELLANEOUS NOTES:
  Moose frequent the area.

MAP REFERENCES:
  *Idaho Atlas & Gazetteer, Page 60 (name not indicated).
  *USGS Topographic Map, Idaho (47116-E4-TF-024-00)
    Rose Lake Quadrangle, 7.5 Minute Series.
  *USGS Topographic Map, Idaho (47116-E1-TM-100-00)
    Coeur d'Alene Quadrangle, 30x60 Minute Series.

## 12   CAVE LAKE

June 29, 1996; Cave Lake, looking southwest.

SIZE: 700 Acres
ELEVATION: 2,127 Feet
MAXIMUM DEPTH: Unknown
COUNTY: Kootenai, Idaho
COORDINATES: T47N R2W Sec4,5
        T48N R2W Sec28,29,32,33

        Longitude: 116d 35m 18s to 116d 37m 46s West
        Latitude: 47d 27m 23s to 47d 28m 45s North

SPECIES, CONFIRMED:
 Black Bullhead Catfish
 Bluegill
 Pumpkinseed Sunfish

SPECIES, REPORTED:
 Crappie
 Largemouth Bass
 Northern Pike
 Yellow Perch

## CHARACTERISTICS:

The lake lies in an area of low, timbered hills.

The area around the lake is a combination of wooded areas and some pastureland. A few homes are scattered randomly around the lake, but most are set well back from the water.

Highway 3 runs along part of the south shore.

A dike on the east side separates Cave Lake from Medicine Lake. A channel through the dike provides a navigable link between the two lakes. Access to Cave Lake is by boat from Medicine Lake through this bridge crossing.

The channel is spanned by a bridge carrying a road that runs atop the dike between the lakes. Very limited shore access is available at the bridge crossing.

The shores on all but the south side of the lake are quite marshy. Most of the lake is shallow, and weed choked close to shore once summer growth is underway.

The bottom is mostly silt, with aquatic vegetation in most areas. The bottom at the bridge area is rock and silt.

The water is murky.

## DIRECTIONS TO:

Take Interstate 90 to exit 34 east of Coeur d'Alene, Idaho. At exit 34, turn south onto Highway 3.

Take Highway 3 south for 12.8 miles to mile 106.7, where Rainy Hill Road enters on the right. The end of the road is signed for "Sportsman's Access" just prior to reaching it.

Turn right onto Rainy Hill Road, and the access area for Medicine Lake will be reached on the left after 0.7 miles. This access provides the only public boat access to Cave Lake. The access area is marked as the "Rainy Hill, Coeur d'Alene National Forest Boat Launch". The public access area is located at the northeast corner of Medicine Lake. It has a large gravel parking area, concrete strip boat ramp, dock and pit toilets. It is day use only, with no overnight camping.

Continue 0.3 miles past the Medicine Lake access to reach an intersection near the bridge over the channel between Medicine and Cave Lakes. You can park here and walk to the limited shore access for the lakes at the channel. Cave Lake can be accessed via water from Medicine Lake by way of the channel through the dike.

An **ALTERNATE ROUTE** to the access areas is from Highway 3 mile 105.1, where Medimont Road enters. Take Medimont Road 1.0 mile north from Highway 3 to reach the bridge and intersection mentioned above.

FISHING TIPS:

My time spent fishing this lake is very limited. Flies cast from shore at the bridge area were effective for Pumpkinseed.

MAP REFERENCES:

*Idaho Atlas & Gazetteer, Page 60.

*USGS Topographic Map, Idaho (47116-D5-TF-024-00)
   Medimont Quadrangle, 7.5 Minute Series.

*USGS Topographic Map, Idaho (47116-A1-TM-100-00)
   St. Maries Quadrangle, 30x60 Minute Series.

## 13  CEDAR LAKE
Also known as: Little Twin Lakes
Little Twin "Lakes"
Lower Twin Lake

May 18, 1996; Cedar Lake, looking north.

SIZE: 6.2 Acres
ELEVATION: 3,719 Feet
MAXIMUM DEPTH: Unknown
COUNTY: Stevens, Washington
COORDINATES: T35N R41E Sec4C

Longitude: 117d 38m 39s to 117d 38m 48s West
Latitude: 48d 34m 7s to 48d 34m 20s North

SPECIES, CONFIRMED:
Cutthroat Trout, Coastal
Cutthroat Trout, West Slope
Rainbow Trout

SPECIES, REPORTED:

CHARACTERISTICS:

The lake is located in a high plateau area, with only low, rolling hills around it.

The area around the lake is all wooded, except for the strip between Cedar and Spruce lakes at the middle of the east side. This is the strip that high water covers to combine the two lakes. This high water condition appears to be the normal condition for these lakes.

There are rocky areas at either side of the flooded strip, and also at the center of the west shore.

A road to the camp area and access for Spruce Lake runs up the west shore, but isn't visible from the lake.

The access to Cedar Lake is found at the south end, and has several campsites, picnic tables, toilets and launch area. The launch area is too shallow for larger, trailered boats, but good for small boats and rafts. Larger boats should use the ramp at the northwest corner of Spruce Lake.

The area out from the access has floating grass bogs. They are also found in other parts of the lake. Some have active beaver lodges built on them.

Just before the flooded strip between lakes is reached, a large beaver lodge is found in open water to the west of the strip.

Shallow mud flats are found on the shoreward sides of the bogs, and have growths of lilypads and other aquatic vegetation. Some of the shallower lakeside bog edges also have lilypads.

The water is clear.

DIRECTIONS TO:

Take Highway 20 to mile 366.7, east of the town of Colville, where Little Twin Lakes Road will be found on the north side of the highway.

Turn onto Little Twin Lakes Road, and take it 4.8 miles to a road on the left. This road runs up the west side of the lakes to the Spruce Lake camp and access area.

Continue 0.1 mile past the road to the Spruce Lake access and you will reach the Cedar Lake camp and access area, on the left.

An **ALTERNATE ROUTE** to Little Twin Lakes is to take Highway 20 to the end of Black Lake-Squaw Creek Road at mile 372.5, on the north side of the highway.

Turn onto Black Lake-Squaw Creek Road, and take it north about 100 yards to a tee intersection, where you will go to the left.

Continue 1.7 miles, and a road on the left that is signed for public fishing will be passed. This is the Black Lake access road. Keep to the right and continue northward.

The road will run up the east side of Black Lake, and around the north end. At the northwest corner, an intersection will be reached. The left fork runs down the west side of Black Lake, and the right fork continues on to Cedar and Spruce (Little Twin Lakes).

Keep to the right, and another intersection will be reached at 1.9 miles past the Black Lake access road (3.6 miles from Highway 2). The right fork goes up the east side of Spruce Lake, and the left goes to the access areas.

Turn left, and go 0.4 miles to the access area at the south end of Cedar Lake, on the right. If you continue past the Cedar access, an intersection will be reached in 0.1 miles. The right fork runs up the west side of the lakes to the Spruce Lake access at its northwest corner.

Because neither route is fully maintained during the winter, one or both may be impassable due to downed trees, washouts or snow until late spring.

FISHING TIPS:

Spinners and flies worked around the bogs and at the strip between the lakes are very effective.

MAP REFERENCES:

*USGS Topographic Map, Washington (48117-E6-TF-024-00)
  Park Rapids Quadrangle, 7.5 Minute Series.
*USGS Topographic Map, Washington (48117-E1-TM-100-00)
  Colville Quadrangle, 30x60 Minute Series.
*Washington Atlas & Gazetteer, Page 118.

# 14   CEDAR LAKE

May 10, 2005; Cedar Lake, looking west from the public access.

SIZE: 51.2 Acres
ELEVATION: 2,135 Feet
MAXIMUM DEPTH: 28 Feet
COUNTY: Stevens, Washington
COORDINATES: T40N R41E Sec26KLPQ

Longitude: 117d 35m 18s to 117d 35m 48s West
Latitude: 48d 56m 24s to 48d 56m 42s North

SPECIES, CONFIRMED:
Rainbow Trout

SPECIES, REPORTED:

CHARACTERISTICS:
  The lake lies in an area of low, timbered hills. The timber stops well away
from the lake, making its closest approach at the west side.
  The area immediately around the lake is open fields.
  A highway runs up the east side of the lake, away from the water except
for a small spot at the northeast corner. It offers no access to the water
except for the public access.

The public access is found on the east side of the lake. It has a gravel boat launch area, gravel parking area and pit toilet. The area is signed for no overnight parking or camping.

The shorelines are mostly lined with aquatic weed growths. Some areas at the southeast corner, where a house is located, are grassy. There are some docks in the area of the house.

The south side has some small bays along a grassy, irregular shoreline. The bays are shallow. The largest bay is the one closest to the house, extending south for a couple of hundred feet.

A small creek exits at the north end.

Fence lines enter the water at the west side and the south end.

The bottom is silt, with a little gravel at the access area.

The water is very clear.

## DIRECTIONS TO:

Cedar Lake is remote, but can be reached via several routes. The major routes are detailed. The route from **COLVILLE** is the primary route.

### FROM COLVILLE:

Take Highway 20 east out of the town of Colville, and watch for Aladdin Road, on the north side of the highway at Highway 20 mile 355.5.

Take Aladdin Road north for 24.8 miles to the intersection with Deep Lake-Boundary Road, on the right at the "town" of Spirit.

Turn onto Deep Lake-Boundary Road, and take it north for 9.5 miles to the public access area for Cedar Lake, on the left.

### FROM NORTHPORT:

Take combined Highway 20 / Highway 395 to mile 239.1, where the intersection with Highway 25 will be reached. The intersection is on the east side of the Columbia River, and at the western side of the town of Kettle Falls.

Turn onto Highway 25 North, and take it about 32 miles to the town of Northport, where the north end of Colville-Aladdin-Northport Road will be found, on the right.

Turn onto Colville-Aladdin-Northport Road, and take it southeast for about nine miles to the intersection with Deep Lake-Boundary Road, on the left at the "town" of Spirit.

Turn onto Deep Lake-Boundary Road, and take it north for 9.5 miles to the public access area for Cedar Lake, on the left.

## **FROM THE NORTH:**

Take combined Highway 20 / Highway 395 to mile 239.1, where the intersection with Highway 25 will be reached. The intersection is on the east side of the Columbia River, and at the western side of the town of Kettle Falls.

Turn onto Highway 25 North, and take it 32.8 miles, through the town of Northport, to where Northport-Waneta Road will be found, on the right, just before you reach the bridge over the Columbia River.

Turn onto Northport-Waneta Road and take it 15.6 miles to the public access area for Cedar Lake, on the right.

FISHING TIPS:

Flies cast to rising fish are very effective for large trout. Especially good is the area along shore at the south side of the lake.

MAP REFERENCES:

*USGS Topographic Map, Washington (48117-H5-TF-024-00)
   Leadpoint Quadrangle, 7.5 Minute Series.
*USGS Topographic Map, Washington (48117-E1-TM-100-00)
   Colville Quadrangle, 30x60 Minute Series.
*Washington Atlas & Gazetteer, Page 118.

## 15   CHASE LAKE

August 22, 2002; Chase Lake, looking east.

SIZE: 194 Acres (estimated)
ELEVATION: 2,495 Feet
MAXIMUM DEPTH: Unknown
COUNTY: Bonner, Idaho
COORDINATES: T59N  R4W  Sec14(southwest 1/4),15JR,23(northwest 1/4)

> Longitude: 116d 49m 1s to 116d 49m 46s West
> Latitude: 48d 27m 5s to 48d 27m 50s North

SPECIES, CONFIRMED:
 Largemouth Bass
 Yellow Perch

SPECIES, REPORTED:
 Pumpkinseed Sunfish

CHARACTERISTICS:

The east side of the lake has low timbered hills above it. The timber cover is sparse in some places, but fairly dense in most.

The other three sides of the lake are fairly low, with the exception of a small but somewhat steep sided rise to the southwest. The rise is also timbered. Hills are visible in the distance to the south, but the skyline is mostly open to the north.

There is little development on the lake. There are places to either side of the public access area near the northwest corner.

An outlet creek exits at the northwest corner, flowing to the south end of Priest Lake.

Marshy shorelines are found at the mouth of the outlet creek, and also at the northeast corner.

The south end of the lake is shallow and weedy, with a marshy shoreline all around it.

There are additional marshy areas along the east side.

The lake has many small islands. The main clusters of them are found at the northwest corner and at the center of the east side. The largest island is at the mouth of a shallow bay on the east side, and covers a little over an acre.

There are extensive beds of aquatic vegetation in the lake. They are mostly dollar pads, but there are also some lilypads. The dollar pad beds extend out a hundred yards or more from shore along most of the west shore. They pretty well cover the entire south end. The beds along the north end are smaller. The east side has pockets of good-sized beds that become larger as you move south.

The center of the lake is open water.

There are some snags along the shorelines, and also scattered randomly on the bottom.

The bottom is deep silt. In addition to the visible aquatic vegetation, the shallows also have bottom hugging growths.

The water is clear, but has a lot of suspended and floating vegetative matter.

DIRECTIONS TO:

Take Highway 2 to mile 5.9, at a stoplight in the middle of the town of Priest River, where Highway 57 / West Side Road will be found on the north side of the highway.

Turn onto Highway 57, and follow it north for 22.5 miles to Dickensheet Road, on the right. The continuation of Highway 57 is signed for Nordman.

Turn right onto Dickensheet Road, and go east for 3.6 miles to Substation Cuttoff Road, on the right.

Turn right onto Substation Cuttoff Road, and go 0.3 miles, to where a "T" intersection with East Side Road will be reached.

Turn left onto East Side Road, and go north 0.1 mile to an unmarked gravel road, on the right.

Turn right onto the gravel road, and go east 0.6 miles to an intersection. The intersection "Y's" into three roads. The center one is signed for "Public Access Area", and runs 0.1 mile to the lake.

FISHING TIPS:

I fished the lake only briefly from the dock at the public access area. Small Largemouth Bass and Yellow Perch could be seen around the weedy shallows, and could be taken on flies.

MISCELLANEOUS NOTES:

Chase Lake produced a state record Pumpkinseed Sunfish of 14 ounces (9.75 inches long) in 1977.

MAP REFERENCES:

*Idaho Atlas & Gazetteer, Page 62.
*USGS Topographic Map, Idaho (48116-D7-TF-024-00)
  Coolin Quadrangle, 7.5 Minute Series.
*USGS Topographic Map, Idaho (48116-A1-TM-100-00)
  Sandpoint Quadrangle, 30x60 Minute Series.

# 16  COCOLALLA LAKE

June 16, 2006; Cocolalla Lake, looking south.

SIZE: 800 Acres
ELEVATION: 2,203 Feet
MAXIMUM DEPTH: Unknown
COUNTY: Bonner, Idaho
COORDINATES: T55N R2W Sec5MNP,6JR,7(southeast 1/2),8(northwest 1/4), 8(east 3/4)

Longitude: 116d 35m 58s to 116d 37m 36s West
Latitude: 48d 6m 30s to 48d 8m 31s North

SPECIES, CONFIRMED:

SPECIES, REPORTED:
 Black Crappie
 Bullhead Catfish
 Channel Catfish
 Cutthroat Trout
 Eastern Brook Trout

German Brown Trout
Largemouth Bass
Pumpkinseed Sunfish
Rainbow Trout
Yellow Perch

## CHARACTERISTICS:

The lake lies in an area of low, timbered hills. The highest hills are visible to the south.

The public access area is located at the northeast corner. It has a concrete strip boat ramp, signed "Attention boaters, launching boats 16 feet or more not recommended, shallow ramp – watch your prop". There is a dock alongside the ramp. Several "pull-in" campsites, designed more for campers and motor homes than tents, are found in the area. There's a small picnic area just east of the boat ramp. It has just a single table, but is pretty close to the water. The area has a fairly large gravel parking area and pit toilets.

The lake is pretty much timbered all around, in spite of many houses found on the west shore.

Railroad tracks run along the east shore, but are separated from the water in most places by a thin strip of scraggly trees. Highway 95 lies on the other side of the railroad tracks. The tracks and highway both make a close approach to the east side of the camp area. Close enough that the sound of cars can be heard quite loudly at times, and since the tracks are even closer, the trains are very loud and even shake the ground in the closest campsites.

The shorelines on the north and west sides have some private docks extending out into the lake. Some homes have manicured lawns running to the water. Many areas have trees and brush to the waters edge.

The entire east shoreline has trees and brush, and also some fairly steep slopes due to the banks lining the railroad tracks at the north end.

Cocolalla Creek enters at the northwest corner, and Fish creek exits at the southeast corner.

The average depth of the lake is reported as 26 feet.

At the end of summer the water is somewhat murky.

## DIRECTIONS TO:

Take Interstate 90 to exit 12 at Coeur d'Alene, Idaho. At exit 12, turn north onto Highway 95.

Take Highway 95 north for about 33 miles to mile 463.9, about ten miles south of the town of Sandpoint, where a narrow road enters on the left. The end of the road is signed for "Sportsman's Access".

Turn left onto the road and head west. The road will drop and pass through a very narrow railroad underpass at 0.1 mile.

At 0.2 miles, a T intersection will be reached. Turn to the left.

At 0.3 miles from Highway 95, you will enter the Cocolalla Lake access area. The pavement ends as you enter the area.

FISHING TIPS:

I did not attempt to fish this lake.

MAP REFERENCES:

*Idaho Atlas & Gazetteer; Page 12, 62.
*USGS Topographic Map, Idaho (48116-A6-TF-024-00)
  Careywood Quadrangle, 7.5 Minute Series.
*USGS Topographic Map, Idaho (48116-A5-TF-024-00)
  Cocolalla Quadrangle, 7.5 Minute Series.
*USGS Topographic Map, Idaho (48116-B5-TF-024-00)
  Sagle Quadrangle, 7.5 Minute Series.
*USGS Topographic Map, Idaho (48116-A1-TM-100-00)
  Sandpoint Quadrangle, 30x60 Minute Series.

## 17  COFFIN LAKE

May 18, 1996; Coffin Lake, looking southeast.

SIZE: 19.6 Acres
ELEVATION: 3,150 Feet
MAXIMUM DEPTH: 31 Feet
COUNTY: Stevens, Washington
COORDINATES: T36N R42E Sec31Q

> Longitude: 117d 33m 2s to 133d 33m 17s West
> Latitude: 48d 34m 27s to 48d 34m 43s North

SPECIES, CONFIRMED:
 Eastern Brook Trout
 Largemouth Bass

SPECIES, REPORTED:
 Cutthroat Trout
 German Brown Trout
 Rainbow Trout
 Tench

## CHARACTERISTICS:

There are wooded hills all around the lake, and Highway 20 runs above the west side. A small cabin is found at the center of the east side.

The Little Pend Oreille River enters the north end of the lake at a large marshy area, and exits the south end at a small flat.

The area at the southwest corner has a rocky shoreline. All other areas have moderate slopes and are brush covered.

There are many snags found along the shorelines. The north end shorelines are shallow and weedy.

The many small trees found along most shores make access difficult, but a rough trail along the west side leads to openings that offer some bank fishing opportunities.

The bottom is silt with a lot of weeds. The water is clear.

## DIRECTIONS TO:

Take Highway 20 to mile 376.5, east of the town of Colville, where a short, gravel loop road is reached on the south side of the highway. The far end of this loop road rejoins Highway 20 at mile 376.7.

Turn onto the gravel road and go to a wide area that provides parking near its south end.

From the parking area, a trail drops over the hill to the west shore of the lake below. It runs less than a hundred yards.

## FISHING TIPS:

Spinners and flies cast along the cover along the shorelines are very effective. The edges of weed beds and submerged logs hold fish.

Best fishing for trout has been at the south end of the lake, and the best bass fishing at the north end.

## MAP REFERENCES:

*USGS Topographic Map, Washington (48117-E5-TF-024-00)
   Lake Gillette Quadrangle, 7.5 Minute Series.
*USGS Topographic Map, Washington (48117-E1-TM-100-00)
   Colville Quadrangle, 30x60 Minute Series.
*Washington Atlas & Gazetteer, Page 118.

## 18   CONGER LAKE
Also known as: Conger Pond #2
Conger Reservoir

June 19, 2006; Conger Lake, looking northwest.

SIZE: 5.3 Acres
ELEVATION: 2,778 Feet
MAXIMUM DEPTH: 10 Feet
COUNTY: Pend Oreille, Washington
COORDINATES: T33N R43E Sec4NP

Longitude: 117d 23m 0s to 117d 23m 13s West
Latitude: 48d 22m 53s to 48d 23m 0s North

SPECIES, CONFIRMED:
Rainbow Trout

SPECIES, REPORTED:
Eastern Brook Trout

CHARACTERISTICS:

The lake lies in an area that is heavily timbered all around.

It is almost pear shaped, running east to west, with the wide end to the east.

The south side and east end have steep banks with timber and brush to the waters edge.

A gravel road reaches the east end, and runs up the north side of the lake. A steep bank that is lined with trees and brush separates the road from the water. The cover on the bank is thin at the east end.

Access to the lake is from the road near the northwest corner, where a steep trail drops to the lake from the road about twenty feet above. The trail comes down from two spots separated by about 75 feet to reach a small, lightly sloped grassy area. The largest "trail" appears to have been used in the past by 4-wheelers, but isn't suitable for getting any large floating device to the water.

The grassy area that provides access is dominated by a very large mound of burnt litter at its center.

A rough trail runs west along the north shore from the access area. It provides limited bank access at a couple of places.

The west end of the lake has a marshy grass area across a low area of shoreline. Trees at that end of the lake are separated from the water by the marsh.

The shorelines have a lot of snags. Most are small, and don't extend out too far from shore.

Trimble Creek enters at the north end of the lake from Conger Pond, and exits at the southeast corner.

The bottom is silt with a covering of aquatic vegetation and some algae.

The water is clear.

DIRECTIONS TO:

Take Highway 20 to mile 417.5, about 19 miles north of the town of Newport, where Kapps Lane will be found on the west side of the highway. The end of the road is signed for "Batey-Bould ORV Area".

Turn onto Kapps Lane, and take it 1.0 mile to a stop sign at the intersection with West Calispell Road.

Turn right onto West Calispell road, and take it 1.9 miles to Sicely Road, on the left. The end of the road is signed for "Batey-Bould ORV Area 1 1/2 Miles".

Turn onto Sicely Road, and take it 2.5 miles to a turnout on the left. From the turnout a short trail drops to the lake.

An **ALTERNATE ROUTE** to Conger Lake is to take Highway 20 to mile 415.4, where West Calispell Road will be found on the west side of the highway.

Turn onto West Calispell Road, and take it 3.0 miles to Sicely Road, on the right. The end of the road is signed for "Batey-Bould ORV Area 1 1/2 Miles".

Turn onto Sicely Road, and take it 2.5 miles to a turnout on the left. From the turnout a short trail drops to the lake.

FISHING TIPS:
Flies and spinners cast from shore will get fish.

MAP REFERENCES:
*USGS Topographic Map, Washington (48117-D4-TF-024-00)
  Tacoma Peak Quadrangle, 7.5 Minute Series.
*USGS Topographic Map, Washington (48117-A1-TM-100-00)
  Chewelah Quadrangle, 30x60 Minute Series.
*Washington Atlas & Gazetteer, Page 105.

## 19  CONGER POND
Also known as: Conger Pond #1

June 19, 2006; Conger Pond, looking north.

SIZE: 3.2 Acres
ELEVATION: 2,836 Feet
MAXIMUM DEPTH: 10 Feet
COUNTY: Pend Oreille, Washington
COORDINATES: T33N R43E Sec4M

   Longitude: 117d 23m 12s to 117d 23m 19s West
   Latitude: 48d 23m 5s to 48d 23m 19s North

SPECIES, CONFIRMED:
  Rainbow Trout

SPECIES, REPORTED:
  Eastern Brook Trout

CHARACTERISTICS:
  The lake is long and quite narrow.
  It lies in a timber covered area, with timber and brush to the waters edge
all around.

A lot of snags are found along the shorelines, as well as on the bottom. One very large snag has its trunk on the eastern shore and its top on the western shore about a quarter of the way up the lake. It forms a very effective obstacle to navigation.

A large weedy area is found just above the snag that spans the lake.

The bottom is mud, and in addition to a lot of submerged snags, has several old stumps.

Trimble Creek exits at the south end, flowing to Conger Lake. It exits at a small beaver dam. The beaver are active as of 2006.

Extremely limited bank access exists at the southwest corner and at the beaver dam. The dense brush along the shores prevents access in other areas.

A gravel logging road runs up the west side of the lake, but is separated from the water by trees and brush. It makes its only close approach at the southwest corner, and then climbs as it runs up the lake.

The west side shorelines become steeper as you move up the lake. The shores of the east side are also fairly steep.

The north end of the lake has a small marshy flat between the open water and the timber at that end of the lake.

The water is clear, but has a slight brownish tinge.

DIRECTIONS TO:

Take Highway 20 to mile 417.5, about 19 miles north of the town of Newport, where Kapps Lane will be found on the west side of the highway. The end of the road is signed for "Batey-Bould ORV Area".

Turn onto Kapps Lane, and take it 1.0 mile to a stop sign at the intersection with West Calispell Road.

Turn right onto West Calispell road, and take it 1.9 miles to Sicely Road, on the left. The end of the road is signed for "Batey-Bould ORV Area 1 1/2 Miles".

Turn onto Sicely Road, and take it 2.6 miles to a fork. The right fork runs to the end of Conger Pond in just 0.1 mile. The pond is on the right.

An **ALTERNATE ROUTE** to Conger Pond is to take Highway 20 to mile 415.4, where West Calispell Road will be found on the west side of the highway.

Turn onto West Calispell Road, and take it 3.0 miles to Sicely Road, on the right. The end of the road is signed for "Batey-Bould ORV Area 1 1/2 Miles".

Turn onto Sicely Road, and take it 2.6 miles to a fork. The right fork runs to the end of Conger Pond in just 0.1 mile. The pond is on the right.

FISHING TIPS:

Flies will get the attention of the small fish, but the heavy brush makes fishing difficult and the fish aren't easy to hook because of their size. Best fishing is from a raft out on the lake, where the small fish will more aggressively take both flies and small spinners.

MAP REFERENCES:

*USGS Topographic Map, Washington (48117-D4-TF-024-00)
  Tacoma Peak Quadrangle, 7.5 Minute Series.
*USGS Topographic Map, Washington (48117-A1-TM-100-00)
  Chewelah Quadrangle, 30x60 Minute Series.
*Washington Atlas & Gazetteer, Page 105.

## 20  COOKS LAKE

July 14, 1999; Cooks Lake, looking northwest.

SIZE: 11.1 Acres
ELEVATION: 3,075 Feet
MAXIMUM DEPTH: Unknown
COUNTY: Pend Oreille, Washington
COORDINATES: T33N R45E Sec19M

> Longitude: 117d 10m 8s to 117d 10m 30s West
> Latitude: 48d 20m 33s to 48d 20m 40s North

SPECIES, CONFIRMED:
 Rainbow Trout

SPECIES, REPORTED:

CHARACTERISTICS:
 Wooded hills rise above the north and south sides of the lake.
 To the west is visible a lower hill, mostly timbered, but bare at the top. Some of the timber cover is sparse on the sides, where rock and grass show through.

The area around the lake is timbered to the shorelines in most places. The immediate shorelines are moderately steep to just plain steep everywhere except at the ends of the lake.

The south side offers almost no bank access. The shores on this side are quite brushy.

The north side has a small point that can be dropped down to from a turnout on the road above. The road is at the top of about a 30 foot bank in this location, which is about 0.1 mile west of the access road. The road runs above the north side of the lake for its entire length. The shores of the north side can be walked from the camp area to the point, which borders deep water.

An unimproved camp area with several sites is located at the east end of the lake. It has a dirt boat launch area. The camp area is situated in a stand of cottonwood and pine. Most of the timber around other parts of the lake is pine and fir.

From the camp area the accessible areas of the lake are mostly shallow, becoming deeper only as you move up the lake.

A small amount of aquatic vegetation is found at the east end in the shallows, but very little is found elsewhere.

The shores of the lake drop to deep water quickly on all but the east end, where a long gradual slope runs from the camping area to the deep water.

The bottom is silt with gravel areas on the east end and at the center of the deep water. The steeper areas above the deep bottom have a rocky bottom.

In the fall of 2000, the water level was 12 to 15 feet below full pool, leaving very little water in the lake. A Department of Wildlife official advised me that this is not an unusual condition at this time of year.

The end of the lake out from the camp area has a bottom of very small rock and silt with a lot of grass.

The water is usually clear, but during the periods of low water becomes turbid and has a brownish color.

DIRECTIONS TO:

The **PRIMARY ROUTE** to Cooks Lake is from the north. Several options from the south are offered below as alternates.

Take Highway 20 to mile 421.0, about 16 miles north of the town of Newport, where Kings Lake Road will be found on the left.

Turn onto Kings Lake Road, and go east through the town of Usk. You will cross a bridge over the Pend Oreille River, and at 1.0 miles from Highway 20 reach a sign that indicates "Skookum Lake 8 Miles", "Browns Lake 11 Miles".

At 2.8 miles from Highway 20, you will find the end of Best Chance Road, on the right.

Turn onto Best Chance Road, which is a gravel road, and take it 8.2 miles to the access and campground road at the east end of Cooks Lake. Signs mark the entrance to the access and camp area.

The access road runs 0.1 mile (when the water level is at full pool), ending at the lake.

To reach the **ALTERNATE ROUTE**, which approaches from the south, take Highway 20 to the town of Newport, where it will end at mile 436.8 at an intersection with Highway 2.

At the stop sign in Newport, turn left onto Highway 2. Take Highway 2 into Idaho and the bridge over the Pend Oreille River.

*As soon as you cross the river, you will need to be in the left lane to turn onto the first road as you leave the bridge. This is LeClerc Creek Road, and enters from the north at Idaho Highway 2 mile 0.5.

Turn left onto LeClerc Creek Road.

**Take LeClerk Creek Road north for 2.7 miles to Marshall Lake Road, which enters on the right. Some maps show this to be Bead Lake Road.

Follow Marshall Lake / Bead Lake Road 6.9 miles to a "Y" intersection. At the intersection, Bead Lake Road continues on the left, becoming gravel, and Bead Lake Drive is on the right. En route to the intersection, you will pass the end of Bench Lake Road at 0.9 miles, the end of Marshall Lake Road at 2.4 miles, and Bead Lake Drive (signed for "Bead Lake Trailhead 1/2 Mile") at 6.0 miles.

***At the "Y" intersection, turn to the left. At 0.2 miles the end of a gravel road on the right will be passed. It is the second road on the right, and the end of the road is signed for "No Name Lake".

Continue on Bead Lake Road, and at 1.4 miles from the "Y" intersection, and just after passing through a slate mining area, you will reach another intersection. Keep to the left here.

At 2.1 miles, and the next intersection, go to the right.

At 2.3 miles, you go to the right again.

At 3.9 miles, you will reach a major intersection. The road to the left is number 5015, and signed as "Cooks Lake Road". The road to the right is marked "Bear Paw Ridge".

Turn left onto Cooks Lake Road, and go 1.5 miles to the access area for Cooks Lake, on the left.

An **ALTERNATE <u>SOUTH</u> ROUTE** to Cooks Lake is from the south on Highway 2.

Take Highway 2 north about 47 miles from Interstate 90 Exit 281 in Spokane to the town of Newport.

Take Highway 2 into Idaho and the bridge over the Pend Oreille River.

From here follow the directions provided above from the point marked with an asterisk(*).

A **SECOND ALTERNATE <u>SOUTH</u> ROUTE** is from the east on Highway 2.

Take Highway 2 west about 28 miles from Highway 95 in the town of Sandpoint to LeClerc Creek Road, which will be on the right at Highway 2 mile 0.5.

At mile 0.5, just before you reach the bridge over the Pend Oreille River, turn right onto LeClerc Creek Road.

From here follow the directions provided above from the point marked with a double asterisk(**).

**NOTE:** In 1997, the Pend Oreille River reached elevations that flooded LeClerc Creek Road. When LeClerc Creek Road is not available, there is another route that can be used for access.

East of Newport at Idaho Highway 2 mile 2.3 is the Albeni Falls Machine Shop on the north side of the road. Freeman Lake Road, a gravel road, heads north next to the shop.

Take this road to access Marshall Lake Road, which will be reached after 6.2 miles. Freeman Lake Road becomes Bench Road before you reach the end.

Turn right, and take Marshall Lake Road 6.0 miles to the "Y" intersection.

From here follow the directions above from the point marked with a triple asterisk(***).

<u>FISHING TIPS</u>:

Bank fishermen using bait favor the point on the north shore because of its access to deep water.

Boat fishermen get fish trolling along the shorelines on the south side of the lake.

Neither of these tips apply when the lake almost dries up.

<u>MAP REFERENCES</u>:

*USGS Topographic Map, Washington (48117-C2-TF-024-00)
   Skookum Creek Quadrangle, 7.5 Minute Series.

*USGS Topographic Map, Washington (48117-A1-TM-100-00)
   Chewelah Quadrangle, 30x60 Minute Series.
*Washington Atlas & Gazetteer, Page 105.

## 21  CRESCENT LAKE

September 18, 2000; Crescent Lake, looking southwest.

SIZE: 21.6 Acres
ELEVATION: 2,503 Feet
MAXIMUM DEPTH: 80 Feet
COUNTY: Pend Oreille, Washington
COORDINATES: T40N R43E Sec12BC

Longitude: 117d 18m 26s to 117d 18m 52s West
Latitude: 48d 59m 6s to 48d 59m 18s North

SPECIES, CONFIRMED:
 Rainbow Trout

SPECIES, REPORTED:

CHARACTERISTICS:
 There are low, heavily timbered hills all around the lake. The hill that rises over the southwest end has areas of exposed vertical tock that show through the timber.
 Highway 31 runs along most of the southeast side of the lake, but is well above the water.

On the north end, where the paved Crescent Lake Road runs, the slopes have been cut for the road.

A gravel road runs the length of the northwest side. The road is separated from the lake by a low bank, and is only two or three feet above the water in most places. The area along the road has a few small trees and bushes, and one large tree at mid lake. There is a lot of bank access in the area.

There was once a campground with boat launch on the south shore. As of the fall of 2000, the road that had reached the camp area was blocked off with boulders about half way down the northwest side of the lake, with only pedestrian access beyond that point.

It was reported that in the winter of 1999-2000 the lake level had risen to flood the campground area.

The shorelines on the southeast side are steep and brushy. There is a clear strip of shore right along the waters edge late in the year when the water level is at its lowest. The strip has rock, gravel and some grass.

Snags extend into the lake in some of the areas bordering timber that runs to the waters edge. Many more lie on the bottom, and some rise almost to the surface or rise above it. The submerged snags have a whitish color from the alkaline water.

There are heavy growths of aquatic vegetation in the shallows around the lake. Very little of it reaches the surface. Most of the bottom is covered with a thick carpet of low, ground hugging vegetation.

The bottom, where not obscured by the mat of weeds, is silt with some rock and gravel.

The water is extremely clear.

## DIRECTIONS TO:

Take Highway 20 about 47 miles north from the town of Newport, to where it makes a 90-degree turn to the left at mile 390.4, and runs west toward the town of Colville. At this corner is the junction with Highway 31, which goes to the north.

Take Highway 31 north for about 26 miles to mile 25.7, where Crescent Lake Road will be found on the left. Highway 31 continues past the lake to reach Canada after just another mile.

Turn onto Crescent Lake Road, which starts at the northeast corner of the lake. Take it to the gravel access road at the northwest corner.

## FISHING TIPS:

Bank fisherman usually fish Powerbait or worms, and they get fish. I caught fish casting a spinner.

MISCELLANEOUS NOTES:

The end of Crescent Lake Road is signed for "Seattle City Light Boundary Dam Viewpoint". The road is paved for the couple of miles to the viewpoint, but is narrow in places. It's worth taking a few minutes to see the dam.

MAP REFERENCES:
*USGS Topographic Map, Washington (48117-H3-TF-024-00)
  Boundary Dam Quadrangle, 7.5 Minute Series.
*USGS Topographic Map, Washington (48117-E1-TM-100-00)
  Colville Quadrangle, 30x60 Minute Series.
*Washington Atlas & Gazetteer, Page 119.

## 22  DAVIS LAKE

May 22, 1995; Davis Lake, looking northwest from Highway 211.

SIZE: 145.9 Acres
ELEVATION: 2,178 Feet
MAXIMUM DEPTH: 146 Feet
COUNTY: Pend Oreille, Washington
COORDINATES: T31/32N R44E Sec31G

Longitude: 117d 17m 15s to 117d 17m 52s West
Latitude: 48d 13m 12s to 48d 13m 55s North

SPECIES, CONFIRMED:
 Rainbow Trout

SPECIES, REPORTED:
 Cutthroat Trout
 Eastern Brook Trout
 Kokanee

CHARACTERISTICS:
 Highway 211 runs down the east side of the lake. Along the highway, the shores are steep with large rock. A turnout at the southeast corner offers good access to the water for bank fishing.

The west shore is mostly steep rock. The south end has low brush and a large marshy area.

Homes are found along the north end, at the southwest corner, and at the center of the east shore.

The lake is surrounded by low hills dotted with pines, and with much exposed rock.

The bottom is rocky.

The water is clear, but has a light brown stain.

## DIRECTIONS TO:

Take Highway 2 to mile 321.2, between Spokane and Newport, where Highway 211 is reached on the west side of the highway. This junction is at Highway 211 mile 0.0.

Turn left onto Highway 211 and go north. A turnout will be reached at Highway 211 mile 9.1. This turnout offers good access for bank fishing at the southeast corner of the lake.

The public access area is at the north end at mile 9.9. It has a boat ramp, gravel parking area and pit toilets.

## FISHING TIPS:

Most bank fishermen use Power Bait. If you get out on the lake, troll spinners or flies. If fish are rising, flies cast to them are very effective.

## MAP REFERENCES:

*USGS Topographic Map, Washington (48117-B3-TF-024-00)
    Sacheen Lake Quadrangle, 7.5 Minute Series.
*USGS Topographic Map, Washington (48117-A1-TM-100-00)
    Chewelah Quadrangle, 30x60 Minute Series.
*Washington Atlas & Gazetteer, Page 105.

## 23   DAWSON LAKE

September 5, 2001; Dawson Lake, looking south.

SIZE: 35 Acres
ELEVATION: 2,959 Feet
MAXIMUM DEPTH: Unknown
COUNTY: Boundary, Idaho
COORDINATES: T63N R2E Sec29MN,32D

Longitude: 116d 14m 14s to 116d 14m 26s West
Latitude: 48d 46m 29s to 48d 46m 55s North


SPECIES, CONFIRMED:
 Black Crappie
 Bluegill
 Pumpkinseed Sunfish
 Yellow Perch

SPECIES, REPORTED:
 Largemouth Bass
 Tiger Muskie

## CHARACTERISTICS:

The lake lies in a fairly flat area with timber covered hills visible to the north, and lower hills over the west side. The surrounding area is completely and heavily timbered with a mixture of fir and pine.

The shorelines on the east and west sides have timber and brush to the waters edge. Most areas are lined with cattails and lilypads.

The south end and northwest half of the lake have many snags. Snags are also scattered along the southwest half, where some along the waters edge are still standing. Many downed snags line the shores, and several extend out into the lake.

The shores at the north and south ends have low marshy areas, large beds of lilypads, and dense beds of aquatic vegetation. Dense aquatic vegetation is found in most shallow shoreline areas.

The first access area is located at the center of the east shore, in a very nice setting of fairly open pines. The area has a fishing dock and two picnic tables, but no boat access or facilities. This area is suitable for launching of float tubes or rafts, but not boats.

The main access area is found at the northeast corner. It has a fishing dock and a concrete strip boat ramp, limited parking at a small gravel parking area, and a pit toilet. The dock at this location isn't as nice as the other one.

Out from the main access area at the northeast corner is a very heavy growth of aquatic vegetation. The lilypad beds north of the main access are very extensive.

An active beaver lodge is found at the center of the north shore, on a grassy strip between the open water and the large lilypad beds further north.

The remains of an old log cabin can be seen in a field a couple of hundred yards north of the main access.

The water has a slight brownish color.

## DIRECTIONS TO:

Take Interstate 90 to exit 12, at the town of Coeur d'Alene.

From exit 12, take Highway 95 north for about 79 miles to mile 510.4, where the intersection with Highway 2 will be reached north of the town of Bonners Ferry.

Turn right onto Highway 2, and go east for 1.9 miles to mile 66.3, where a road will be found on the left. The end of the road is signed for "Sportsman's Access" and "Dawson Lake".

Turn left onto the road, and go north for 4.1 miles to a turnout above the center of Dawson Lake, on the left. This turnout provides parking for the first access area.

To reach the main access area at the northeast corner of the lake, continue on another 0.2 miles. The main access area is also on the left.

FISHING TIPS:

During summer months the panfish will take small jigs and spinnerbaits fished off the edges of the weed beds. There are nice Crappie present.

Bait fishermen soaking worms at the fishing docks also get some fish.

MAP REFERENCES:

*Idaho Atlas & Gazetteer, Page 48, 62.

*USGS Topographic Map, Idaho (48116-G2-TF-024-00)
  Meadow Creek Quadrangle, 7.5 Minute Series.

*USGS Topographic Map, Idaho (48116-E1-TM-100-00)
  Bonners Ferry Quadrangle, 30x60 Minute Series.

# 24  DEEP LAKE

May 10, 2005; Deep Lake, looking southwest from the public access.

SIZE: 198.1 Acres
ELEVATION: 2,025 Feet
MAXIMUM DEPTH: 48 Feet
COUNTY: Stevens, Washington
COORDINATES: T39N R40E Sec22R,23N,26DEM,27(east 1/2),34BC

Longitude: 117d 35m 53s to 117d 36m 56s West
Latitude: 48d 51m 0s to 48d 52m 3s North

SPECIES, CONFIRMED:
Cutthroat Trout, West Slope

SPECIES, REPORTED:
Eastern Brook Trout
Rainbow Trout

CHARACTERISTICS:
The lake lies in an area of low, timbered hills. At the north end the timber cover becomes more sparse, and the hills have a lot more rock showing through.

There is a fairly large community at the south end of the lake, as well as scattered but heavy development up both the east and west sides of the lake. There are homes along shore and also set back into the trees above.

The north end of the lake has large undeveloped meadow areas. An inlet stream enters at the center of the north end.

The north end of the lake has a shallow, mud bottomed flat. Beds of lily-pads and aquatic weed are found along the shorelines.

The lake has both a public access, located near the northeast corner, and a resort, located south of the public access. The public access has a good-sized gravel parking area, pit toilets and a concrete strip boat ramp. The area is signed for no overnight parking or camping.

A paved two-lane road runs the length of the east side of the lake, but is well away from the water everywhere except at the northeast corner. It offers no access to the water.

The shorelines are mostly steep. The slopes are a little more gentle on the east side than the west. There are a few snags along the wooded shorelines, but few elsewhere.

The bottom is mostly silt, with some rock and gravel. There are some growths of aquatic vegetation in the shallows.

The water is very clear.

## DIRECTIONS TO:

Deep Lake is fairly remote, but can be reached via several routes. The major routes are detailed. The route from **COLVILLE** is the primary route.

### FROM COLVILLE:

Take Highway 20 east out of the town of Colville, and watch for Aladdin Road, on the north side of the highway at Highway 20 mile 355.5.

Take Aladdin Road north for 24.8 miles to the intersection with Deep Lake-Boundary Road, on the right at the "town" of Spirit.

Turn onto Deep Lake-Boundary Road, and take it north for 3.7 miles to the public access area for Deep Lake, on the left.

### FROM NORTHPORT:

Take combined Highway 20 / Highway 395 to mile 239.1, where the intersection with Highway 25 will be reached. The intersection is on the east side of the Columbia River, and at the western side of the town of Kettle Falls.

Turn onto Highway 25 North, and take it about 32 miles to the town of Northport, where the north end of Colville-Aladdin-Northport Road will be found, on the right.

Turn onto Colville-Aladdin-Northport Road, and take it southeast for about nine miles to the intersection with Deep Lake-Boundary Road, on the left at the "town" of Spirit.

Turn onto Deep Lake-Boundary Road, and take it north for 3.7 miles to the public access area for Deep Lake, on the left.

### FROM THE NORTH:

Take combined Highway 20 / Highway 395 to mile 239.1, where the intersection with Highway 25 will be reached. The intersection is on the east side of the Columbia River, and at the western side of the town of Kettle Falls.

Turn onto Highway 25 North, and take it 32.8 miles, through the town of Northport, to where Northport-Waneta Road will be found, on the right, just before you reach the bridge over the Columbia River.

Turn onto Northport-Waneta Road and take it 21.4 miles to the public access area for Deep Lake, on the right.

The access for Cedar Lake will be passed at 15.6 miles, also on the right.

FISHING TIPS:

Flies trolled at the north end are effective.

MAP REFERENCES:

*USGS Topographic Map, Washington (48117-G5-TF-024-00)
   Deep Lake Quadrangle, 7.5 Minute Series.
*USGS Topographic Map, Washington (48117-E1-TM-100-00)
   Colville Quadrangle, 30x60 Minute Series.
*Washington Atlas & Gazetteer, Page 118.

## 25  DEER LAKE

May 23, 2002; Deer Lake, looking southeast.

SIZE: 1,162.8 Acres
ELEVATION: 2,478 Feet
MAXIMUM DEPTH: 75 Feet
COUNTY: Stevens, Washington
COORDINATES: T30N R41E Sec1(south 1/2),11(east 2/3),12(southwest 1/2), 13(north 1/2),14(northeast 1/4)

Longitude: 117d 34m 3s to 117d 36m 18s West
Latitude: 48d 5m 56s to 48d 7m 46s North

SPECIES, CONFIRMED:

SPECIES, REPORTED:
 Black Crappie
 Brown Bullhead Catfish
 Eastern Brook Trout
 Kokanee
 Largemouth Bass
 Mackinaw
 Rainbow Trout
 Smallmouth Bass

Yellow Perch

## CHARACTERISTICS:

The lake lies in an area of low hills. Deer Lake Mountain rises to the south. It is timbered, but heavily logged above the lake. The hills in the distance to the east include Blue Grouse Mountain. Blue Grouse is timbered, densely in some places and sparsely in others. Roads are visible cutting some of the hills. Bald Mountain rises to the north.

The lake has an almost rectangular shape, broken up by two good-sized points extending from the west half of the south end. There is also a large arm that reaches for almost a mile toward the northeast from the northeast corner of the lake.

The public access area, located at the center of the west side, has a large gravel parking area, pit toilets and a concrete strip boat ramp.

The area south of the public access is heavily developed. The homes are separated from the access area by a large marshy area. The lake drains at this marsh.

There is development all around the lake, with just scattered undeveloped shoreline areas remaining. Most of the homes have docks extending out into the lake.

There is a bog covering about 100 acres at the northeast end. There is a seasonal inlet that enters through the marsh.

An inlet stream enters at the end of the arm to the northeast. Other small, seasonal inlet streams enter at various places around the lake.

The bottom is mostly silt, with small rock and gravel.

The water is clear.

## DIRECTIONS TO:

Take Highway 395 to mile 193.7, between the towns of Deer Park and Chewelah, where you will find North Deer Lake Road on the east side of the highway. North Deer Lake Road is about 35 miles south of the town of Colville.

Turn onto North Deer Lake Road, and go east for 1.7 miles to an intersection that is signed for public access.

Turn left at the intersection, and go 0.1 mile to the entrance to the public access area, on the right.

**NOTE:** The maps and signs use both "North Deer Lake Road" and "Deer Lake Road North". The discrepancy is confusing since the difference can be meaningful in most places, but here it is the same road.

## FISHING TIPS:

I did not attempt to fish this lake.

MAP REFERENCES:
*USGS Topographic Map, Washington (48117-B5-TF-024-00)
 Nelson Peak Quadrangle, 7.5 Minute Series.
*USGS Topographic Map, Washington (48117-A5-TF-024-00)
 Deer Lake Quadrangle, 7.5 Minute Series.
*USGS Topographic Map, Washington (48117-A1-TM-100-00)
 Chewelah Quadrangle, 30x60 Minute Series.
*Washington Atlas & Gazetteer, Page 104.

## 26  EAST ROMAN NOSE LAKE
Also known as: First Roman Nose Lake

August 21, 2002; East Roman Nose Lake, looking south.

SIZE: 12 Acres (estimated)
ELEVATION: 5,891 Feet
MAXIMUM DEPTH: Unknown
COUNTY: Boundary, Idaho
COORDINATES: T61N R2W Sec15R

      Longitude: 116d 34m 12s to 116d 34m 24s West
      Latitude: 48d 37m 54s to 48d 38m 3s North


SPECIES, CONFIRMED:
 Cutthroat Trout, West Slope
 Rainbow Trout

SPECIES, REPORTED:

CHARACTERISTICS:
 Vertical rock rises over the south end of the lake. It gives way to near vertical rock and boulder fields. At the bottom of the hill are broken rock

slopes. There are some areas among the rock that are covered with low brush. There are very few trees in this area.

The steep slopes continue around the southeast corner and down the east side of the lake. As you move north the amount of vegetation present gradually increases, until you get to the north end of the lake where there are a lot of very small fir trees.

The west side also has rocky slopes, but they are lower with a lot more brush and timber cover.

The slopes drop away quickly to the northwest, and more gradually to the northeast, where the road and trail to the lake come in.

A dense stand of large fir trees is found at the southwest corner. In all other areas the firs around the lake are much smaller.

The area was burned in the Sundance fire of 1967, and standing snags can be seen on most of the slopes.

An outlet creek exits at the north end, flowing to Caribou Creek. The parking area for access to this lake, and to the trailhead for the other two, is located next to the creek and about 150 yards north of the lake. A nice boardwalk runs the entire distance from the parking area to the lake. It also branches to a fishing platform found at the northeast corner. The parking area is day use only, and has a concrete pit toilet.

The camping area for Roman Nose Lakes is located on a spur road on the hillside above the northeast corner. A trail runs from the fishing platform at the northeast corner to the camping area.

On the ridgeline to the west is a small saddle about 350 feet above the lake. It has many large boulders scattered on it, as well as a lot of low brush and a sparse covering of small timber. This saddle is where the trail to the other lakes crosses.

The shorelines are mostly gently sloped, with exceptions at the southeast corner where broken rock reaches to the waters edge, and at the extreme south end where there are large boulders.

The shorelines at the north end are fairly open.

The shorelines along the east and west sides are brushy, although most of the brush is fairly low. These shorelines also have a lot of boulders and snags on them. There are trees to the waters edge in places.

There are a lot of snags around the lake. The shorelines are almost completely lined with them. The fewest snags are found at the rocky shores of the southeast corner.

A large concentration of snags has drifted into the mouth of the outlet stream at the north end, with a small logjam spanning the creek. A large number of snags are submerged in the area.

The bottom is silt with a lot of rock showing through it. Most of the rock is large.

The water is extremely clear.

## DIRECTIONS TO:

### From the north:

Take Highway 95 to mile 507.5, at the town of Bonners Ferry, where Riverside Road will be found on the west side of the highway just south of the bridge over the Kootenai River. The end of the road is signed for "Kootenai Wildlife Refuge 6 Miles".

Turn onto Riverside, and head west out of Bonners Ferry, keeping to the right as the road follows the banks of the river.

At 5.0 miles from Highway 95 the road will reach the base of the foothills, and a "Y" intersection.

Turn to the left, onto the gravel road, West Side Road, which will run south.

Go approximately 2.8 miles to the end of Forest Service Road 402, on the right. As you start up Road 402 a sign indicates "Cooks Pass 13", "Little Creek 18", and "Roman Nose Lakes 20".

*Turn onto Road 402, Snow Creek Road, and go 16.2 miles to Ruby Pass, staying on the main road for the distance. Some parts of the road, especially where it climbs, are badly washboarded.

At Ruby Pass, you will come to Road 2667, on the right. The end of the road is signed for "Roman Nose Lakes 2 Miles". The continuation of the road straight ahead is signed "Naples 13 Miles".

Turn right onto Road 2667, and in 0.5 miles you will come to an intersection with Road 294, on the left. The road to the right is signed "1.7 Miles to East Roman Nose Lake" and "3 Miles to Lower Roman Nose Lake".

Keep to the right, and at 1.3 miles from Ruby Pass you will reach another intersection. Keep to the right again.

At 1.8 miles is another road on the left. This one is signed for "Camp Area", and "Narrow Steep Road, No Trailers". This road runs 0.2 miles, with campsites and a pit toilet along it.

Keep to the right to reach the parking area for the trailheads for Roman Nose Lakes. This parking lot is posted "No Overnight Camping". It has a concrete pit toilet, and a signboard with a map of the trail system.

There are two trails that exit from the parking area.

From the far end of the parking lot, to the left of the pit toilet, is a board-walk that runs the entire distance to East Roman Nose Lake. The distance is about 150 yards or so. Take this "trail".

The second trail leaves from the center of the parking lot, on the right. It runs to Upper Roman Nose Lake and Lower Roman Nose Lake.

**From the south:**

Take Interstate 90 to exit 12, at the town of Coeur d'Alene.

From exit 12, take Highway 95 north for about 67 miles to mile 496.8, where a road on the left exits for the town of Naples.

Turn off of Highway 95 here, and go 6.3 miles to West Side Road, on the left. The end of the road is signed "Snow Creek Road 2 Miles", "Kootenai National Wildlife Refuge 5 Miles".

Turn left onto West Side Road, and go 2.0 miles to Forest Service Road 402, Snow Creek Road, on the left.

From here, follow the direction above from the point marked with an asterisk(*).

FISHING TIPS:

Flies cast from shore are very effective.

MISCELLANEOUS NOTES:

Planting records indicate that the lake received 1,155 Hayspur Triploid Rainbow Trout on September 16, 2000.

On my visit to this lake in August 2002, a bull moose fed along the shores of the lake, spending the entire evening in the area before bedding down within sight of the parking area.

MAP REFERENCES:

*Idaho Atlas & Gazetteer, Page 62 (name not indicated).
*USGS Topographic Map, Idaho (48116-F5-TF-024-00)
  Roman Nose Quadrangle, 7.5 Minute Series.
*USGS Topographic Map, Idaho (48116-E1-TM-100-00)
  Bonners Ferry Quadrangle, 30x60 Minute Series.

## 27  ELBOW LAKE, NORTH
Also known as: Crown Lake

May 10, 2005; Elbow Lake, North, lower end looking northwest.

SIZE: 7.1 Acres
ELEVATION: 2,880 Feet
MAXIMUM DEPTH: Unknown
COUNTY: Stevens, Washington
COORDINATES: T40N R38E Sec21KQ

Longitude: 117d 58m 55s to 117d 59m 10s West
Latitude: 48d 56m 57s to 48d 57m 5s North

SPECIES, CONFIRMED:

SPECIES, REPORTED:
Eastern Brook Trout

CHARACTERISTICS:
Elbow Lake consists of two separate lakes, separated by a marshy area. The northern lake covers 7.1 acres, and drains through the marsh at its south end to the southern lake, which covers 6.4 acres.

The lake has a campground located at its southeastern corner. The campground has just a few sites. The sites have fire pits and parking, but no picnic tables. There is a new (cast date 11-14-2003) pit toilet at the center of the loop road. The campground is in a deteriorating state of repair that suggests it is no longer as popular as it once was. A good trail, about 200 feet long, drops from the campground to near the northeast corner of the south lake, but no good trails run to the north lake.

The lake is the headwaters of the west fork of Crown Creek. An outlet exits at the south end of the lake, flowing to the southern lake. A strip of scrub trees and timber separate the northern lake from the one to the south.

The north lake has the "elbow" shape that gives the lakes their name. It runs north to south, and has a hook to the east at the north end. The portion of the lake that runs east extends about 150 yards from the main body of the lake. The lake has a fairly uniform width for its entire length.

The northeast corner of the lake has a large marshy area at its end, with a dense growth of grasses lining the shorelines.

A steep ridge that rises over the west side wraps around the north end of the lake, and then runs to the east. The southeast side of the lake folds around a knob that forms the end of a ridge. The slopes of the knob form the steep ground that rises over the east side of the lake, and the south side of its east to west run.

The entire lake is shallow and snag filled. The lower hundred yards of the lake has a large concentration of snags both on the surface and lying on the bottom. The deepest spots are found along the west side of the lake, but they are also shallow.

Small beds of lilypads are scattered randomly around the lake, although most are along the east shore. Timber and brush reach to the waters edge at all but the ends of the lake.

The bottom is silt, covered with a growth of aquatic vegetation.

The water is very clear.


DIRECTIONS TO:

Elbow Lake can be reached from two major routes, both of which have Highway 20 as a starting point. They are from the west from Highway 395, and from the east from Highway 25. The road conditions are better from the west.


**FROM THE EAST:**

Take combined Highway 20 / Highway 395 to mile 239.1, where the intersection with Highway 25 will be reached. The intersection is on the east side of the Columbia River, and at the western side of the town of Kettle Falls.

Turn onto Highway 25 North, and take it 33.6 miles, through the town of Northport and over the Columbia River, to Sheep Creek Road, on the left at mile 114.7.

This intersection is a double intersection, with paved Flat Creek Road to the hard left, and unpaved Sheep Creek Road to the left. The intersection is signed for "Sheep Creek Campground".

Turn left, onto Sheep Creek Road, and follow it west.

At 0.5 miles you will pass a dirt race track, on the left.

At 3.0 miles you will pass a well used road, on the left.

At 4.2 miles you will pass Sheep Creek Campground, on the right.

At 4.3 miles you will pass a Placer Mining historical marker, on the right.

At 8.4 miles you will reach a major intersection. As of 2005, the number "9" was painted on the trees here. Keep to the left.

At 8.5 miles is a marker identifying the road as Forest Service Road 15.

At 9.8 miles, just past a cattleguard, is milepost 14.

At 9.9 miles is a road to the right, keep left.

At 10.6 miles is a marker saying you are entering the Colville National Forest.

At 10.7 miles is milepost 13.

At 11.1 miles is another cattleguard.

At 11.2 miles is a large cross intersection. The road to the right is marked as FS 670. The road to the left is unmarked. Continue straight ahead.

At 11.3 miles is an unnamed lake, to the right.

At 12.1 miles is another cattleguard.

At 12.3 miles is a road on the left, the end of which is signed for Elbow Lake.

Turn here, and take the road 0.3 miles to the entrance to the old Elbow Lake Campground. The loop road reaches its far end in another 0.1 mile.

The end of the road at Elbow Lake is a total of 12.7 miles from Highway 25, and 46.3 miles from where you left Highway 20.

### **FROM THE WEST:**

Take Highway 20 to the junction with Highway 395 on west end of the bridge over the Columbia River at Kettle Falls. The junction is at Highway 395 mile 241.9.

From the junction, go north on Highway 395 for 22 miles to Rock Cut Road, on right at mile 263.8. Rock Cut Road is reached 3.6 miles past Main Street of the town of Orient. On the opposite side of the road from the end of Rock Cut Road is Little Boulder Road. The end of Rock Cut Road is signed for Pierre Lake.

Turn onto Rock Cut Road, and take it northeast. It will pass through a single lane railroad underpass, then cross the Kettle River before climbing. At 0.4 miles from Highway 395, the road you are on becomes Sand Creek Road, and Rock Cut Road turns to the left.

Stay on Sand Creek Road until, at 3.9 miles from Highway 395, it reaches an intersection at a 90-degree corner and pavement starts. Here Sand Creek Road becomes Pierre Lake Road and turns to the south. At this intersection, the gravel road on the left is Churchill Mine Road.

Turn onto Churchill Mine Road, and you will immediately pass the end of Box Canyon Road, on the left. The end of Box Canyon Road is signed for Summit Lake.

Take Churchill Mine Road east for 1.3 miles to a large four-way intersection. Straight ahead is signed "Sheep Creek 12", "Northport 22". To the left is signed "Sheep Creek 14", Northport 24", "Forest Service Road 15". The road to the right is unmarked.

Turn left, onto Forest Service Road 15.
At 3.5 miles is milepost 5.
At 7.1 miles you will cross a cattleguard.
At 7.4 miles is milepost 9.
At 8.0 miles is an intersection with two roads on the right. Keep left, remaining on the main road.
At 8.1 miles is another intersection. Here the right is identified as FS 15, and signed "Elbow Lake" and "Northport". Take the right, remaining on FS 15.
At 8.4 miles is milepost 10.
At 9.7 miles is a road on the right signed for Elbow Lake.
Turn here, and take the road 0.3 miles to the entrance to the old Elbow Lake Campground. The loop road reaches its far end in another 0.1 mile.

The end of the road at Elbow Lake is a total of 15.3 miles from Highway 395, and 37.3 miles from where you left Highway 20.

A good trail drops from the campground area to the south lake. To reach the north lake you can just head north through the trees, or go up the near shore at the northeast corner of the south lake. Either way is an easy walk.

FISHING TIPS:
I did not attempt to fish this lake. On my one visit there I saw no evidence of fish presence, but the substantial amount of cover and the presence of Eastern Brook in the south lake makes it likely they are also in this water.

MAP REFERENCES:
*USGS Topographic Map, Washington (48117-H8-TF-024-00)
  Belshazzar Mountain Quadrangle, 7.5 Minute Series.
*USGS Topographic Map, Washington (48117-E1-TM-100-00)
  Colville Quadrangle, 30x60 Minute Series.
*Washington Atlas & Gazetteer, Page 118.

## 28  ELBOW LAKE, SOUTH
Also known as: Crown Lake

May 10, 2005; Elbow Lake, South, looking south.

SIZE: 6.4 Acres
ELEVATION: 2,875 Feet
MAXIMUM DEPTH: Unknown
COUNTY: Stevens, Washington
COORDINATES: T40N R38E Sec21KQ

> Longitude: 117d 58m 53s to 117d 59m 3s West
> Latitude: 48d 56m 42s to 48d 56m 55s North

SPECIES, CONFIRMED:
 Eastern Brook Trout

SPECIES, REPORTED:

CHARACTERISTICS:
 Elbow Lake consists of two separate lakes, separated by a marshy area. The northern lake covers 7.1 acres, and drains through the marsh at its south end to the southern lake, which covers 6.4 acres.

The lake has a campground located at its northeastern corner. The campground has just a few sites. The sites have fire pits and parking, but no picnic tables. There is a new (cast date 11-14-2003) pit toilet at the center of the loop road. The campground is in a deteriorating state of repair that suggests it is no longer as popular as it once was. A good trail, about 200 feet long, drops from the campground to near the northeast corner of the lake.

The lake is the headwaters of the west fork of Crown Creek, which exits at the south end of the lake. An inlet from the northern lake enters at the north end.

The lake is long and narrow, running from north to south in a steep walled canyon. The skyline is open to the south, and closed by a ridgeline to the north.

The shorelines are steep, except at the north and south ends of the lake. The north end shorelines are grassy. A strip of scrub trees and timber separate the southern lake from the one to the north. The north end also has a shallow flat with beds of lilypads and several snags, both floating and submerged.

The south end has shallows with a large number of surface snags, some of which completely span the lake and isolate the extreme south end.

The east side has trees and brush to the waters edge, below steep slopes that also hold trees and brush.

The west side has trees and brush at the waters edge at the northern half, and slopes of broken rock in the southern half. Above the broken rock of the west shores are steep slopes with sparse timber and areas of vertical and near vertical rock.

There are a lot of snags scattered randomly along both shores. Where the trail reaches the lake near the northeast corner is a large snag, still holding large limbs, that extends straight out into the lake and is mostly submerged.

The center of the lake is deep water.

The bottom is silt in most places, and rock along the southwest slopes.

The water is very clear.

## DIRECTIONS TO:

Elbow Lake can be reached from two major routes, both of which have Highway 20 as a starting point. They are from the west from Highway 395, and from the east from Highway 25. The road conditions are better from the west.

## **FROM THE EAST:**

Take combined Highway 20 / Highway 395 to mile 239.1, where the intersection with Highway 25 will be reached. The intersection is on the east side of the Columbia River, and at the western side of the town of Kettle Falls.

Turn onto Highway 25 North, and take it 33.6 miles, through the town of Northport and over the Columbia River, to Sheep Creek Road, on the left at mile 114.7.

This intersection is a double intersection, with paved Flat Creek Road to the hard left, and unpaved Sheep Creek Road to the left. The intersection is signed for "Sheep Creek Campground".

Turn left, onto Sheep Creek Road, and follow it west.

At 0.5 miles you will pass a dirt race track, on the left.

At 3.0 miles you will pass a well used road, on the left.

At 4.2 miles you will pass Sheep Creek Campground, on the right.

At 4.3 miles you will pass a Placer Mining historical marker, on the right.

At 8.4 miles you will reach a major intersection. As of 2005, the number "9" was painted on the trees here. Keep to the left.

At 8.5 miles is a marker identifying the road as Forest Service Road 15.

At 9.8 miles, just past a cattleguard, is milepost 14.

At 9.9 miles is a road to the right, keep left.

At 10.6 miles is a marker saying you are entering the Colville National Forest.

At 10.7 miles is milepost 13.

At 11.1 miles is another cattleguard.

At 11.2 miles is a large cross intersection. The road to the right is marked as FS 670. The road to the left is unmarked. Continue straight ahead.

At 11.3 miles is an unnamed lake, to the right.

At 12.1 miles is another cattleguard.

At 12.3 miles is a road on the left, the end of which is signed for Elbow Lake.

Turn here, and take the road 0.3 miles to the entrance to the old Elbow Lake Campground. The loop road reaches its far end in another 0.1 mile.

The end of the road at Elbow Lake is a total of 12.7 miles from Highway 25, and 46.3 miles from where you left Highway 20.

### FROM THE WEST:

Take Highway 20 to the junction with Highway 395 on west end of the bridge over the Columbia River at Kettle Falls. The junction is at Highway 395 mile 241.9.

From the junction, go north on Highway 395 for 22 miles to Rock Cut Road, on right at mile 263.8. Rock Cut Road is reached 3.6 miles past Main

Street of the town of Orient. On the opposite side of the road from the end of Rock Cut Road is Little Boulder Road. The end of Rock Cut Road is signed for Pierre Lake.

Turn onto Rock Cut Road, and take it northeast. It will pass through a single lane railroad underpass, then cross the Kettle River before climbing. At 0.4 miles from Highway 395, the road you are on becomes Sand Creek Road, and Rock Cut Road turns to the left.

Stay on Sand Creek Road until, at 3.9 miles from Highway 395, it reaches an intersection at a 90-degree corner and pavement starts. Here Sand Creek Road becomes Pierre Lake Road and turns to the south. At this intersection, the gravel road on the left is Churchill Mine Road.

Turn onto Churchill Mine Road, and you will immediately pass the end of Box Canyon Road, on the left. The end of Box Canyon Road is signed for Summit Lake.

Take Churchill Mine Road east for 1.3 miles to a large four-way intersection. Straight ahead is signed "Sheep Creek 12", "Northport 22". To the left is signed "Sheep Creek 14", Northport 24", "Forest Service Road 15". The road to the right is unmarked.

Turn left, onto Forest Service Road 15.

At 3.5 miles is milepost 5.

At 7.1 miles you will cross a cattleguard.

At 7.4 miles is milepost 9.

At 8.0 miles is an intersection with two roads on the right. Keep left, remaining on the main road.

At 8.1 miles is another intersection. Here the right is identified as FS 15, and signed "Elbow Lake" and "Northport". Take the right, remaining on FS 15.

At 8.4 miles is milepost 10.

At 9.7 miles is a road on the right signed for Elbow Lake.

Turn here, and take the road 0.3 miles to the entrance to the old Elbow Lake Campground. The loop road reaches its far end in another 0.1 mile.

The end of the road at Elbow Lake is a total of 15.3 miles from Highway 395, and 37.3 miles from where you left Highway 20.

FISHING TIPS:

Fish take both flies and spinners very readily. Flies were especially effective in the evening when the fish were actively feeding. In the cool morning, when there was almost no surface activity, small spinners were more effective.

MAP REFERENCES:

*USGS Topographic Map, Washington (48117-H8-TF-024-00)
  Belshazzar Mountain Quadrangle, 7.5 Minute Series.
*USGS Topographic Map, Washington (48117-E1-TM-100-00)
  Colville Quadrangle, 30x60 Minute Series.
*Washington Atlas & Gazetteer, Page 118.

## 29  LAKE ELSIE

September 6, 1997; Lake Elsie, looking south.

SIZE:  8 Acres
ELEVATION: 5,070 Feet
MAXIMUM DEPTH: Unknown
COUNTY: Shoshone, Idaho
COORDINATES: T47N R3E Sec13C

Longitude: 116d 1m 13s to 116d 1m 28s West
Latitude: 47d 25m 32s to 47d 25m 43s North

SPECIES, CONFIRMED:
 Eastern Brook Trout
 Rainbow Trout

SPECIES, REPORTED:
 Cutthroat Trout

CHARACTERISTICS:

The lake has hills rising over the east, west and south sides, and visible in the distance to the north. They are fairly low, with the highest to the south. The hills are timbered. Those to the south are the most sparsely covered, and have a lot of exposed rock. Some of the exposed rock is vertical.

The shorelines have vertical rock in some areas of the south side, where rocky slopes reach to the waters edge from the large rock above. A couple of smaller vertical rock areas are found in other sections of the shorelines. The north side has a wooded flat and the road that reaches the lake. The road runs to camp areas located along the east shore.

The north end of the lake has a large, shallow flat with dense weed beds. Few of the weeds reach to the surface. In some places snags rise through the weeds. The cover in this area holds fish.

The center and south end of the lake is deep water. On the south side, the shorelines drop off quickly. A shallow cove is found at the southeast corner, and a shallow strip lines the shores along the camp area on the east side. The shallows all have some weed growth. The growth is heavy in some places.

An inlet stream enters the center of the west side, and a seasonal inlet enters the west side through the middle of the camp area. An outlet exits the center of the north side.

There are many snags in the lake, with the heaviest concentration at the north end. The northwest corner has some very large snags that rise above the surface.

The bottom is silt with weeds, and has a large number of snags lying in the mud.

The shorelines are mostly grass and brush, except at the rocky areas of the south side. Access to the water is good at all but the south end and south-west corner.

The water is very clear.

DIRECTIONS TO:

Take Interstate 90 to exit 54, between the towns of Kellogg and Osburn, Idaho.

At exit 54, turn south onto Big Creek Road. Big Creek Road will eventually become Forest Service Road 2354.

Take Road 2354 south for 12.4 miles to lake. Much of the road is rough and narrow and some stretches between turnouts are long.

On road 2354, you will pass the Sunshine Mining Company at 2.3 miles. At this point the road narrows, and is marked for CB channel 7.

You will pass a trailhead marker for Trail #113 on the right at 6.5 miles, and another marker at 6.7 miles.

An access road for Cedars Campground will be passed on the right at 6.9 miles. Road 2354 continues on the left, and is signed "Narrow road not suited for trailer traffic".

The road crests at 11.9 miles from I-90, and drops to reach the north end of the lake at 12.4 miles.

When you reach the lake, keep to the left to enter the camp area after another 0.1 mile.

FISHING TIPS:

Flies worked over the shallow flat and along the outer edges of the weed bed at the north end will get fish. The shorelines also produce some fish, but not many are usually found along the rocky sections. The lakes deeper water is not very productive.

MAP REFERENCES:

*Idaho Atlas & Gazetteer, Page 61 (lake not shown).

*USGS Topographic Map, Idaho (47116-D1-TF-024-00)
  Polaris Peak Quadrangle, 7.5 Minute Series.

*USGS Topographic Map, Idaho (47116-A1-TM-100-00)
  St. Maries Quadrangle, 30x60 Minute Series.

## 30  FAN LAKE

May 23, 2002; Fan Lake, looking northwest.

SIZE: 72.9 Acres
ELEVATION: 1,921 Feet
MAXIMUM DEPTH: 74 Feet
COUNTY: Pend Oreille, Washington
COORDINATES: T30N R43E Sec29N,32(northwest 1/4)

> Longitude: 117d 24m 9s <u>to</u> 117d 24m 45s West
> Latitude: 48d 3m 11s <u>to</u> 48d 3m 48s North

SPECIES, CONFIRMED:
 Yellow Perch

SPECIES, REPORTED:
 Cutthroat Trout
 Rainbow Trout

CHARACTERISTICS:
 The lake lies in an area of low timbered hills. The hills have a mix of fir and pines. The highest hill is to the northwest.

On the hill directly across from the public access area the upper areas are sparsely timbered, and a cross marks a tree near the top. Some rock shows through the sparse timber cover.

The lake is developed along the southwest corner, where Camp Reed is located. A walk gate is found between Camp Reed and the west side of the public access, offering easier access to the area for the Camp Reed patrons.

The shorelines are moderately steep in most places. They are gentle along part of the southeast corner and at the north end.

A road runs close by the southeast corner, but is separated from the water by a cyclone fence and a strip of aquatic weeds.

A narrows at the center of the lake separates a larger and deeper southern section from a smaller and shallower northern section.

After you pass through the narrows to enter the northern section, a large shallow flat lined with cattails and aquatic vegetation is found on the right, on the eastern side of the lake. A smaller shallows holding an old beaver house and a smaller lilypad bed is found on the west side.

The north end is lined with a very heavy bed of cattails and other aquatic vegetation. Open fields are found beyond the shores, and an old barn is visible in the distance. Hills form the background.

The north end shorelines are very brushy. The hills above are timber covered, though sparsely in most places.

A dirt road runs up the east side of the north end, but is well away from the water.

The southern section of the lake has small bays at the south end and the northwest and northeast corners.

A small island is located out from the point next to the small bay at the northeast corner. The island barely rises above the surface of the lake, and is grass covered.

Cattails line most of the shallow shoreline areas, especially at the ends of the small bays.

In some places trees reach to the waters edge, but they set well back from the water in most places, with a border of brush between the trees and the water.

Most of the snags in the lake are found very close to the shores. Very large ones are found on the east side just south of the narrows.

The public access area, located near the southeast corner of the lake, has a good-sized paved parking area, a concrete strip boat launch with a paved approach, and pit toilets. The area is signed for no overnight parking or camping, and as closed from 10 PM to 4 AM. Trails lead to the right from the boat launch, running about a hundred yards and offering limited bank access along the way.

The bottom is primarily silt, with some rock.

The water is very clear.

## DIRECTIONS TO:

Take Highway 2 north from the City of Spokane for about 20 miles to Eloika Lake Road, on the left at mile 312.7.

Turn onto Eloika Lake Road and go west for 3.3 miles to Division Road, a gravel road on the right.

Turn right onto Division Road, and take it 1.5 miles to Insert Road, on the right.

Turn right onto Insert Road, and go east for 0.4 miles to an intersection with Hatch Road. Insert Road ends at this intersection, with Hatch Road both straight ahead and to the right.

Keep to the left, and take Hatch Road 1.2 miles to the entrance to the Fan Lake public access area.

The entrance is on the left, and found just before and to the right of the very well marked entrance to Camp Reed.

The access road runs 0.1 mile to the lake.

An **ALTERNATE ROUTE** to Fan Lake is to take Eloika Lake Road just 2.1 miles from Highway 2, to where Eloika Road will be found on the right.

Turn right onto Eloika Road, and go north for 0.6 miles, to where Eloika Road turns to the left, and Perry Road goes straight ahead.

Turn onto Perry Road, and continue north for 0.5 miles to a 90-degree corner to the right, where the road becomes Oregon Road.

Go west on Oregon Road for 0.5 miles to a second 90-degree corner, this one to the right, where the road now becomes Hatch Road.

Go north on Hatch Road for 0.5 miles to a rough "T" intersection, where Insert Road goes to the left and Hatch Road continues to the right.

Turn right, staying on Hatch Road, and go 1.2 miles to Fan Lake.

This more direct route to Fan Lake is presented as an alternate because it can be very confusing when roads keep changing names every time you turn a corner.

## FISHING TIPS:

Small jigs fished along the weeds at the north end will attract an occasional Perch. On my one visit to this lake fishing was slow.

MAP REFERENCES:
*USGS Topographic Map, Washington (48117-A4-TF-024-00)
  Fan Lake Quadrangle, 7.5 Minute Series.
*USGS Topographic Map, Washington (48117-A1-TM-100-00)
  Chewelah Quadrangle, 30x60 Minute Series.
*Washington Atlas & Gazetteer, Page 105.

## 31  FERNAN LAKE

September 16, 2001; Fernan Lake, looking east.

SIZE: 300 Acres
ELEVATION: 2,125 Feet
MAXIMUM DEPTH: Unknown
COUNTY: Kootenai, Idaho
COORDINATES: T50N R3W Sec16,17(south 1/2),18(southeast 1/4),19AH,20D

> Longitude: 116d 42m 15s to 116d 44m 58s West
> Latitude: 47d 40m 10s to 47d 40m 49s North

SPECIES, CONFIRMED:
 Pumpkinseed Sunfish

SPECIES, REPORTED:
 Bullhead Catfish
 Channel Catfish
 Crappie
 Cutthroat Trout
 Eastern Brook Trout
 Largemouth Bass

Northern Pike
Rainbow Trout
Yellow Perch

## CHARACTERISTICS:

The only major development at the lake is at its northwest corner, where the west end access is located. Here, a heavy concentration of homes is found, and an abundance of docks line the shores.

Fernan Lake Road runs the entire length of the north side. It's close to the water most of the way, but separated from the water by a very steep bank in most places. The banks have a few trees, including some large pines.

The north side has only a couple of homes on it. One is found near the center of the north side at the north end of a small bay, and another at the point of land just to the west.

The north side has many small bays and points. The bays have some large concentrations of snags, many of which extend out into the lake from shore.

The south side of the lake has steep slopes dotted with timber and brush. Some areas have some pretty heavy timber cover, but in most places it's sparse.

Shorelines are very steep and rocky on both the north and south sides of the lake. The shores drop off quickly in all areas except the east and west ends, where shallows are found. The most extensive shallows are at the east end. The east end has a huge bed of lilypads out from the access area found at the northeast corner. A very narrow channel runs through the weeds between the boat ramp and open water.

Power lines cross high over the west end of the lake. One set of lines is equipped with large orange balls for visibility.

The average depth of the lake is reported by the Idaho Department of Fish and Game to be 12 feet.

The water is slightly murky, with a light greenish tinge.

## DIRECTIONS TO:

Take Interstate 90 to exit 15 in Coeur d'Alene, Idaho. At exit 15, Sherman Street, go to the stoplight at the east side of the freeway. If you are westbound, this is the one at the end of the exit lane.

From the westbound exit lane, turn right onto Sherman Drive. If you're eastbound, after you have passed under the freeway, to reach the stoplight go straight ahead.

From the stoplight, go just 0.1 mile to the end of Theis Drive, found on the right just before a "Y" intersection.

Turn onto Theis Drive and take it 0.1 mile to a stop sign.

Go straight at the stop sign, and you will enter the west end public access area in just a hundred yards. This access has a very nice boat ramp and fishing docks, and a paved parking area.

To reach the public access at the east end of the lake:

On Sherman Drive continue past the end of Theis Drive to the "Y" intersection.

At the "Y", take the left fork, Fernan Lake Road. Fernan Lake Road winds its way along the north shore of the lake for 2.5 miles to reach the east end public access area. This access has a poor boat launch, a dock, portable toilets, and a gravel parking area. I don't know if the portable toilets are seasonal or maintained year around.

On its run along the north side of the lake, Fernan Lake Road has several side of the road turnouts that offer bank access, including one at 2.2 miles that is a Department of Fish and Game site with a fishing dock.

FISHING TIPS:

Pumpkinseed can be seen in the shallows along shore, and will respond to small jigs and flies.

On summer weekends the lake attracts a lot of people. Because I prefer less crowded fishing, I didn't spend much time here on my one visit.

MAP REFERENCES:
 *Idaho Atlas & Gazetteer, Page 60.
 *USGS Topographic Map, Idaho (47116-F6-TF-024-00)
  Fernan Lake Quadrangle, 7.5 Minute Series.
 *USGS Topographic Map, Idaho (47116-E1-TM-100-00)
  Coeur d'Alene Quadrangle, 30x60 Minute Series.

## 32   FRATER LAKE

August 22, 2002; Frater Lake, looking west.

SIZE: 11.1 Acres
ELEVATION: 3,205 Feet
MAXIMUM DEPTH: 15 Feet
COUNTY: Pend Oreille, Washington
COORDINATES: T36N R42E Sec3AB

> Longitude: 117d 28m 53s to 117d 29m 11s West
> Latitude: 48d 39m 18s to 48d 39m 26s North

SPECIES, CONFIRMED:

SPECIES, REPORTED:
 Cutthroat Trout

CHARACTERISTICS:
 The lake lies in an area of low, timbered hills.
 There are trees around almost all of the lake, with a grassy area found at a portion of the west shore.
 Almost the entire lake perimeter is brushy with no access. An exception is the southwest corner, where trails from the parking area reach an open point that provides limited bank fishing access.

A small grassy point extends out from the south side.

Shoreline areas are shallow, and have growths of aquatic weed. Beds of lilypads and dollar pads are found in many areas.

The bottom is gravel and silt. The water is clear.

## DIRECTIONS TO:

Take Highway 20 to mile 384.0, east of the town of Colville, where an access area for Frater Lake is located next to the north side of the highway.

The access area has a pit toilet, a nice picnic area, and a large parking area. There is also a boat launch area, but no ramp for trailer access. The access area is posted for no overnight camping.

## FISHING TIPS:

The lake has a small population of fish, and while I have managed to hook a couple on flies, I have yet to land one of them.

## MAP REFERENCES:

*USGS Topographic Map, Washington (48117-F4-TF-024-00)
  Ione Quadrangle, 7.5 Minute Series.
*USGS Topographic Map, Washington (48117-E1-TM-100-00)
  Colville Quadrangle, 30x60 Minute Series.
*Washington Atlas & Gazetteer, Page 119.

## 33  FREEMAN LAKE

May 18, 1997; Freeman Lake, looking north.

SIZE: 30 Acres
ELEVATION: 2,560 Feet (estimated)
MAXIMUM DEPTH: Unknown
COUNTY: Bonner, Idaho
COORDINATES: T56N R6W Sec1PQ,12BC

Longitude: 117d 1m 30s to 117d 1m 56s West
Latitude: 48d 13m 15s to 48d 13m 38s North

SPECIES, CONFIRMED:
 Black Bullhead Catfish
 Black Crappie
 Largemouth Bass
 Pumpkinseed Sunfish
 Rainbow Trout
 Yellow Perch

SPECIES, REPORTED:
  Channel Catfish
  Northern Pike
  Tench
  Tiger Muskie

CHARACTERISTICS:
  There are hills around the lake on all but the south side, which is open. The hills are mostly wooded, but the east side has smaller trees due to old logging activity.
  A gravel road runs along most of the east shore, but is private and provides no access. In some areas the road is just a few feet above the water.
  A house sets above the southeast corner, and another sets far back from the north end of the lake. The house at the southeast corner has a dock at the old access area. The area is now private.
  The public access is found about one third of the way up the west side. It has a grassy camp area, an old pit toilet, a gravel boat ramp and a dock. Bank fishing is available at the access area and at the point to the north, which is reached by trail from the access area.
  The entire lake is fairly shallow. The south end has a large mud flat that is shallower than most other areas. Large beds of lilypads are found in the shallowest areas, and at the lake corners. Large areas are also covered with dollar pads.
  The shorelines at the north and south ends are marshy and lined with cattails. The northeast corner also fits this description, and has an active beaver hut at its center.
  The bottom is silt with heavy growths of aquatic weed in most places. The water is clear.

DIRECTIONS TO:
  From the north, take Highway 20 to the town of Newport, where it will end at mile 436.8 at an intersection with Highway 2.
  At the stop sign in Newport, turn left onto Highway 2. Take Highway 2 into Idaho and the bridge over the Pend Oreille River.

*As soon as you cross the river, you will need to be in the left lane to turn onto the first road as you leave the bridge. This is LeClerc Creek Road, and enters from the north at Idaho Highway 2 mile 0.5.
  Turn left onto LeClerc Creek Road.

**Take LeClerk Creek Road north for 2.7 miles to Marshall Lake Road, which enters on the right. Some maps show this to be Bead Lake Road.

Turn onto Marshall Lake Road, and go 0.9 miles to Bench Road, which will be on the right.

Turn onto Bench Road, and go southeast for 1.7 miles to a gravel road that enters on the left. The end of the road is at the state line, and is poorly marked as a State of Idaho fisherman's access.

Turn onto the gravel road and go north for 0.3 miles to a fork. Take the right fork 0.2 miles to the public access for Freeman Lake.

An **ALTERNATE ROUTE** to Freeman Lake is from the south on Highway 2.

Take Highway 2 north about 47 miles from Interstate 90 Exit 281 in Spokane to the town of Newport.

Take Highway 2 into Idaho and the bridge over the Pend Oreille River.

From here follow the directions provided above from the point marked with an asterisk(*).

A **SECOND ALTERNATE ROUTE** is from the east on Highway 2.

Take Highway 2 west about 28 miles from Highway 95 in the town of Sandpoint to LeClerc Creek Road, which will be on the right at Highway 2 mile 0.5.

At mile 0.5, just before you reach the bridge over the Pend Oreille River, turn right onto LeClerc Creek Road.

From here follow the directions provided above from the point marked with a double asterisk(**).

**NOTE:** In 1997, the Pend Oreille River reached elevations that flooded LeClerc Creek Road. When LeClerc Creek Road is not available, there is another route that can be used for access.

East of Newport at Idaho Highway 2 mile 2.3 is the Albeni Falls Machine Shop on the north side of the road. Freeman Lake Road, a gravel road, heads north next to the shop.

Take Freeman Lake Road 4.5 miles to a gravel road on the right. The end of the road is at the state line, and is poorly marked as a State of Idaho fisherman's access.

Turn onto the gravel road and go north for 0.3 miles to a fork. Take the right fork 0.2 miles to the public access for Freeman Lake.

FISHING TIPS:

Best fishing is at the northeast corner of the lake, from the road edge to the corner on the left. The edges of the lilypads out from the beaver house are best.

Bass and perch can be caught in most areas of the lake on traditional bass gear. Spinners and spinnerbaits are best.

Crappie, including many large ones of 11 to 12 inches, can be caught in the northeast corner on jigs and flies. While they can be found along the lilypads, they also rise over the submerged weeds further out in the lake on spring evenings.

Large Pumpkinseed can be found in the same corner, but are usually in the heavier weeds of the lilypad beds and on the inside edge between the pads and shore. They can also be caught in the flat at the south end of the lake. They will often measure to over eight inches and weigh nearly half a pound.

Trout are planted in the lake, and can be caught in most areas on flies. Most productive are the flat north of the access area, and out from the northeast corner. Trout fishing is best early in the season.

Bait fishermen fishing worms on the bottom get occasional catfish.

The dock at the access area is heavily used by bank fishermen.

MISCELLANEOUS NOTES:

A state record Tench of 3.82 pounds (19 1/4 inches long) was caught in Freeman Lake in 1994.

Planting records indicate that Channel Catfish were planted in 1999 (2,670 at 3-6 inches) and 2000 (448 at 6 inches plus).

MAP REFERENCES:
*Idaho Atlas & Gazetteer; Page 62.
*USGS Topographic Map, Washington (48117-B1-TF-024-00)
  Newport Quadrangle, 7.5 Minute Series.
*USGS Topographic Map, Washington (48117-A1-TM-100-00)
  Chewelah Quadrangle, 30x60 Minute Series.
*Washington Atlas & Gazetteer, Page 105.

## 34  GAMBLE LAKE
Also known as: Gamblin Lake

June 17, 2006; Gamble Lake, looking south.

SIZE: 130 Acres
ELEVATION: 2,079 Feet
MAXIMUM DEPTH: Unknown
COUNTY: Bonner, Idaho
COORDINATES: T56N R1E Sec6P,7BCFGK

   Longitude: 116d 22m 46s to 116d 23m 34s West
   Latitude: 48d 12m 55s to 48d 13m 46s North

SPECIES, CONFIRMED:
 Black Crappie

SPECIES, REPORTED:
 Largemouth Bass
 Pumpkinseed Sunfish
 Yellow Perch

CHARACTERISTICS:
 Low, timbered hills surround the lake, with higher hills visible in the distances all around.
 The lake is heavily timbered on the south and west sides. Homes are visible above the lake on the north and east sides.

There are marshy shorelines with a lot of aquatic vegetation at the southeast corner.

The north end has low, grassy shorelines, also lined with aquatic vegetation. Above the north end are fields dotted with small trees. The grassy area is separated from the water by heavy growths of aquatic weed.

At the northwest corner of the lake are some small beds of lilypads.

A road runs down the east side of the lake, right next to the water. It provides all access, including limited bank fishing access.

The shallow areas of the lake are all dotted with beds of dollar pads.

The bottom is mud.

The water is clear.

## DIRECTIONS TO:

Take Interstate 90 to exit 12 at Coeur d'Alene, Idaho. At exit 12, turn north onto Highway 95.

Take Highway 95 north for about 39 miles to mile 468.2, where Sagle Road will be found on the east side of the highway.

Turn onto Sagle Road, and go east for 12.5 miles to Glengary Road, on the right. At this intersection Martin Bay Road goes straight ahead, and the right onto Glengary Road is the continuation of the main road.

Take Glengary Road south for 0.3 miles to a roadside turnout that provides the public access for Gamble Lake. There is no boat launch, but small craft can be launched along the road.

**NOTE:** If you continue past Gamble Lake, at 0.7 miles from the Martin Bay Road intersection you will come to the "Gamblin Lake BLM Recreation Area". It has a small parking area and pit toilet, and provides access to a trail system. The area is posted as a day use area with no camping.

## FISHING TIPS:

On my one visit to the lake I only cast small jigs from shore at the "public access" area. It was effective for nice crappie.

As of 2006, the lake has special regulations, including "electric motors only". See the current regulations before fishing.

## MAP REFERENCES:
*Idaho Atlas & Gazetteer, Page 62.
*USGS Topographic Map, Idaho (48116-B4-TF-024-00)
  Talache Quadrangle, 7.5 Minute Series.
*USGS Topographic Map, Idaho-Montana (48116-A1-TM-100-00)
  Sandpoint Quadrangle, 30x60 Minute Series.

## 35   LAKE GILLETTE

August 22, 2002; Lake Gillette, looking northwest
from near the access area.

SIZE: 48.0 Acres
ELEVATION: 3,147 Feet
MAXIMUM DEPTH: 87 Feet
COUNTY: Stevens, Washington
COORDINATES: T36N R42E Sec19A

Longitude: 117d 32m 18s to 117d 32m 43s West
Latitude: 48d 36m 43s to 48d 37m 7s North

SPECIES, CONFIRMED:
 Cutthroat Trout, West Slope
 Pumpkinseed Sunfish
 Yellow Perch

SPECIES, REPORTED:
 Eastern Brook Trout
 Rainbow Trout
 Tiger Trout

## CHARACTERISTICS:

A campground and access area is located on the east shore. The area has a large campground to the left as you enter, and picnic areas and boat launch to the right. If you continue past the entrance to the access area, several other campgrounds are found further down the road.

The west and south shores, plus portions of the north shore, have homes on them.

Even with the homes, the area surrounding the lake is primarily timbered. Low, rolling hills can be seen in the distance to the west.

The shoreline areas have low scrub trees where there aren't homes. There are also some grassy areas and developed beach areas. The access area has a dock that extends well out into the lake next to a concrete strip boat ramp.

The bottom is silt and gravel, with some aquatic vegetation around the lake. There are some lilypad beds around the shorelines.

A major inlet stream, the Little Pend Oreille River, enters at the northwest corner, flowing from Lake Thomas, and exits at the south end to Lake Sherry. The channels between the lakes at either end are navigable by small boats.

The channel to Lake Sherry is crossed by a bridge, and has a cobbled, rocky bottom.

A smaller inlet stream enters at the center of the bay to the right of the boat launch area. A small, sandy delta has formed out from its mouth, but the water drops off very quickly to deep water all around.

A point is found between the bay to the right of the access area and the inlet stream channel from Lake Thomas. While it has a lot of fairly open area, it is posted as private property and offers no access.

Good-sized weed beds are found near the mouths of the channels. The channel at the north end, leading to Lake Thomas, has the remnants of an old bridge approach on each side. The bridge no longer exists.

The water is clear.

## DIRECTIONS TO:

Take Highway 20 to mile 379.2, east of the town of Colville, where Lake Pend Oreille Road will be found on the south side of the highway.

Turn onto Lake Pend Oreille Road and follow it 0.5 miles to the public access area for Lake Gillette, on the left. The area has a campground, boat ramp, picnic area and beach.

## FISHING TIPS:

Flies worked along the shorelines are extremely effective. The best areas are around any weed beds and at the stream channels. Spinners, small plugs, and other hardware are also effective cast in the same areas, as well as trolled in the more open water.

Cutthroat make up most of the catch, but small Perch and Pumpkinseed are occasionally caught in all areas. Most of the spiny ray fish are caught in the channel areas.

MISCELLANEOUS NOTES:

As of 2006, there is a "parking fee" of $3.00 per day to use the access area.

MAP REFERENCES:

*USGS Topographic Map, Washington (48117-E5-TF-024-00)
  Lake Gillette Quadrangle, 7.5 Minute Series.
*USGS Topographic Map, Washington (48117-E1-TM-100-00)
  Colville Quadrangle, 30x60 Minute Series.
*Washington Atlas & Gazetteer, Page 118.

## 36  GRANITE LAKE

June 16, 2006; Granite Lake, looking southeast.

SIZE: 20 Acres
ELEVATION: 2,145 Feet
MAXIMUM DEPTH: Unknown
COUNTY: Bonner, Idaho
COORDINATES: T54N R3W Sec27BCFG

Longitude: 116d 41m 1s <u>to</u> 116d 41m 23s West
Latitude: 48d 0m 8s <u>to</u> 48d 0m 23s North

SPECIES, CONFIRMED:
 Largemouth Bass
 Rainbow Trout

SPECIES, REPORTED:
 Bullhead Catfish
 Cutthroat Trout, West Slope
 Kokanee

CHARACTERISTICS:

The lake lies in an area of low, mostly timbered hills.

The south side of the lake has timber and brush to the waters edge on moderately steep slopes.

The north side has a road running down it, although most of it is at the top of a very steep bank. The road starts out high above the east end of the lake, and drops to the level of the lake at the west end where the public access is found.

On the north side of the lake are high bluffs of vertical rock. Below the vertical areas are steep slopes of rock, with some broken rock toward the west end. There are also some broken rock slopes at the southwest corner.

The public access area is located at the northwest corner of the lake. It has a gravel boat ramp and a fishing dock. There is also a small, undeveloped camp area on the opposite side of the road.

The west end of the lake has a large marshy area covered with cattails. The growths start at the access area and spread across the whole area.

At the east end of the lake are several large concrete footings. They are spaced across the end of the lake, and run up the hill on the north side. They appear to be from an old railroad bridge that once crossed the end of the lake. A new grade with railroad tracks visible at the top is visible in the distance to the east.

A small house sets in a grassy flat at the southeast corner. A couple other small buildings are found above the lake in the same corner. A large house overlooks the lake from the top of the hill at the northeast corner.

The shallow areas of the lake have heavy concentrations of aquatic weeds. They extend out for a good distance from the dock at the access area.

Some snags are scattered along the shorelines, mostly on the south side of the lake.

The water is clear.


DIRECTIONS TO:

Take Interstate 90 to exit 12 at Coeur d'Alene, Idaho. At exit 12, turn north onto Highway 95.

Take Highway 95 north for about 22 miles to mile 452.9, where Granite Loop Road will be reached, on the left. The end of the road is signed for "Granite Lake".

Turn onto Granite Loop Road, and go west for 0.8 miles to a stop sign at Kelso Lake Road. The intersection is signed for "Sportsman's Access" and "Kelso Lake Resort 1.5 Miles" to the left.

Turn left onto Kelso Lake Road, and go 0.5 miles to the public access area for Granite Lake. A gravel boat launch and fishing dock are on the left, and a small parking / camp area with porta-potty are on the right side of the road.

FISHING TIPS:

Spinners worked along the shorelines on the far side of the lake are effective for both bass and trout.

Bait fishermen fishing from the dock get planted Rainbow.

As of 2006, the lake has special regulations, including "no motors". Check the current regulations before fishing.

MAP REFERENCES:

*Idaho Atlas & Gazetteer, Page 62.

*USGS Topographic Map, Idaho (48116-A6-TF-024-00)
  Careywood Quadrangle, 7.5 Minute Series.

*USGS Topographic Map, Idaho-Montana (48116-A1-TM-100-00)
  Sandpoint Quadrangle, 30x60 Minute Series.

# 37  HALF MOON LAKE
Also known as: Moon Lake
New Moon Lake

July 14, 1999; Half Moon Lake, looking south.

SIZE: 13.9 Acres
ELEVATION: 3,398 Feet
MAXIMUM DEPTH: 30 Feet
COUNTY: Pend Oreille, Washington
COORDINATES: T34N R44E Sec26N,35D

Longitude: 117d 12m 48s to 117d 13m 0s West
Latitude: 48d 24m 31s to 48d 24m 51s North

SPECIES, CONFIRMED:
Cutthroat Trout, West Slope
Eastern Brook Trout

SPECIES, REPORTED:

## CHARACTERISTICS:

There are low hills all around the lake. They are timbered, although sparsely in some places. Where timber cover is sparse, the underbrush is heavy.

To the south rise two small hills of nearly identical shape. The hill on the east side is cut by a road.

The north end has a knob hill dominating the skyline. Part of the knob is timbered.

The lake is long and narrow, with a slight dish at the east side and a small hook to the east at the south end.

A gravel road runs along the east side of the lake. It is above the lake at the top of a steep bank for the full run, in most places 20 to 50 feet up. Trees cover the area between the road and the water. The lake is visible through the trees from the road.

A wide, but steep, gravel ramp area drops from the road to the water's edge at the east side of the north end. The gravel area is about 20 feet wide, dropping from the road about 20 feet above. It is suitable for launching a small boat, raft or float tube, but could be trouble trying to launch a trail-ered boat.

A tiny inlet stream passes through the draw in which the parking area is located, and enters the lake at the northeast corner.

The shorelines are timbered and lined with dense brush in almost all areas. They are also very steep. There are a couple of open spots on more gently sloped ground at the north end, but they are not easily accessible on foot.

There are logjams at both ends of the lake, and a lot of snags along the other shores. The bottom is rocky with silt deposits, and also has many snags on it. The bottom at the north end is primarily silt.

There is some aquatic vegetation out from shore at the north end. Most of the growth consists of tall weeds that rise from the bottom, but don't reach the surface.

The water is very clear.

## DIRECTIONS TO:

Take Highway 20 to mile 421.0, about 16 miles north of the town of New-port, where Kings Lake Road will be found on the east side of the highway.

Turn onto Kings Lake Road, and go east through the town of Usk. You will cross a bridge over the Pend Oreille River, and at 1.0 miles from Highway 20 reach a sign that indicates "Skookum Lake 8 Miles", "Browns Lake 11 Miles".

At 5.0 miles, the pavement ends.

At 7.2 miles, you will reach an intersection with Road 5030, on the left. Road 5030 goes to Half Moon Lake and Browns Lake. If you continue straight ahead, the road goes to Skookum Lakes and Kings Lake.

Turn left, and go north for 1.9 miles to the parking area at the north end of Half Moon Lake. The parking area is on the right, and the lake on the left.

The parking area has no facilities, and room for only two or three vehicles. A steep gravel slope opposite the parking area provides access to the water.

FISHING TIPS:

Spinners trolled or cast anywhere on the lake are very effective.

Flies are particularly effective at the ends of the lake around the floating logs and bottom snags, but will get fish in all areas. Casts to rising fish will almost always get hits.

Eastern Brook are less common than Cutthroat, following attempts by the Department of Wildlife in the mid 1990's to eradicate them by rehabilitating the lake. They are still present, and can be best caught by fishing bait on the bottom. The best areas are next to shore at the center section of the lake.

MISCELLANEOUS NOTES:

Half Moon Lake produced a state record West Slope Cutthroat for me on September 17, 2000. The fish was 14.75 inches long with a girth of 8.75 inches, and weighed 1.44 pounds. The fish was caught at 1820 in the evening on a fly near the south end. It broke the previous record of 0.84 pounds, which I had set in Rainy Lake, Chelan County, on August 23, 2000.

MAP REFERENCES:

*USGS Topographic Map, Washington (48117-D2-TF-024-00)
   Browns Lake Quadrangle, 7.5 Minute Series.
*USGS Topographic Map, Washington (48117-A1-TM-100-00)
   Chewelah Quadrangle, 30x60 Minute Series.
*Washington Atlas & Gazetteer, Page 105.

## 38   HAUSER LAKE

May 12, 1996; Hauser Lake, looking south.

SIZE: 550 Acres
ELEVATION: 2,300 Feet (estimated)
MAXIMUM DEPTH: Unknown
COUNTY: Kootenai, Idaho
COORDINATES: T51N R5W Sec7(west 1/2),18BCD
        T51N R6W Sec12(east 1/2)

        Longitude: 117d 0m 26s to 117d 1m 55s West
        Latitude: 47d 46m 11s to 47d 47m 18s North

SPECIES, CONFIRMED:
 Rainbow Trout

SPECIES, REPORTED:
 Bullhead Catfish
 Channel Catfish
 Crappie
 Cutthroat Trout
 Eastern Brook Trout

German Brown Trout
Green Sunfish
Kokanee
Largemouth Bass
Northern Pike
Pumpkinseed Sunfish
Tiger Muskie
Yellow Perch

## CHARACTERISTICS:

The lake lies in an area of fir and pine covered rolling hills, which can be seen in the distance.

The shape is nearly oval, with an indentation on the north side formed by a rocky point.

The coves found in the corners at the north end have beds of lilypads in them, and small willows lining much of the shoreline. The shoreline areas of the south side, southeast corner, and west side have large beds of cattails.

There are homes around most of the lake, but most are set back away from the water. Several have small docks and floats. The road runs right along the water down the northeast shore, but most is posted as private property.

The home at the center of the north shore, on the west side of the point, is the old Wright family homestead, where my grandmother was born.

The visible bottom areas are gavel and silt. The water is clear.

## DIRECTIONS TO:

Take Interstate 90 to exit 5 in Idaho. At exit 5, Spokane Street, turn left and go north for 2.2 miles to a tee intersection with Prairie Avenue.

Turn left onto Prairie Avenue and head west. After 1.5 miles you will reach a stop sign at McGuire Road. Go straight through, and continue west for another 1.7 miles to the tee intersection with Highway 53.

At Highway 53, turn right and go 0.2 miles to the end of Cloverleaf Road, on the left.

Turn left onto Cloverleaf Road, and go north for 1.7 miles to a fork. The left fork is West Hauser Lake Road, and the right fork is East Hauser Lake Road.

If you take a right and continue north on East Hauser Lake Road, a public access, with boat ramp, will be reached on the left after another 1.8 miles.

At 0.4 miles past the public access you will come to a rocky point which extends into the lake from the north side. The road passes around the point next to the water, and offers about 0.2 miles of shoreline access.

If you take West Hauser Lake Road from the intersection, it is 3.1 miles to the public access, and West Hauser Lake Road becomes North Hauser Lake Road after 2.0 miles.

FISHING TIPS:

Small spoons trolled out from the north shores will get an occasional trout.

MISCELLANEOUS NOTES:

Hauser Lake has a long history of producing state record Tiger Muskies. It has the following records to its credit:
   *17 pounds 4 ounces (39 inches), caught in the lake outlet in 1995.
   *21 pounds 8 ounces (41 inches) in 1997.
   *29 pounds 10 ounces (45 inches) in 1998 was the third and largest
      new record caught that year.
   *34 pounds 8 ounces (49.375 inches, 21 inch girth) in 1999.
   *35 pounds in 2000.
   *37 pounds 13 ounces (49.375 inches) later in 2000.
   *38 pounds 7 ounces (48.25 inches) in June 2001.
   In addition to the numerous Muskie records, Hauser also produced a state record Green Sunfish of 5 ounces (7 3/8 inches long) in 1994.

MAP REFERENCES:
   *Idaho Atlas & Gazetteer, Page 12, 60.
   *USGS Topographic Map, Washington (47117-G1-TF-024-00)
      Newman Lake Quadrangle, 7.5 Minute Series.
   *USGS Topographic Map, Washington (47117-E1-TM-100-00)
      Spokane Quadrangle, 30x60 Minute Series.

## 39  HAYDEN LAKE

May 12, 1996; Hayden Lake, looking southwest.

SIZE: 4,000 Acres
ELEVATION: 2,238 Feet
MAXIMUM DEPTH: 185 Feet
COUNTY: Kootenai, Idaho
COORDINATES: T51N R3W Sec3,9-11,14-18,19-22
        T52N R3W Sec33,34

        Longitude: 116d 39m 58s to 116d 45m 28s West
        Latitude: 47d 44m 48s to 47d 49m 0s North

SPECIES, CONFIRMED:
 Largemouth Bass

SPECIES, REPORTED:
 Black Crappie
 Bullhead Catfish
 Cutthroat Trout
 Eastern Brook Trout

Kokanee
Northern Pike
Pumpkinseed Sunfish
Rainbow Trout
Smallmouth Bass
Splake
Whitefish
Yellow Perch

## CHARACTERISTICS:

The lake is large and of a very irregular shape. Many bays, points and arms break the shorelines. The northern portions of the lake are narrow, with the largest body of open water found across the south end.

Most of the shores are wooded, but developed, with homes in most places. Many of the homes have docks extending into the lake.

The north end of the lake, in the area of the public access, is mostly shallow water with weed beds.

Algae is suspended during periods of bloom. The usually clear water is tinged slightly green during these periods.

The bottom is mud, but not usually visible due to the covering of aquatic vegetation.

## DIRECTIONS TO:

Take Interstate 90 to exit 12 at Coeur d'Alene, Idaho. At exit 12, turn north onto Highway 95.

Take Highway 95 north for 6.1 miles to mile 436.8, where Lancaster Road enters on the right.

Turn right onto Lancaster Road, and go east for 6.2 miles to Park Drive, on the right. The end of Park Drive is signed for "Hayden Lake Sportsman Park" and "Public Fishing and Camping Area".

Turn right onto Park Drive, and go 0.2 miles to a gravel road on the right.

Turn onto the gravel road, which will drop down to a parking area in 0.1 miles. The parking area is located just above the boat ramp. The ramp is concrete, with a dock alongside.

## FISHING TIPS:

Spinners cast along the weed beds will get an occasional bass.

MISCELLANEOUS NOTES:

A state record Rainbow of 19 pounds was caught in Hayden in 1947.

A state record Splake of 4 pounds 8 ounces (22 1/2 inches long) was caught in the Hayden Lake outlet in 1996.

A Northern Pike of 38 pounds 9 ounces (49.75 inches long) caught in Hayden tied a State record on March 19, 2002.

It is reported that the first planting of Smallmouth Bass was in 1983.

MAP REFERENCES:

*Idaho Atlas & Gazetteer; Page 32, 60.

*USGS Topographic Map, Idaho (47116-G7-TF-024-00)
  Hayden Quadrangle, 7.5 Minute Series.

*USGS Topographic Map, Idaho (47116-E1-TM-100-00)
  Coeur d'Alene Quadrangle, 30x60 Minute Series.

# 40  LAKE HERITAGE

May 27, 2003; Lake Heritage, looking northeast.

SIZE: 71.1 Acres
ELEVATION: 3,163 Feet
MAXIMUM DEPTH: 18 Feet
COUNTY: Stevens, Washington
COORDINATES: T36N R42E Sec8(southeast 1/4),9DE

> Longitude: 117d 30m 58s <u>to</u> 117d 31m 51s West
> Latitude: 48d 37m 52s <u>to</u> 48d 38m 27s North

SPECIES, CONFIRMED:
 Cutthroat Trout, West Slope
 Pumpkinseed Sunfish
 Yellow Perch

SPECIES, REPORTED:
 Eastern Brook Trout
 Rainbow Trout
 Tiger Trout

CHARACTERISTICS:

The lake is long and narrow, and the area around it is mostly heavily timbered. It lies in an area of low, timbered hills.

There is development on both the east and west shores, but less than is found on any of the other lakes in the chain. The east side is the most heavily developed of the two, but the west side also has a couple of large homes. Most of the homes have docks extending out into the lake.

The outlet stream, the Little Pend Oreille River, exits from Heritage Lake at the southwest corner, flowing very gently to Lake Thomas. As you enter Heritage from Thomas, a buoy marks Lake Heritage as a "No Wake" zone.

Large beds of lilypads are found on both sides of the mouth of the outlet channel, with the largest one on the east side. Smaller beds are found in almost every shallow pocket and bay.

The channel from Lake Heritage to Lake Thomas is undeveloped as of the spring of 2003, but there are signs of clearing being done up from the east side of the upper end of the channel. The channel has brushy, boggy shores, with timber back from the brush. It winds through large beds of lilypads that fill the shallows surrounding the deeper main channel. A large beaver house is located on the west bank about half way between Thomas and Heritage.

The upper end of the lake, at the northeast corner, has large beds of lilypads and brushy shorelines.

The shorelines in the undeveloped areas have brush and or trees to the waters edge in most places.

The bottom is heavy silt and mud, with a good deal of aquatic vegetation.

The water is clear, but has a slight brownish color at times.

DIRECTIONS TO:

Take Highway 20 to mile 379.2, east of the town of Colville, where Lake Pend Oreille Road will be found on the south side of the highway.

Turn onto Lake Pend Oreille Road and follow it 0.5 miles to the public access area for Lake Gillette, on the left. The area has a campground, boat ramp, picnic area and beach.

Launch on Lake Gillette, and go to the right to reach the channel between Lakes Gillette and Thomas.

To reach Lake Heritage you have to run the full length of Lake Thomas by water, angling toward the far right corner where the entrance to the channel between Lakes Thomas and Heritage is found.

Unlike the very short channels found between Lakes Sherry and Gillette, and Lakes Gillette and Thomas, this one is considerably longer. It winds about a quarter of a mile to reach the south end of Lake Heritage.

FISHING TIPS:

Flies worked around the weed beds are very effective. An especially good area is the mouth of the channel to Lake Thomas.

MISCELLANEOUS NOTES:

As of 2006, there is a "parking fee" of $3.00 per day to use the access area at Lake Gillette.

MAP REFERENCES:

*USGS Topographic Map, Washington (48117-F5-TF-024-00)
  Aladdin Mountain Quadrangle, 7.5 Minute Series.
*USGS Topographic Map, Washington (48117-E1-TM-100-00)
  Colville Quadrangle, 30x60 Minute Series.
*Washington Atlas & Gazetteer, Page 118.

## 41   HORSESHOE LAKE

May 23, 2002; Horseshoe Lake, western arm, looking north.

SIZE: 128.0 Acres
ELEVATION: 1,970 Feet
MAXIMUM DEPTH: 140 Feet
COUNTY: Pend Oreille, Washington
COORDINATES: T30N R43E Sec7(east 1/3),8(west 1/3)

      Longitude: 117d 24m 25s to 117d 25m 17s West
      Latitude: 48d 6m 18s to 48d 6m 59s North

SPECIES, CONFIRMED:
 Kokanee
 Rainbow Trout

SPECIES, REPORTED:
 Black Crappie
 Largemouth Bass
 Mackinaw
 Yellow Perch

CHARACTERISTICS:

As its name suggests, the lake has the shape of a rough horseshoe, with a large peninsula extending from the south to separate the lake into east and west sections. A small point also extends from the north side of the lake toward the larger peninsula, to create a channel between the two. The channel is fairly wide, but forms a distinct boundary between the east and west arms of the lake.

For a lake that isn't overly large, it is quite distinct from most others because the east and west arms of the lake differ so greatly. They almost seem to be two completely separate lakes, and the surrounding areas are different enough that they could be miles apart. Because of the differences, I'll describe the characteristics for each arm separately.

Homes are found on both the north point and the southern peninsula, and power lines cross over the channel between the east and west arms of the lake.

The west arm has the public access area located near its southwest corner. The access area has a gravel parking area, a gravel boat launch, and pit toilets. The area is signed for no overnight parking or camping.

Westbrook Resort is located just north of the public access.

The west arm is by far the larger of the two sections of the lake.

It is all deep water, with the exception of along the south end and southeast corner, and a small area at the northeast corner.

The west arm has a house in a small cove at the center of the peninsula that forms its eastern shore, as well as several at the north end of the peninsula.

Vertical rock bluffs are visible in the distance to the north through the lower areas found at the north end of the lake.

Steep hills rise high over the entire length of the west side of the lake. They have a lot of exposed rock and broken rock slopes. They are dotted with trees, sparsely in most places and more heavily in others.

A gravel road, Horseshoe Lake Road, runs along the base of the slopes, but is separated from the water everywhere except at the northwest corner. At the corner the road is close to the water, but at the top of a very steep gravel bank.

The west side is pretty heavily developed. Homes on this shore are found along the very steep slopes. Some of the homes have docks. There are trees on the west side, but cover is sparse and there is little brush in most places.

The north end of the west arm has some homes in the northwest corner, west of where Buck Creek enters. Buck Creek enters almost at the center of the north shore. The remaining area is deciduous tree covered and brushy to the shorelines. The area is low and flat.

The peninsula side, the eastern side of the west arm, is heavily wooded with some open area. A dirt road runs up it to the homes on the north end. All of the west side of the peninsula is private property with no access.

Some shorelines of the peninsula are brush covered to the waters edge. Most are steep and rocky.

The south end of the western arm has steep rocky areas with some low ground between them.

There is a section of marshy shoreline at the southeast corner.

A steep ridge of low rock runs along the west half of the south end. It rises 20 to 25 feet, and trails over the center and around the east end provide the route to Blue Lake.

The east arm is undeveloped except at the north end of the peninsula on its west side.

The hills around the east arm are sparsely timbered with a lot of steep rock. The slopes are moderately steep to very steep, including much vertical rock.

There is a good deal of exposed rock along the shorelines. Most shoreline areas are fairly open, but steep and rocky.

The east arm has the largest inlet stream found on the lake. The West Branch of the Little Spokane River enters near the northeast corner at an impressive waterfall. It flows into the lake around a low finger of rock that extends from the south bank. A grassy flat formed by sediment deposits forms the north shore of the stream mouth. A shallow area with a silt bottom surrounds the mouth of the inlet.

The West Branch of the Little Spokane River exits at the south end of the east arm.

A good-sized bay is found at the northwest corner, north of the Little Spokane inlet.

North of the inlet is a very high, nearly vertical rock ridge with very few trees on it. The slopes are vertical and almost vertical until you reach the extreme north end of the east arm, where there is a low brushy area.

In the corner of a bay located at the northeast corner is a small rise dotted with grass and trees. Another small, low area is found between this rise and the small point that extends from the north shore toward the large southern peninsula.

South from the inlet is a narrow neck, only about 40 feet wide, with vertical rock walls rising high over the east side, and steep timber covered slopes over the west side. Many snags extend from the west side out into the narrows, reducing the navigable area to about ten feet wide. The area also has a noticeable current.

The lake gradually widens as you move south, with the vertical rock shore on the east side giving way to very steep slopes.

A small point is found on the east bank, about 200 yards south of the neck. It is timbered, but has little brush. The point provides a good place to beach your boat for a picnic, and also provides the start of a short trail to the Devil's Well (see miscellaneous notes below).

The first large bay, on the east side about 300 yards south of the neck, has a good-sized mud bottomed flat and snags, both along shore and out from the bay.

Half way down the east arm the lake widens considerably, and the hills over the west side become vertical rock at the upper reaches, with very steep slopes between the vertical rock and the water. Trees grow along the top of the rock cliffs.

The hills on the east side in the same area have a lot of exposed rock, but the slopes are broken by more gently sloped strips that have trees growing on them.

The hills become much gentler in the southern half of the east arm, especially on the peninsula side to the west. The east side stays pretty steep, but without as much vertical rock.

The shorelines in the southern half remain steep except at the southwest corner.

The bottom is rock and silt.

The water, of both arms, is usually very clear.

## DIRECTIONS TO:

Take Highway 2 north from the City of Spokane for about 20 miles to Eloika Lake Road, on the left at mile 312.7.

Turn onto Eloika Lake Road and go west 3.3 miles to Division Road, a gravel road on the right.

Turn right onto Division Road, and take it 7.3 miles to the public access area for Horseshoe Lake, on the right.

Somewhere during this 7.3 mile run, Division Road becomes Horseshoe Lake Road.

## FISHING TIPS:

Flatfish plugs, in size F4 with a green frog finish, are very effective trolled very close to the shores.

Even more effective are flies cast to rising fish. Most of the active fish I encountered on my only visit were in the eastern arm, south of the narrow neck, and at the southeast corner of the west arm.

## MISCELLANEOUS NOTES:

The Devil's Well is listed as a "Unique Natural Feature" in the Washington Atlas & Gazetteer. It is an almost perfectly circular hole, about 20 feet in diameter, found in solid rock.

It is flooded with extremely clear water and holds several large trees that have dropped in from the slopes above over the years. Unfortunately, it also holds cans and bottles tossed in by visitors with limited intelligence.

The sides of the well are vertical rock, rising about eight feet over the lowest side, and towering more that 30 feet over the uphill side.

The view of the well is well worth the short hike of about 150 yards and the climb of about a hundred feet from Horseshoe Lake.

## MAP REFERENCES:
*USGS Topographic Map, Washington (48117-A4-TF-024-00)
  Fan Lake Quadrangle, 7.5 Minute Series.
*USGS Topographic Map, Washington (48117-A1-TM-100-00)
  Chewelah Quadrangle, 30x60 Minute Series.
*Washington Atlas & Gazetteer, Page 105.

## 42  JEWEL LAKE

June 17, 2006; Jewel Lake, looking northeast from the public access area.

SIZE: 35 Acres
ELEVATION: 2,477 Feet
MAXIMUM DEPTH: Unknown
COUNTY: Bonner, Idaho
COORDINATES: T55N R3W Sec4M,5J

Longitude: 116d 42m 51s to 116d 43m 19s West
Latitude: 48d 8m 19s to 48d 8m 36s North

SPECIES, CONFIRMED:
 Black Crappie
 Bluegill
 Rainbow Trout

SPECIES, REPORTED:
 Channel Catfish
 Cutthroat Trout, West Slope
 Kokanee
 Yellow Perch

CHARACTERISTICS:

The lake is long and almost rectangular, running from southwest to north-east.

The area around the lake has low, timbered hills with some bare rocky spots showing through. The timber cover is dense in most places.

Immediately around the lake the timber and brush reaches to the waters edge on the east side. Near the center of the east shore is a large rock, about 15 feet high, that sets on the waters edge. It is lined by a thin strip of lily-pads.

Above the north end of the lake is a large farm. It has large, open fields, a barn and several other buildings.

There are also buildings in other areas around the lake, including at the southeast corner and above the center of the west side. Both are away from the water, and the one on the west side even has a road between it and the water.

Jewel Lake Road runs down the west side of the lake, but is separated from the water by trees and brush.

An inlet stream enters at the southwest end, and an outlet is found at the marshy northeast end of the lake.

The shorelines are almost all lined with at least a thin strip of cattails. The corners of the lake at the south end have wider beds of cattails than other areas.

The north end of the lake has a very heavy bed of lilypads that forms a green barrier across that end of the lake. The strip of dense lilypads is about a hundred feet wide, and there is more open water beyond them. Past the northernmost open water, at the true north end of the lake, are additional lilypads and a shoreline strip of aquatic weeds.

The public access area is located at the south end of the lake. It has a shallow boat launch of fine gravel, a fishing dock, a gravel parking area and a porta-potty.

The mud bottom has a lot of aquatic vegetation covering it, although the water drops off quickly enough in most places that it doesn't approach the surface.

The water is clear.

DIRECTIONS TO:

Take Interstate 90 to exit 12 at Coeur d'Alene, Idaho. At exit 12, turn north onto Highway 95.

Take Highway 95 north for about 36 miles to mile 465.6, where Dufort Road will be reached, on the left.

Turn onto Dufort Road, and go 6.2 miles to Jewel Lake Road, on the left.

Turn onto Jewel Lake Road, and you will see a sign for "Jewel Lake 3 Miles". Take Jewel Lake Road 3.1 miles to an intersection, where Schneiders Road goes to the left, and Jewel Lake Road turns to the right.

Keep right, remaining on Jewel Lake Road, and go another 0.7 miles to the Jewel Lake sportsman's access road, on the left.

The access road runs 0.1 mile to the boat launch area.

Jewel Lake is reached a total of 10.1 miles from Highway 95.

## FISHING TIPS:

Flies are very effective for both trout and panfish.

The dock at the access area is very popular, with most people fishing either Berkley Power Bait or worms, depending on whether they are after trout or warm water fish.

## MISCELLANEOUS NOTES:

The lake access is a day use only area, with camping no longer permitted as of 2006.

## MAP REFERENCES:

*Idaho Atlas & Gazetteer, Page 62.

*USGS Topographic Map, Idaho (48116-B6-TF-024-00)
  Morton Quadrangle, 7.5 Minute Series.

*USGS Topographic Map, Idaho-Montana (48116-A1-TM-100-00)
  Sandpoint Quadrangle, 30x60 Minute Series.

## 43   JUMPOFF JOE LAKE
Also known as: Jumpoff Lake.

June 23, 1997; Jumpoff Joe Lake, looking southwest.

SIZE: 105.1 Acres
ELEVATION: 2,030 Feet
MAXIMUM DEPTH: 24 Feet
COUNTY: Stevens, Washington
COORDINATES: T31N R40E Sec36R

Longitude: 117d 41m 0s to 117d 41m 51s West
Latitude: 48d 7m 56s to 48d 8m 23s North

SPECIES, CONFIRMED:
Eastern Brook Trout
German Brown Trout

SPECIES, REPORTED:
Bluegill
Largemouth Bass
Rainbow Trout
Yellow Perch

## CHARACTERISTICS:

There are timbered hills to the east and west. The south side is timbered and has several houses, many with docks extending into the lake. The north side has a large, flat grassy field with one house. A large farm is found on the west side.

A resort on the southeast shore has both docks and a cordoned swimming area.

The public access is found at the northeast corner. It has a gravel boat launch, a large gravel parking area and pit toilets. Because of the heavy growths of cattails lining the shores in the area, no bank fishing is available.

On the west side, the center of the lake has a point covered with small trees. The bay at the southwest corner is shallow, with a silt bottom covered with aquatic weed.

Much of the lake has cattails on the shorelines, especially the north side. There is a lot of aquatic vegetation in the shallows along the shorelines.

The center of the lake has the deepest water, and is mostly weed free.

The water is clear.

## DIRECTIONS TO:

Take Highway 395 to mile 198.0, south of the town of Chewelah and north of Spokane, where Jumpoff Joe Road enters from the west.

Turn onto Jumpoff Joe Road and go 0.9 miles to the public access area for Jumpoff Joe Lake, on the right.

## FISHING TIPS:

Spinners trolled around the center area of the lake in late spring will get fish.

## MAP REFERENCES:

*USGS Topographic Map, Washington (48117-B6-TF-024-00)
  Valley Quadrangle, 7.5 Minute Series.
*USGS Topographic Map, Washington (48117-A1-TM-100-00)
  Chewelah Quadrangle, 30x60 Minute Series.
*Washington Atlas & Gazetteer, Page 104.

## 44  KELSO LAKE

June 16, 2006; Kelso Lake, looking southwest
from the public access area.

SIZE: 60 Acres
ELEVATION: 2,150 Feet
MAXIMUM DEPTH: Unknown
COUNTY: Bonner, Idaho
COORDINATES: T54N R3W Sec21(south 1/3)

Longitude: 116d 41m 52s to 116d 42m 51s West
Latitude: 48d 0m 29s to 48d 0m 42s North

SPECIES, CONFIRMED:
 Rainbow Trout

SPECIES, REPORTED:
 Bluegill
 Bullhead Catfish
 Cutthroat Trout, West Slope
 Eastern Brook Trout
 German Brown Trout
 Kokanee
 Largemouth Bass

## CHARACTERISTICS:

The lake lies in a timber covered area, although development is heavy on the north side.

The area around the east end of the lake has low, timbered hills. There are several houses along the northeast corner, and some tucked in the timber at that end of the lake.

The only low, open skyline around the lake is to the west.

The east end of the lake has a large bed of lilypads covering it. On the open water side of the lilypads is a bed of dollar pads about 50 to 60 yards wide.

The west end also has a line of lilypads running the length of the shore. Behind the pads at the west end of the lake is a heavy growth of cattails.

One break in the otherwise brushy, tree lined shores is at the west end of the lake where a large rock formation rises about 20 feet above the water. Deep water is found right off the rock. Cattails start at the west side of the rock, and then extend in an unbroken line around the west end of the lake.

The only other breaks in the shoreline brush are where homes have lawn areas that reach the water. Some of the homes also have docks extending out into the lake.

The lake drains at the northeast corner, flowing to Round Lake.

Kelso Lake Road runs the length of the north side of the lake. It offers access to the water only at the public access area or the Kelso Lake Resort.

The public access area is located at the center of the north side of the lake. It has a crude boat launch area and a nice fishing dock on the lakeside, and a good-sized parking area and a pit toilet on the opposite side of the road.

The water is very clear.

## DIRECTIONS TO:

Take Interstate 90 to exit 12 at Coeur d'Alene, Idaho. At exit 12, turn north onto Highway 95.

Take Highway 95 north for about 22 miles to mile 452.9, where Granite Loop Road will be reached, on the left. The end of the road is signed for "Granite Lake".

Turn onto Granite Loop Road, and go west for 0.8 miles to a stop sign at Kelso Lake Road. The intersection is signed for "Sportsman's Access" and "Kelso Lake Resort 1.5 Miles" to the left.

Turn left onto Kelso Lake Road, and go 1.6 miles to the public access area for Kelso Lake. Parking is on the right side of the road.

The Kelso Lake access area is reached a total of 2.4 miles from Highway 95.

Kelso Lake Resort is reached 0.2 miles before the public access area. It offers camping and boat launching.

FISHING TIPS:
The lake receives regular plants of Rainbow Trout. The dock at the public access area is very popular with bait fishermen.
Casting spinners was effective for me, especially off the rock at the northwest corner of the lake.
As of 2006, the lake has special regulations, including "no motors". See the current regulations before fishing.

MISCELLANEOUS NOTES:
Planting records indicate that the following plants:
Bluegill in 1982;
Eastern Brook from 1994 to 1997;
German Brown from 1981 to 1989;
Cutthroat from 1970 to 1978.

MAP REFERENCES:
*Idaho Atlas & Gazetteer, Page 62.
*USGS Topographic Map, Idaho (48116-A6-TF-024-00)
  Careywood Quadrangle, 7.5 Minute Series.
*USGS Topographic Map, Idaho-Montana (48116-A1-TM-100-00)
  Sandpoint Quadrangle, 30x60 Minute Series.

## 45  KILLARNEY LAKE

June 29, 1996; Killarney Lake, looking south.

SIZE: 500 Acres
ELEVATION: 2,100 Feet
MAXIMUM DEPTH: Unknown
COUNTY: Kootenai, Idaho
COORDINATES: T48N R2W Sec2,3,10,11,14,15

Longitude: 116d 32m 54s to 116d 35m 8s West
Latitude: 47d 30m 26s to 47d 32m 9s North

SPECIES, CONFIRMED:
 Black Bullhead Catfish
 Northern Pike

SPECIES, REPORTED:
 Black Crappie
 Largemouth Bass
 Pumpkinseed Sunfish
 Yellow Perch

## CHARACTERISTICS:

The area around the north end of the lake is mostly steep and wooded, while the south end is low and marshy.

A public access is found at the southeast corner. It has a boat ramp, two docks, picnic tables, pit toilet, and a camping area. The access is a fee area. Additional limited shore access is found at the center of the east shore.

The lake is almost all shallow and weedy, especially at the south end and the bays of the north end. The shallower areas have very heavy weed growth.

The steep and brushy shores offer very little bank access. Most of what is available is found at the public access area.

A gravel road runs the length of the east shore and around the north end, but is well above and away from the water.

A narrow point at the north end separates a marshy area to the west from the main body of the lake. A small wooded island, Popcorn Island, is found at the north end. It has a public picnic area on it, with boat access and a dock on the north side.

The bottom is silt at the south end, and somewhat rocky along the steeper shores. The water is clear.

## DIRECTIONS TO:

Take Interstate 90 to exit 34 east of Coeur d'Alene, Idaho. At exit 34, turn south onto Highway 3.

Take Highway 3 south for 5.1 miles to mile 114.4, where Killarney Lake Road enters on the right. The end of the road is signed for "Killarney Boat Launch Area 3 1/2 Miles", and "Picnic Area 4 Miles".

Turn right onto Killarney Lake Road and go 3.1 miles to a fork.

The left fork enters the public access area with boat ramp, which is reached in another 0.3 miles. A sign is posted at the left side of the road to identify it.

The right fork climbs above the public access, which will be visible below, to continue up the east side of the lake to a wide spot on the left after another 0.8 miles. This wide spot provides parking for a picnic area that is reached down a short trail. The picnic area has a pit toilet, a couple of picnic tables, and a small fishing dock. In the spring of 1996 the dock was in a poor state of repair.

The road continues past the east bank access, but no other access points are reached.

FISHING TIPS:

Many people fish for pike from the docks and shoreline areas at the public access. While most of the fishing is done with bait suspended below a bobber, my son caught his first pike here casting a spoon.

MAP REFERENCES:

*Idaho Atlas & Gazetteer, Page 60.

*USGS Topographic Map, Idaho (47116-E5-TF-024-00)
  Lane Quadrangle, 7.5 Minute Series.

*USGS Topographic Map, Idaho (47116-E1-TM-100-00)
  Coeur d'Alene Quadrangle, 30x60 Minute Series.

## 46   LEDBETTER LAKE

Also known as: Leadbetter Lake
Loon Lake

June 8, 2005; Ledbetter Lake, looking southeast
from the access area at the center of the west side.

SIZE: 22.7 Acres
ELEVATION: 2,528 Feet
MAXIMUM DEPTH: 20 Feet
COUNTY: Pend Oreille, Washington
COORDINATES: T39N R43E Sec34Q
      T40N R43E Sec3B

    Longitude: 117d 21m 5s to 117d 21m 24s West
    Latitude: 48d 54m 56s to 48d 55m 9s North

SPECIES, CONFIRMED:

SPECIES, REPORTED:
Eastern Brook Trout
Rainbow Trout

## CHARACTERISTICS:

Hills are visible in the distance to the north, over fields that can be seen from the lake.

The lake lies in a timbered area, and timbered hills rise over the west side and wrap around to the south. In other directions the hills are lower.

A large marshy area with heavy growths of aquatic weeds is found at the north end.

The other shorelines are fairly open, but have brush and grass to the waters edge in most places. Most shorelines are marshy. Timber is close to the shorelines at all but the north end.

Where the road reaches the lake at the center of the west side is limited parking and an old dock at the launch area. The dock is reached by a hodgepodge of debris that has been placed to span an area of shallow water and deeper mud. A narrow channel over the deep, soft mud passes through aquatic weeds and along the dock to finally reach open water. The mud in the launch area is much deeper than the water, which makes access difficult.

Shallow water out from the dock makes bank fishing, even from the dock, of limited effectiveness.

The center of the lake is deep. The shallows found along the shorelines don't extend out very far in most places. The shallows are most extensive at the north and south ends, and at the launch area.

The bottom is silt and mud, with a covering of low, bottom hugging aquatic vegetation.

The water is extremely clear.

## DIRECTIONS TO:

Take Highway 20 about 47 miles north from the town of Newport, to where it makes a 90-degree turn to the left at mile 390.4, and runs west toward the town of Colville. At this corner is the junction with Highway 31, which goes to the north.

Turn north onto Highway 31, and take it about 13 miles to the town of Metaline. At mile 13.1, Boundary Road will be found on the left.

Turn left onto Boundary Road and follow it north for 6.2 miles to an unmarked gravel road on the right. At 4.0 miles up Boundary Road you will pass a "Y" intersection with a large gravel road signed "Van Dyke", on the right.

Turn onto the unmarked gravel road and go 0.2 miles to another gravel road that goes to the right at a 90-degree turn, dropping downhill and turning back to the right.

Take this branch 0.2 miles to the lake.

The 0.4 miles from the paved road to the lake seems longer because the road is steep, rough and narrow with very few turnouts.

FISHING TIPS:

Spinners trolled along the far shore hooked fish on my one visit. The day I fished the lake the wind was blowing so hard that as soon as I would drop the oars to pick up the fishing rod to fight a fish, I was whipped down the lake so fast it was impossible to land anything. I can confirm the trout are there and what they'll hit, but can't tell you what kind they are because I never got one that close.

MAP REFERENCES:

*USGS Topographic Map, Washington (48117-H3-TF-024-00)
  Boundary Dam Quadrangle, 7.5 Minute Series.
*USGS Topographic Map, Washington (48117-E1-TM-100-00)
  Colville Quadrangle, 30x60 Minute Series.
*Washington Atlas & Gazetteer; Page 119.

## 47   LAKE LEO

May 22, 1995; Lake Leo, looking southwest from the access area.

SIZE: 39.3 Acres
ELEVATION: 3,165 Feet
MAXIMUM DEPTH: 37 Feet
COUNTY: Pend Oreille, Washington
COORDINATES: T36N R42E Sec3LM

Longitude: 117d 29m 30s to 117d 30m 6s West
Latitude: 48d 38m 45s to 48d 39m 1s North

SPECIES, CONFIRMED:
 Cutthroat Trout, West Slope
 Pumpkinseed Sunfish

SPECIES, REPORTED:
 Eastern Brook Trout
 German Brown Trout
 Rainbow Trout
 Tiger Trout

## CHARACTERISTICS:

The lake is completely surrounded by timber covered hills and flats. There are slight rises on the south and west sides.

There is a fairly open area immediately around the lake, especially at the ends. The areas that lack timber cover are filled with low scrub trees in many places.

A campground runs nearly the full length of the north shore, offering good access along that whole side of the lake. There is also an open area with access at the eastern half of the south side.

The shoreline areas are shallow. Many of the shallow spots have beds of lilypads and other aquatic vegetation.

The bottom is silt covered with a light layer of aquatic vegetation.

The water is clear.

## DIRECTIONS TO:

Take Highway 20 to mile 383.2, east of the town of Colville, where a paved road will be found on the south side of the highway. A sign at the end of the road indicates "Colville National Forest Campground, Lake Leo".

Turn onto this road, and take it 0.3 miles to the camp area at the shores of Lake Leo.

The area has toilets, a total of eight nice campsites, and a good concrete boat ramp.

## FISHING TIPS:

Flies worked along the shores work very well for both Cutthroat and Pumpkinseed.

## MAP REFERENCES:

*USGS Topographic Map, Washington (48117-F4-TF-024-00)
  Ione Quadrangle, 7.5 Minute Series.
*USGS Topographic Map, Washington (48117-F5-TF-024-00)
  Aladdin Mtn Quadrangle, 7.5 Minute Series.
*USGS Topographic Map, Washington (48117-E1-TM-100-00)
  Colville Quadrangle, 30x60 Minute Series.
*Washington Atlas & Gazetteer, Page 119.

# 48  LONG MOUNTAIN LAKE

September 6, 2001; Long Mountain Lake, looking northeast.

SIZE: 8 Acres (estimated)
ELEVATION: 6,705 Feet
MAXIMUM DEPTH: Unknown
COUNTY: Boundary, Idaho
COORDINATES: T63N R2W Sec9D

> Longitude: 116d 36m 32s to 116d 36m 37s West
> Latitude: 48d 49m 57s to 48d 50m 1s North

SPECIES, CONFIRMED:

SPECIES, REPORTED:
 Arctic Grayling
 Golden Trout

CHARACTERISTICS:
 Long Mountain rises to a height of 400 to 600 feet over the east side of
the lake. The mountain is very rocky, with a lot of low vegetation and grass
in boulder fields covering its slopes. It is dotted with a scattering of small
alpine firs.

The lake lies in a very small flat with ridges coming down from Long Mountain on both the north and south sides. The bowl the lake lies in is open to the northeast.

The northeast side of the lake has a skyline bordered by about a 20 foot high rock formation. The rocky area is dotted with a few trees, and has one large boulder that sets on top of it near the center. Mountains are visible in the distance to the northeast.

The shorelines have boulders, low shrubbery and scattered trees to the waters edge. The exception is the northeast side, where it's all rock.

There are a lot of snags along the shores, most of them submerged and lying on the bottom.

The water is shallow along and out from the shores in most places. The exceptions are at the east side of the lake, and the middle of the south side, where the water drops off more quickly. Looking down from Long Mountain, a couple of very large boulders can be seen lying on the bottom out from the south side.

The water is very clear.

The trail reaches the lake at the southwest corner, where a campsite is found. The campsite is fairly open, lying in a thin stand of small pines.

## DIRECTIONS TO:

Take Interstate 90 to exit 12, at the town of Coeur d'Alene.

From exit 12, take Highway 95 north for about 77 miles to mile 507.5, at the town of Bonners Ferry, where Riverside Road will be found on the west side of the highway just south of the bridge over the Kootenai River. The end of the road is signed for "Kootenai Wildlife Refuge 6 Miles".

Turn onto Riverside, and head west out of Bonners Ferry, keeping to the right as the road follows the banks of the river.

At 5.0 miles from Highway 95 the road will reach the base of the foothills, and a "Y" intersection. Keep to the right, and the road will begin running to the north. Past the "Y" about a quarter mile, you will pass the Kootenai Wildlife Refuge headquarters. The pavement ends in another 6.5 miles.

At 14.9 miles from Highway 95 you will reach the end of Forest Service Road 634, also shown on some maps as Trout Creek Road. The end of the road is signed "Junction Trail 6 Miles, Trail 12 7 Miles, Trail 13 9 Miles".

*Turn onto Road 634, and follow it 8.8 miles to a parking area, on the left, for the trailhead, which is on the right. The road ends in another 0.2 miles at a horse facility and camp area.

On the 8.8 mile run to the trailhead, you will reach an intersection at 4.5 miles, where you keep to the left.

You will pass the Fisher Peak trailhead, on the right, at 5.2 miles.

You will pass the Russell Peak Trail #12 parking area, on the left, at 6.1 miles. There are signs here for the trailhead that indicate "Russell Peak 2 1/2 Miles", and for the continuation of the road to the right indicating "Junction Trail #92 3 Miles".

The trailhead provides access to several lakes in the area, found off various branches of the trail system. The lakes include Pyramid, Upper Ball, Lower Ball, Trout, Big Fisher, Long Mountain, and Parker.

To reach Long Mountain Lake, take the trail about 0.5 miles (elevation gain approximately 450 feet) to a fork. Take the right fork.

Go about 0.75 miles (gain about 150 feet) to the next fork. This fork is reached at a wooden footbridge, to the right of which is a sign indicating that the trail to the right is to Trout Lake and Big Fisher Lake, and providing distances. The trail to the left is unmarked. Take the trail to the left.

Go about 1.0 mile to a saddle on the ridgeline to the west (gain about 450 feet).

From the saddle, the trail drops about 250 feet over a distance of about 0.5 miles before reaching the next fork in the trail. The main trail continues straight, and is signed with distance to a forest road on Long Canyon Creek. The trail you need branches off to the right, and is unmarked. Take the right.

The trail now becomes steeper and rougher than what you've been on so far. It climbs about 600 feet over a distance of about 0.75 miles to the top of the ridge. Once the ridge top is gained, the trail becomes better and runs along it for about 0.25 miles to the branch that drops to Long Mountain Lake.

The trail to Long Mountain Lake is marked with signs propped on top of a boulder just before you reach it. Two signs are placed back to back, giving approximate distances in both directions.

Take the branch to the right and the trail will become narrow and steeper again as it drops about 300 feet over about 0.5 miles to Long Mountain Lake.

An **ALTERNATE ROUTE** to the Trout Creek trail system would be to take Highway 95 to mile 523.0, north of the town of Bonners Ferry, where Highway 1 will be found on the left.

Turn onto Highway 1, and continue north for 1.1 miles to a road on the left at the town of Copeland. The end of the road is signed for "Sportsman's Access" and "National Forest Entrance".

Turn left onto the road, and head west. At 1.6 miles you will reach a bridge over the Kootenai River. At 3.4 miles from Highway 1 you will reach a "T" intersection with West Side Road. There is a sign opposite the end of the road you are on that indicates "Maravia 20 Miles" to the left, and "Smith Creek Road and Boundary Creek Road 9 Miles" to the right.

At West Side Road, turn left and go south for 2.9 miles to a 90-degree corner. The paved road turns to the left, and a gravel road leaves the pavement straight ahead. Contrary to appearances, the gravel road is the continuation of West Side Road.

Take the gravel road, and after 1.8 miles you will reach the end of Forest Service Road 634, also shown on some maps as Trout Creek Road, on the right. The end of the road is signed "Junction Trail 6 Miles, Trail 12 7 Miles, Trail 13 9 Miles".

From here, follow the directions provided above from the point marked with an asterisk(*).

FISHING TIPS:

I'm unable to offer any tips due to a lack of success in this lake. I fished it only once, in the fall of 2001. On my one visit I spent about an hour at the lake, walking completely around it while casting randomly. No evidence of fish was seen during the entire period.

MAP REFERENCES:
*Idaho Atlas & Gazetteer, Page 48 (lake not shown).
*USGS Topographic Map, Idaho (48116-G5-TF-024-00)
   Pyramid Peak Quadrangle, 7.5 Minute Series.
*USGS Topographic Map, Idaho (48116-E1-TM-100-00)
   Bonners Ferry Quadrangle, 30x60 Minute Series.

## 49  LOON LAKE

May 23, 2002; Loon Lake, north end,
looking southeast from the public access.

SIZE: 1,118.5 Acres
ELEVATION: 2,381 Feet
MAXIMUM DEPTH: 104 Feet
COUNTY: Stevens, Washington
COORDINATES: T29N R41E Sec2EN,3,4AB,10AB,11DE
             T30N R41E Sec33(southeast 1/4),34(southwest 1/4)

             Longitude: 117d 36m 14s to 117d 38m 34s West
             Latitude: 48d 1m 40s to 48d 3m 28s North

SPECIES, CONFIRMED:

SPECIES, REPORTED:
 Black Crappie
 Bluegill
 Brown Bullhead Catfish
 Eastern Brook Trout
 German Brown Trout
 Kokanee
 Largemouth Bass
 Mackinaw

Rainbow Trout
Smallmouth Bass
Warmouth
Yellow Perch

## CHARACTERISTICS:

The lake is 2.6 miles long, lying in an area of mostly low, rolling, timbered hills.

It has a shape that is hard to describe, with the first word that comes to mind being "sprawling". It is a large, open water lake, with many small bays and points, as well as two larger bays at the northwest corner.

Deer Lake Mountain rises to the northeast. It is sparsely timbered, and like so many other hills has sprouted cell phone towers at its top.

The north end is heavily developed, with the town of Loon Lake located on that end. The rest of the area around the lake is also developed, but not as heavily in most places. Even with the development, a lot of trees remain around the lake.

Because of the extensive development around the lake, the shores are lined with a lot of private docks.

The public access area, located near the northwest corner, has a large gravel parking area, pit toilets and a concrete strip boat ramp. A small channel about 50 feet wide runs about 150 yards from the boat ramp to open water. Two snags rise well above the surface out from the end of the channel.

The northwest corner, north of the public access, has marshy shores lined with cattails, and large fields beyond the shores. A very large, dense bed of lilypads is found at the northwest corner. The area south of the access is heavily developed.

Beaver Creek enters at the extreme south end. Other seasonal inlet streams enter at various places.

There is a regulating gate at the outlet, where Sheep Creek exits at the northwest corner.

The water is very clear.

## DIRECTIONS TO:

Take Highway 395 to mile 190.5, between the towns of Deer Park and Chewelah, where the junction with Highway 292 will be reached. The end of Highway 292 is signed for Shore Acres Resort, Loon Lake, and Springdale. The Highway 292 junction is about 38 miles south of the town of Colville.

Turn onto Highway 292, and go west for 1.8 miles, through the town of Loon Lake, to Shore Acres Road, on the left. The end of the road is signed for fishing and boat ramp.

Turn left, and go 0.3 miles to a large "Y" intersection. A large gravel road goes to the left, and the paved road continues to the right.

Keep to the right, and at 1.0 miles from Highway 292 you will reach Arnold Road, on the left. The end of the road is signed for public fishing.

Turn left onto Arnold Road, and go east for 0.4 miles to the boat ramp at the northwest corner of the lake.

FISHING TIPS:

I did not attempt to fish this lake.

MISCELLANEOUS NOTES:

Loon Lake produced a state record Mackinaw of 30 pounds 4 ounces in June of 1966.

MAP REFERENCES:

*USGS Topographic Map, Washington (48117-A6-TF-024-00) Springdale Quadrangle, 7.5 Minute Series.

*USGS Topographic Map, Washington (48117-A5-TF-024-00) Deer Lake Quadrangle, 7.5 Minute Series.

*USGS Topographic Map, Washington (48117-A1-TM-100-00) Chewelah Quadrangle, 30x60 Minute Series.

*Washington Atlas & Gazetteer, Page 104.

## 50   LOWER BALL LAKE

September 9, 2000; Lower Ball Lake, looking northwest.

SIZE: 3 Acres (estimated)
ELEVATION: 6,605 Feet
MAXIMUM DEPTH: Unknown
COUNTY: Boundary, Idaho
COORDINATES: T63N R2W Sec20Q

Longitude: 116d 37m 6s to 116d 37m 11s West
Latitude: 48d 47m 24s to 48d 47m 27s North

SPECIES, CONFIRMED:
 Cutthroat Trout, West Slope

SPECIES, REPORTED:

CHARACTERISTICS:
 Upper Ball Lake is at the headwaters of Spanish Creek. Its outlet stream
flows into the west side of Lower Ball Lake. The outlet creek at Lower Ball
exits at its southeast corner.

A mountain rises over the northwest corner of the lake. It has a lot of vertical rock and broken rock slopes. A large field of broken rock lies above the north end of the lake, east from the higher slopes of the mountain, and in the direction in which the upper lake lies.

From the rocky crest of the mountain, a ridge comes down the west side of the lake, tapering off just above the south end. The ridge is composed of mostly broken rock, but also has some vertical areas.

The trail to the lake reaches it through the small fir trees on the east side.

There are trees to the waters edge along the south side and around the east side up to where the inlet creek enters at the north end. The other shorelines are open with very large, broken rock.

A lot of rock lines shores in all areas, and many rise from the water along the edges. The south end, between where the trail comes in and the outlet creek, has several fairly flat rocks rising out of the lake that provide some very good places to fish from.

The bottom is almost all big rock, with some silt deposits between the rocks. There are a few very small snags along the south side.

The water is very clear.

DIRECTIONS TO:
Take Interstate 90 to exit 12, at the town of Coeur d'Alene.

From exit 12, take Highway 95 north for about 77 miles to mile 507.5, at the town of Bonners Ferry, where Riverside Road will be found on the west side of the highway just south of the 95 bridge over the Kootenai River. The end of the road is signed for "Kootenai Wildlife Refuge 6 Miles".

Turn onto Riverside, and head west out of Bonners Ferry, keeping to the right as the road follows the banks of the river.

At 5.0 miles from Highway 95 the road will reach the base of the foothills, and a "Y" intersection. Keep to the right, and the road will begin running to the north. Past the "Y" about a quarter mile, you will pass the Kootenai Wildlife Refuge headquarters. The pavement ends in another 6.5 miles.

At 14.9 miles from Highway 95 you will reach the end of Forest Service Road 634, also shown on some maps as Trout Creek Road. The end of the road is signed "Junction Trail 6 Miles, Trail 12 7 Miles, Trail 13 9 Miles".

*Turn onto Road 634, and follow it 8.8 miles to a parking area, on the left, for the trailhead, which is on the right. The road ends in another 0.2 miles at a horse facility and camp area.

On the 8.8 mile run to the trailhead, you will reach an intersection at 4.5 miles, where you keep to the left.

You will pass the Fisher Peak trailhead, on the right, at 5.2 miles.

You will pass the Russell Peak Trail #12 parking area, on the left, at 6.1 miles. There are signs here for the trailhead that indicate "Russell Peak 2 1/2 Miles", and for the continuation of the road to the right indicating "Junction Trail #92 3 Miles".

The trailhead provides access to several lakes in the area, found off various branches of the trail system. The lakes include Pyramid, Upper Ball, Lower Ball, Trout, Big Fisher, Long Mountain, and Parker.

To reach Lower Ball Lake, take the trail about 0.5 miles (elevation gain approximately 450 feet) to a fork. Take the left fork.

Pyramid Lake will be reached after about 0.3 miles, and the trail will run along its east side. Pass Pyramid, and the trail will switchback up the steep grade to the south, providing a great look down on Pyramid, and then resume a more gradual run on top.

At about 1.3 miles (elevation gain about 750 feet) from the last fork in the trail, another fork will be reached about 50 yards from the east side of Upper Ball Lake.

The fork to the right makes the short run to Upper Ball Lake, while the fork to the left makes a gradual drop and switches back to Lower Ball Lake after about a quarter of a mile.

The total hike to Lower Ball Lake is about two miles.

An **ALTERNATE ROUTE** to the Trout Creek trail system would be to take Highway 95 to mile 523.0, north of the town of Bonners Ferry, where Highway 1 will be found on the left.

Turn onto Highway 1, and continue north for 1.1 miles to a road on the left at the town of Copeland. The end of the road is signed for "Sportsman's Access" and "National Forest Entrance".

Turn left onto the road, and head west. At 1.6 miles you will reach a bridge over the Kootenai River. At 3.4 miles from Highway 1 you will reach a "T" intersection with West Side Road. There is a sign opposite the end of the road you are on that indicates "Maravia 20 Miles" to the left, and "Smith Creek Road and Boundary Creek Road 9 Miles" to the right.

At West Side Road, turn left and go south for 2.9 miles to a 90-degree corner. The paved road turns to the left, and a gravel road leaves the pavement straight ahead. Contrary to appearances, the gravel road is the continuation of West Side Road.

Take the gravel road, and after 1.8 miles you will reach the end of Forest Service Road 634, also shown on some maps as Trout Creek Road, on the right. The end of the road is signed "Junction Trail 6 Miles, Trail 12 7 Miles, Trail 13 9 Miles".

From here, follow the directions provided above from the point marked with an asterisk(*).

FISHING TIPS:
 Flies cast from shore will get fish.

MAP REFERENCES:
 *Idaho Atlas & Gazetteer, Page 48 (lake not shown).
 *USGS Topographic Map, Idaho (48116-G5-TF-024-00)
    Pyramid Peak Quadrangle, 7.5 Minute Series.
 *USGS Topographic Map, Idaho (48116-E1-TM-100-00)
    Bonners Ferry Quadrangle, 30x60 Minute Series (name not indicated).

# 51  LOWER GLIDDEN LAKE

July 1, 1996; Lower Glidden Lake, looking southwest.

SIZE: 12 Acres
ELEVATION: 5,608 Feet
MAXIMUM DEPTH: 13 Feet
COUNTY: Shoshone, Idaho
COORDINATES: T48N R6E Sec8Q

Longitude: 115d 43m 40s to 115d 43m 53s West
Latitude: 47d 30m 53s to 47d 31m 8s North

SPECIES, CONFIRMED:
 Arctic Grayling
 Cutthroat Trout, West Slope
 Eastern Brook Trout
 Rainbow Trout

SPECIES, REPORTED:

CHARACTERISTICS:
 The lake lies in a ring of steep hills open to the north.

The slopes above are mostly timber covered, although sparsely in some areas due to exposed rock. There are also some meadow areas.

Thick stands of small trees grow right up to the waters edge in most places. The inlet area and northeast corner are open.

A small inlet creek enters at the south end, and an outlet creek exits at the northwest corner. Snags are found at both locations. A large area of shallow water and marsh grass is found on the west side of the inlet creek.

The road to the lake reaches it at the north end, and runs around the east side. In most places it is separated from the water by small trees, but stays within a hundred yards of the lake.

Most of the lake is shallow, with the deepest water found at the center of the north half. The center area of the north half of the lake maintains a pretty uniform depth of around 12 feet, with the deepest water found being 13 feet. The west side of the north section is mostly eight to ten feet deep, and shallows up to a depth of six feet between the points at the center of the lake that divide the lake into north and south halves.

The maximum depth of the south half is nine feet, with a lot of shallow water at the extreme south end and along the shores, where the depth drops very gradually. The center area of the south section is mostly eight to nine feet deep.

The small bay where the inlet stream enters at the southeast corner has an unexpectedly deep center, with a depth of six to seven feet. Shallows of only two to three feet deep separate it from the main body of the lake. The area has a heavy covering of bottom hugging vegetation.

The bottom is mostly silt deposits, and has some scattered snags. There are several snags found scattered on the bottom in the area of the shallows that separate the deeper water of the north and south sections.

The water is very clear.

Old mine tailings can be seen about half way up the slopes above the south end of the lake. The old road that runs up the east side of the lake continues past the lake to reach the site of the old mine, providing a nice view looking back over the lake.

The large quantity of tailings would indicate that the mine was fairly large. The entrance is mostly closed now, and a sign in the area indicates that it is too dangerous to enter.

DIRECTIONS TO:
Take Interstate 90 to exit 62 at Wallace, Idaho, where Highway 4 enters from the north.

Follow Highway 4 through the many small, side of the road "towns" to the town of Burke, where it will become the Burke-Can Creek Road.

Continue east on Burke-Can Creek Road, and a power station will be reached on the left at 7.7 miles from Interstate 90.

Continue past the power station to the intersection with Road 615, on the right at 11.1 miles from the interstate.

Turn right onto Road 615. It will drop downhill and reach power lines after 0.1 mile.

At the power lines, keep to the left until you reach a small wooden bridge.

Cross the bridge and continue up the road to reach Lower Glidden Lake at 1.1 miles from the start of Road 615, 12.2 miles from the interstate.

When the lake becomes visible on your right, a parking area will be found on the left. Additional parking is available on both sides of the road in another 0.1 mile. A large, sloped area right next to the water provides the main access.

The road runs around the east side of the lake to reach the upper end in another 0.2 miles. The last of the camp / access areas are found here.

The road ends 0.2 miles past the end of the lake at an old mine, but the last part of the road is steep, rough and narrow. It's best to park below and walk up to the mine.

FISHING TIPS:

Spinners and flies cast from shore will get fish. Because of the brushy nature of the west side, shore access is from the other three. On the north end, you can cross the creek to reach an open area at the northwest corner. On the east side, old roads running the length of the shore not too far from the water offer access at many places.

The same lures worked over the shallow flats from a boat are also very productive.

Planting records indicate that 2,800 Arctic Grayling fry (0-3 inches long) were planted on August 8, 2001. On September 12, 2002 I caught one measuring seven inches long. It was the only Grayling taken out of 281 fish caught in the lake for the season, so I don't know about the survival rate of the fry. It may be that it was just one of the larger of the fish planted, and therefore one of the few capable of taking a fly. In the 2003 season, I caught none, but one other fisherman reported catching one.

The only Cutthroat I have caught in the lake was caught in 2003. It measured 6 1/4 inches long.

MISCELLANEOUS NOTES:

On the morning of June 28, 2004, while fishing in the upper end of the lake, a large mountain goat stood on the shores of the lake watching me fish. Heavy thunderstorms the evening before had driven everyone else home, so the area had been much quieter than usual for a while.

On August 8, 2006, a large bull moose spent the day at the lake. He was at the lake for two hours after daylight, returned in the middle of the day, then returned again in late afternoon and spent the entire evening feeding around the southwest end of the lake.

MAP REFERENCES:
  *Idaho Atlas & Gazetteer, Page 61.
  *Montana Atlas & Gazetteer, Page 80.
  *USGS Topographic Map, Montana-Idaho (47115-E6-TF-024-00)
    Thompson Pass Quadrangle, 7.5 Minute Series.
  *USGS Topographic Map, Montana-Idaho (47115-E1-TM-100-00)
    Thompson Falls Quadrangle, 30x60 Minute Series.

# 52   LOWER LEAD KING LAKE

May 18, 1997; Lower Lead King Lake, looking north.

SIZE: 2.4 Acres
ELEVATION: 2,550 Feet
MAXIMUM DEPTH: Unknown
COUNTY: Pend Oreille, Washington
COORDINATES: T40N R43E Sec27F

> Longitude: 117d 21m 17s to 117d 21m 21s West
> Latitude: 48d 56m 28s to 48d 56m 32s North

SPECIES, CONFIRMED:
 Cutthroat Trout, Coastal
 Pumpkinseed Sunfish

SPECIES, REPORTED:

CHARACTERISTICS:
 The area has low hills to the east and west, and is open to the north and
south.
 An old cabin is located on a rise above the north end, but is barely visible.

A paved road runs up the east side, but provides no access. Power lines cross to the north of the lake, and run down the west side. The gravel road that accompanies the power lines provides limited access to the water at the northwest corner. There are no suitable bank fishing areas, and launching of any floating device is difficult.

Small trees are found at the waters edge in many areas. Cattails and lily-pads ring the shores. All shoreline areas have heavy growths of aquatic vegetation. There are a few fairly open shoreline areas, particularly on the east side near the road. The only open area close to the water is at the south-east corner opposite a lilypad bed.

The center portion of the lake is deepest, and has the only open water. The open water makes up only about half of the total surface area.

An inlet stream enters at the northwest corner from the upper lake. An out-let stream exits the south end of the lake, but the actual outlet is lost in the heavy weed growth.

There is an active beaver lodge on the center of the west side of the lake. The visible bottom is silt and algae. The water is clear.

## DIRECTIONS TO:

Take Highway 20 about 47 miles north from the town of Newport, to where it makes a 90-degree turn to the left at mile 390.4 and runs west toward the town of Colville. At this corner is the junction with Highway 31, which goes to the north.

Turn north onto Highway 31, and take it about 13 miles to the town of Metaline. At mile 13.1, Boundary Road will be found on the left.

Turn left onto Boundary Road and follow it north for 8.3 miles to a gravel road on the left. You will pass both Lower and Upper Lead King Lakes before you reach the gravel road at the north end of the lakes.

Turn left onto the gravel road. The road runs toward the trees, then turns back to the south and passes under the power lines along the west side of the lakes.

Access for the upper lake will be reached at 0.3 miles, and consists of small, little used branches of road.

Access for the lower lake is another 0.3 miles, at 0.6 miles down the gravel road, and is also by a small branch road.

## FISHING TIPS:

Flies fished along the edges of the lilypads will get trout. For sunfish, work the edges of the shallower areas.

MISCELLANEOUS NOTES:

For an interesting side trip while in the area, visit the Gardiner Cave at Crawford State Park. The park is just north of the lakes. As of 1997 the park opened at 0900, with guided cave tours every even hour. The tour lasts about 30 to 40 minutes, is provided by the park service, and is free of charge.

MAP REFERENCES:

*USGS Topographic Map, Washington (48117-H3-TF-024-00)
   Boundary Dam Quadrangle, 7.5 Minute Series.
*USGS Topographic Map, Washington (48117-E1-TM-100-00)
   Colville Quadrangle, 30x60 Minute Series (lake not shown).
*Washington Atlas & Gazetteer, Page 119 (lake not shown).

## 53  LOWER ROMAN NOSE LAKE

August 21, 2002; Lower Roman Nose Lake, looking west.

SIZE: 10 Acres (estimated)
ELEVATION: 5,921 Feet
MAXIMUM DEPTH: Unknown
COUNTY: Boundary, Idaho
COORDINATES: T61N R2W Sec15F

> Longitude: 116d 34m 52s to 116d 35m 4s West
> Latitude: 48d 38m 23s to 48d 38m 30s North

SPECIES, CONFIRMED:
 Eastern Brook Trout

SPECIES, REPORTED:

CHARACTERISTICS:
 The lake lies on a shelf with steep hills over the north side, and a steep drop to the east.

The north and south shores are very different from one another. The south shore is all timbered, has quite a bit of brush, and is gently sloped. On the north shore the hillside rises very swiftly to fill the skyline. It is extremely rocky, with a lot of vertical rock and huge boulder fields.

The area was burned in the Sundance fire of 1967, and many standing snags still dot the rocky slopes to the north. The slopes have fields of brush and are dotted with fir trees.

On the west side, the heavy timber cover of the south side of the lake wraps around the base of a steep slope rising above the lake. The bowl at the top of these slopes above the southwest corner holds Upper Roman Nose Lake. The slopes are timbered, but also have a lot of rock.

On the ridgeline about 300 feet above the southeast side is a saddle where the trail from East Roman Nose Lake crosses.

The northwest corner has steep slopes of broken rock between the timbered slopes to the south and the steep rock to the north.

The east side of the lake is lowest, where the skyline is open and skylight can be seen through the thin strip of trees that line the area between the lake and the cliffs that fall away to the east.

There are a lot of snags in the lake. They are concentrated very heavily at the outlet end, but are found everywhere around the shores.

An inlet creek, Caribou Creek, flows down from the upper lake to enter at the southernmost point of the lake near the southwest corner. It exits at the east side. A good sized logjam covers the outlet end of the lake, providing an excellent platform for fishing the deep water out from it.

The bottom is silt with rock, and has a lot of boulders along the north side of the lake.

The water is extremely clear.

## DIRECTIONS TO:

### From the north:

Take Highway 95 to mile 507.5, at the town of Bonners Ferry, where Riverside Road will be found on the west side of the highway just south of the bridge over the Kootenai River. The end of the road is signed for "Kootenai Wildlife Refuge 6 Miles".

Turn onto Riverside, and head west out of Bonners Ferry, keeping to the right as the road follows the banks of the river.

At 5.0 miles from Highway 95 the road will reach the base of the foothills, and a "Y" intersection.

Turn to the left, onto the gravel road, West Side Road, which will run south.

Go approximately 2.8 miles to the end of Forest Service Road 402, on the right. A sign as you start up Road 402 indicates "Cooks Pass 13", "Little Creek 18", and "Roman Nose Lakes 20".

*Turn up Road 402, Snow Creek Road, and go 16.2 miles to Ruby Pass, staying on the main road for the distance. Some parts of the road, especially where it climbs, are badly washboarded.

At Ruby Pass, you will come to Road 2667, on the right. The end of the road is signed for "Roman Nose Lakes 2 Miles". The continuation of the road straight ahead is signed "Naples 13 Miles".

Turn right onto Road 2667, and in 0.5 miles you will come to an intersection with Road 294, on the left. The road to the right is signed "1.7 Miles to East Roman Nose Lake" and "3 Miles to Lower Roman Nose Lake".

Keep to the right, and at 1.3 miles from Ruby Pass you will reach another intersection. Keep to the right again.

At 1.8 miles is another road on the left. This one is signed for "Camp Area", and "Narrow Steep Road, No Trailers". This road runs 0.2 miles, with campsites and a pit toilet along it.

Keep to the right to reach the parking area for the trailheads for Roman Nose Lakes. This parking lot is posted "No Overnight Camping". It has a concrete pit toilet, and a signboard with a map of the trail system.

There are two trails that exit from the parking area.

From the far end of the parking lot, to the left of the pit toilet, is a boardwalk that runs the entire distance to East Roman Nose Lake. The distance is about 150 yards or so.

The second trail, Trail 160, exits from the center of the parking lot, on the right. It runs to Upper Roman Nose Lake and Lower Roman Nose Lake.

Take this trail, and it will switchback to the top of the low saddle to the west.

Before reaching the top, you will come to a fork in the trail. Turn uphill to the left at this fork.

About 50 feet past the fork you will come to another. This is the "scenic loop" trail. Go to the right here.

After cresting the saddle the trail will begin to drop down the other side and run to the left, reaching another fork about a mile from the trailhead.

Take the right fork here, and the trail will drop a short distance to yet another fork.

At this fork, the left goes about 0.5 miles Upper Roman Nose Lake, and the right goes about 0.5 miles to Lower Roman Nose Lake.

Take the right fork, and the trail will switchback down before angling to the right.

After a short, fairly straight stretch, the trail will come out onto a large slab of hard rock. The trail is easily lost here (can't leave tracks in solid rock). Look slightly to the left for the largest boulder along the edge of the slab of rock. The trail resumes just to the right of the boulder.

From the rocky area, the trail drops down through timber and brush, angling to the right again, to reach the lake at the east side near the outlet creek. This section of trail has low brush that closes in on the trail enough to soak your legs pretty thoroughly if it's wet.

As you reach the lake, a spur trail that comes in on the right will be passed. Coming in it is easily missed, but it is much more obvious when you leave the lake. Be sure to keep to the right here when you leave.

**From the south:**
Take Interstate 90 to exit 12, at the town of Coeur d'Alene.

From exit 12, take Highway 95 north for about 67 miles to mile 496.8, where a road on the left exits for the town of Naples.

Turn off of Highway 95 here, and go 6.3 miles to West Side Road, on the left. The end of the road is signed "Snow Creek Road 2 Miles", "Kootenai National Wildlife Refuge 5 Miles".

Turn left onto West Side Road, and go 2.0 miles to Forest Service Road 402, Snow Creek Road, on the left.

From here, follow the direction above from the point marked with an asterisk(*).

FISHING TIPS:
Flies cast from shore along the logjam at the outlet end of the lake are very effective.

MAP REFERENCES:
*Idaho Atlas & Gazetteer, Page 62 (name not indicated).
*USGS Topographic Map, Idaho (48116-F5-TF-024-00)
   Roman Nose Quadrangle, 7.5 Minute Series.
*USGS Topographic Map, Idaho (48116-E1-TM-100-00)
   Bonners Ferry Quadrangle, 30x60 Minute Series.

## 54  LOWER TWIN LAKE

June 25, 2004; Lower Twin Lake, looking south from Twin Lakes Road.

SIZE: 350 Acres
ELEVATION: 2,306 Feet
MAXIMUM DEPTH: Unknown
COUNTY: Kootenai, Idaho
COORDINATES: T52N R4W Sec5,6,8,17
        T53N R4W Sec31

        Longitude: 116d 51m 23s to 116d 53m 33s West
        Latitude: 47d 51m 30s to 47d 53m 34s North

SPECIES, CONFIRMED:
 Pumpkinseed Sunfish

SPECIES, REPORTED:
 Black Crappie
 Bullhead Catfish
 Cutthroat Trout
 Eastern Brook Trout
 German Brown Trout
 Kokanee

Largemouth Bass
Rainbow Trout
Yellow Perch

## CHARACTERISTICS:

The lake is long and narrow, winding from the inlet at the west end to the southeast.

The inlet is a narrow channel from Upper Twin Lake, found at the extreme west end of the lake. The shorelines of the channel are rocky.

The lake is heavily developed all around, but does still have some undeveloped sections of shoreline.

The public access area for the lake is located near the west end. The access has extremely limited bank access, a paved parking area, concrete boat ramp, small dock, picnic table and toilets. It lies in an area with houses all around it.

A channel runs about a hundred yards from the boat launch to the open water of the west end of the lake. The channel is about 30 feet wide and lined by beds of lilypads.

The area of the lake out from and west of the access is shallow and mostly covered by lilypads. Narrow channels wind through the weeds, and a main channel runs close to the south shore to reach the narrows between Upper Twin and Lower Twin Lakes.

Just east of the public access, an old bridge spans a narrows. The main body of the lake, with the deeper water, opens up east of the bridge.

Once away from the bridge, the lake winds to the southeast, then turns back to the east. The south shore becomes much less developed as you go east.

The bottom is heavy silt in most areas, rock in some places.

The water is murky in the summer months.

## DIRECTIONS TO:

Take Interstate 90 to exit 7, just east of Post Falls, Idaho, where Highway 41 enters from the north.

Take Highway 41 north for 12.5 miles to mile 12.5, where Twin Lakes Road will be reached, on the left. The intersection is signed for "Sportsman's Access".

Turn left onto Twin Lakes Road, and there is a sign for "Upper Twin 2.5 Miles" and "Lower Twin 1.5 Miles".

Go 1.6 miles to the access area for Lower Twin Lake, on the left.

An **ALTERNATE ROUTE** to Twin Lakes is to leave Interstate 90 at exit 12 at Coeur d'Alene.

From exit 12, turn left and go north 8.2 miles to mile 438.9, where Highway 53 will be found on the left.

Turn onto Highway 53 and go west about four miles to an intersection with Highway 41, reached at Highway 41 mile 7.7.

Turn right, and go north on Highway 41 for about five miles to Highway 41 mile 12.5, where Twin Lakes Road will be reached, on the left. The intersection is signed for "Sportsman's Access".

Turn left onto Twin Lakes Road, and there is a sign for "Upper Twin 2.5 Miles" and "Lower Twin 1.5 Miles".

Go 1.6 miles to the access area for Lower Twin Lake, on the left.

A **SECOND ALTERNATE ROUTE** is to take Highway 2 to the town of Newport, Washington / Old Town, Idaho, located on the state line. The junction of Highway 2 and Highway 41 is stoplighted.

At the junction of Highways 2 and 41, turn south onto Highway 41. Go south on Highway 41 for 26.5 miles to mile 12.5, where Twin Lakes Road will be reached, on the right. The intersection is signed for "Sportsman's Access".

Turn right onto Twin Lakes Road, and there is a sign for "Upper Twin 2.5 Miles" and "Lower Twin 1.5 Miles".

Go 1.6 miles to the access area for Lower Twin Lake, on the left.

FISHING TIPS:

I have visited the lake only once, and fished it very briefly, so can't offer many tips.

Micro jigs cast from shore at the access area were effective for Pumpkinseed Sunfish.

MAP REFERENCES:

*Idaho Atlas & Gazetteer, Page 60.
*USGS Topographic Map, Idaho (47116-G7-TF-024-00)
  Hayden Quadrangle, 7.5 Minute Series.
*USGS Topographic Map, Idaho (47116-H7-TF-024-00)
  Spirit Lake East Quadrangle, 7.5 Minute Series.
*USGS Topographic Map, Idaho (47116-H8-TF-024-00)
  Spirit Lake West Quadrangle, 7.5 Minute Series.
*USGS Topographic Map, Idaho (47116-E1-TM-100-00)
  Coeur d'Alene Quadrangle, 30x60 Minute Series.

# 55  MARSHALL LAKE

May 22, 2002; Marshall Lake, looking north.

SIZE: 188.7 Acres
ELEVATION: 2,724 Feet
MAXIMUM DEPTH: 92 Feet
COUNTY: Pend Oreille, Washington
COORDINATES: T32N R45E Sec14R,23(east 1/2),24E

Longitude: 117d 3m 53s to 117d 4m 51s West
Latitude: 48d 15m 21s to 48d 16m 16s North

SPECIES, CONFIRMED:
 Cutthroat Trout, West Slope

SPECIES, REPORTED:

CHARACTERISTICS:
 The lake lies in a mountainous area, with steep wooded hills all around.
 The lowest ground in the area is at the southwest corner, where the public access and a resort with a very large campground are located.

The shape is very irregular, with large arms extending to the north and to the east from the main body of the lake, and small bays to the northwest and southeast. There is a small point at the southeast corner, plus a very large point at the northeast corner between the two main arms.

The lake is developed at the southwest corner, and there are also some homes at the southeast corner. There are some docks in the developed areas along the east side.

Most shorelines are steep. The exceptions are the southwest corner and the ends of the large arms. There are trees and brush to the waters edge in most places, but the steepest shores are rocky and sparsely covered. The shores of the point at the southeast corner are open, but steep and rocky.

Snags rise close along shorelines in some places. Most are at the ends of the large arms.

The inlets are Marshall Creek, at the end of the north arm, and Burnt Creek, at the end of east arm. The inlet areas have flats of relatively shallow water extending out from them for some distance. The flats have some aquatic vegetation and scattered snags on the bottom.

Marshall Creek flows out at a small dam at the south end.

The visible bottom areas are gravel in the access area, rocky along the steep shorelines, and silt in the shallow flats found at the ends of the arms where the inlet streams enter.

The center of the lake is all deep water, with a fairly flat bottom and a depth that varies slightly between 90 and 92 feet.

The water is very clear.

DIRECTIONS TO:

From the north, take Highway 20 to the town of Newport, where it will end at mile 436.8 at an intersection with Highway 2.

At the stop sign in Newport, turn left onto Highway 2. Take Highway 2 into Idaho and the bridge over the Pend Oreille River.

*As soon as you cross the river, you will need to be in the left lane to turn onto the first road as you leave the bridge. This is LeClerc Creek Road, and enters from the north at Idaho Highway 2 mile 0.5.

Turn left onto LeClerc Creek Road.

**Take LeClerk Creek Road north for 2.7 miles to Marshall Lake Road, which enters on the right. Some maps show this to be Bead Lake Road.

Turn right onto Marshall Lake / Bead Lake Road, and go 2.4 miles to Marshall Lake Road, a gravel road on the right.

***Turn onto this Marshall Lake Road, and go 1.3 miles to Marshall Lake. The public access is not obvious when you reach the area. You drive through the camp area of a resort and come to a small office with a sign telling you to stop to check in. The public access is just beyond this office, so keep going unless you plan to camp there.

The public access has a large gravel parking area, pit toilets and a large gravel launch area. There is no overnight parking or camping at the access area.

An **ALTERNATE ROUTE** to Marshall Lake is from the south on Highway 2.

Take Highway 2 north about 47 miles from Interstate 90 Exit 281 in Spokane to the town of Newport.

Take Highway 2 into Idaho and the bridge over the Pend Oreille River.

From here follow the directions provided above from the point marked with an asterisk(*).

A **SECOND ALTERNATE ROUTE** is from the east on Highway 2.

Take Highway 2 west about 28 miles from Highway 95 in the town of Sandpoint to LeClerc Creek Road, which will be on the right at Highway 2 mile 0.5.

At mile 0.5, just before you reach the bridge over the Pend Oreille River, turn right onto LeClerc Creek Road.

From here follow the directions provided above from the point marked with a double asterisk(**).

**NOTE:** In 1997, the Pend Oreille River reached elevations that flooded LeClerc Creek Road. When LeClerc Creek Road is not available, there is another route that can be used for access.

East of Newport at Idaho Highway 2 mile 2.3 is the Albeni Falls Machine Shop on the north side of the road. Freeman Lake Road, a gravel road, heads north next to the shop.

Take this road to access Marshall Lake Road, which will be reached after 6.2 miles. Freeman Lake Road becomes Bench Road before you reach the end.

Turn right, and take Marshall Lake Road 1.8 miles to the gravel Marshall Lake Road, on the right.

From here follow the directions above from the point marked with a triple asterisk(***).

## FISHING TIPS:

Flies cast to rising fish are effective. For best results, work the flats at the inlet areas at the ends of the arms to the north and east. Both flies and spinners worked over the flats, and around the snags found there, are very effective for decent sized fish.

## MAP REFERENCES:
*USGS Topographic Map, Washington (48117-C1-TF-024-00)
  Bead Lake Quadrangle, 7.5 Minute Series.
*USGS Topographic Map, Washington (48117-A1-TM-100-00)
  Chewelah Quadrangle, 30x60 Minute Series.
*Washington Atlas & Gazetteer, Page 105.

## 56  MCARTHUR LAKE
Also known as: McArthur Reservoir

September 9, 2000; McArthur Lake, looking south.

SIZE: 200 Acres
ELEVATION: 2,085 Feet (at spillway)
MAXIMUM DEPTH: Unknown
COUNTY: Boundary, Idaho
COORDINATES: T60N R1W Sec27(south 1/2),34(northwest 1/2)

Longitude: 116d 26m 27s to 116d 27m 22s West
Latitude: 48d 30m 26s to 48d 31m 17s North


SPECIES, CONFIRMED:
 Yellow Perch

SPECIES, REPORTED:
 Eastern Brook Trout
 Rainbow Trout

CHARACTERISTICS:

The lake lies right alongside Highway 95, which runs up the east side.

The lake is found in a wide valley that runs from north to south. Rolling, timbered hills are found on both the east and west sides of the valley.

The lake has timber around it, but the trees are mostly well away from the water. The shorelines are brushy and marshy.

The lake is very shallow with a lot of weed beds. By late summer weeds are at the surface in most places, and very close to the surface almost everywhere.

The public access is located at the northeast corner. It has a gravel boat ramp with a small launching dock. South of the boat ramp about fifty yards is a fishing dock that extends out from the east shore. The fishing dock is reached by a trail across a grassy area.

Beyond the fishing dock, further south, is a large concrete spillway. Power lines cross the northeast corner.

A few homes are located above the east side of the lake, between Highway 95 and the water. They are on the northern half of the east side.

The bottom is thick silt and mud, covered by dense growths of aquatic weeds.

The water is clear.

In the summer of 2002, for reasons unknown to me, the reservoir was drained. It was refilled that fall.

DIRECTIONS TO:

Take Interstate 90 to exit 12, at the town of Coeur d'Alene.

From exit 12, take Highway 95 north for about 63 miles to mile 493.3, where a road at the north end of the lake will be reached.

Turn left onto the road and go east 0.1 mile to the end of a gravel access road, on the left.

Turn left onto the access road and go 0.1 mile to the public access area. The access has a large gravel parking area, pit toilet, boat ramp with launching dock, and a fishing dock.

FISHING TIPS:

Jigs fished from the fishing dock will get an occasional Perch.

MISCELLANEOUS NOTES:

In September 2000, Idaho Fish & Game had a notice posted that tagged Rainbow are present.

MAP REFERENCES:
*Idaho Atlas & Gazetteer, Page 62.
*USGS Topographic Map, Idaho (48116-E4-TF-024-00)
  Naples Quadrangle, 7.5 Minute Series.
*USGS Topographic Map, Idaho (48116-E1-TM-100-00)
  Bonners Ferry Quadrangle, 30x60 Minute Series.

## 57   MCDOWELL LAKE

May 17, 1997; McDowell Lake, looking northwest from the access area.

SIZE: 33.0 Acres
ELEVATION: 2,325 Feet
MAXIMUM DEPTH: Unknown
COUNTY: Stevens, Washington
COORDINATES: T34N R41E Sec6R

Longitude: 117d 40m 27s <u>to</u> 117d 40m 58s West
Latitude: 48d 27m 51s <u>to</u> 48d 28m 12s North

SPECIES, CONFIRMED:

SPECIES, REPORTED:
 Eastern Brook Trout
 German Brown Trout
 Rainbow Trout
 Tench

## CHARACTERISTICS:

The lake is surrounded by low, wooded hills. In some areas the tree cover is sparse and the slopes are grassy.

Most shoreline areas have small trees at the waters edge, and bank access is limited.

Most areas of the lake are shallow. The southeast end has boggy areas and a small island near a point on the south shore.

There are many snags on the bottom, and several rising from the bottom along the shorelines and in the shallower areas.

The bottom is silt. The water is clear.

## DIRECTIONS TO:

Take Highway 20 to mile 364.9, east of the town of Colville, where Starvation Lake Road will be found on the south side of the highway.

Turn onto Starvation Lake Road and go south. At 0.9 miles a gravel road on the right enters the public access area for Starvation Lake.

Continue past the access on Starvation Lake Road, and at 1.3 miles from Highway 20 you will reach an intersection.

Go to the right. At 0.4 miles you will cross a cattleguard and a sign indicating "Little Pend Oreille Wildlife Refuge" will be seen on the right side of the road. Just a little further, at 0.5 miles, will be another intersection.

Turn right. After another 0.7 miles you will reach the next intersection.

Turn left. After another 1.6 miles you will pass a road on the left, just before crossing the Little Pend Oreille River and entering a camp area after another 0.1 mile.

Pass through the camp area, where the road will angle to the left before it begins to climb above the camp and turns back to the right. The McDowell Lake access area will be reached 1.1 miles from the camp, a total of 5.3 miles from Highway 20. The access has a small gravel parking area overlooking the south end of the lake. From the parking area, trails drop down to the water.

## FISHING TIPS:

The lake is fly fishing only, and catch and release only, with no motors allowed. Check the current regulations before fishing.

## MAP REFERENCES:

*USGS Topographic Map, Washington (48117-D6-TF-024-00)
  Cliff Ridge Quadrangle, 7.5 Minute Series.
*USGS Topographic Map, Washington (48117-A1-TM-100-00)
  Chewelah Quadrangle, 30x60 Minute Series.
*Washington Atlas & Gazetteer, Page 104.

## 58  MEDICINE LAKE

June 29, 1996; Medicine Lake, looking southeast.

SIZE: 340 Acres
ELEVATION: 2,134 Feet
MAXIMUM DEPTH: Unknown
COUNTY: Kootenai, Idaho
COORDINATES: T47N R2W Sec3CD
        T48N R2W Sec27,28,33,34

        Longitude: 116d 34m 35s to 116d 35m 42s West
        Latitude: 47d 27m 34s to 47d 28m 40s North

SPECIES, CONFIRMED:
 Black Bullhead Catfish
 Bluegill
 Pumpkinseed Sunfish

SPECIES, REPORTED:
 Black Crappie
 Largemouth Bass
 Northern Pike
 Yellow Perch

## CHARACTERISTICS:

The lake lies in an area of low, timbered hills.

The north and south ends of the lake are very shallow and weed choked. The center and south end of the east side are deeper with steeper shores. A large point extends into the east side.

Highway 3 runs along part of the southeast corner. A gravel road, Rainy Hill Road on the north and Medimont Road on the west, runs around the lake. The road at the northwest corner runs atop a rock dike that separates Medicine and Cave Lakes. A bridge in this road spans a navigable channel that connects the two lakes.

The public access area is located at the northeast corner of the lake. It has a large gravel parking area, concrete strip boat ramp, a small dock, and pit toilets. It is day use only, with no overnight camping. The access area also provides some bank fishing opportunities.

A narrow channel runs to the right from the access area to the Coeur d'Alene River. It is navigable, but limited to boats small enough to pass through the low and narrow bridge crossing.

A small portion of Medicine Lake, cut off by Rainy Hill Road, is found on the northwest corner. This portion of the lake is almost entirely weeded.

The bottom is rocky in the shoreline areas at the access area, and along the road at the northwest corner. The bottom is mostly silt in other areas.

Most shorelines are grass and / or brush covered to the waters edge. One major exception is the steep rocky shore along Medimont Road.

The water is usually murky.

## DIRECTIONS TO:

Take Interstate 90 to exit 34 east of Coeur d'Alene, Idaho. At exit 34, turn south onto Highway 3.

Take Highway 3 south 12.8 miles to mile 106.7, where Rainy Hill Road enters on the right. The end of the road is signed for "Sportsman's Access" just prior to reaching it.

Turn right onto Rainy Hill Road, and the access area for Medicine Lake will be reached on the left after 0.7 miles. The access area is marked as the "Rainy Hill, Coeur d'Alene National Forest Boat Launch".

Continue 0.3 miles past the Medicine Lake access to reach an intersection near the bridge over the channel between Medicine and Cave Lakes. You can park here and walk to the limited shore access for the lakes at the channel. Cave Lake can also be accessed via water from Medicine Lake thanks to the channel through the dike.

An **ALTERNATE ROUTE** to the access areas is from Highway 3 mile 105.1, where Medimont Road enters. Take Medimont Road 1.0 mile north from Highway 3 to reach the intersection mentioned above. There are a few places along Medimont Road that offer additional, although limited, bank access to Medicine Lake.

FISHING TIPS:
  My time spent fishing this lake is very limited. Flies cast from shore at the access area were effective for Bluegill and Pumpkinseed.

MAP REFERENCES:
  *Idaho Atlas & Gazetteer, Page 60.
  *USGS Topographic Map, Idaho (47116-D5-TF-024-00)
    Medimont Quadrangle, 7.5 Minute Series.
  *USGS Topographic Map, Idaho (47116-A1-TM-100-00)
    St. Maries Quadrangle, 30x60 Minute Series.

# 59   MIRROR LAKE

June 16, 2006; Mirror Lake, looking southeast from the resort.

SIZE: 90 Acres
ELEVATION: 2,368 Feet
MAXIMUM DEPTH: Unknown
COUNTY: Bonner, Idaho
COORDINATES: T56N R1W Sec30N,31(northwest 1/4)
      T56N R2W Sec25R

      Longitude: 116d 29m 34s to 116d 30m 11s West
      Latitude: 48d 9m 35s to 48d 10m 8s North

SPECIES, CONFIRMED:
 Eastern Brook Trout
 Rainbow Trout

SPECIES, REPORTED:
 Cutthroat Trout, West Slope
 German Brown Trout
 Kokanee

CHARACTERISTICS:
 The lake lies in an area of heavily timbered mountains that rise up almost all around. Higher hills are visible in the distance to the south.

The shorelines have timber and brush to the waters edge all around the lake. Breaks in the shoreline cover are minimal, and only at the few developed areas. A couple of houses set in the trees over the northwest corner of the lake, and a Kiwanis camp is located at the south end of the lake. Each has a dock.

Access is at a private resort at the north end of the lake. Mirror Lake Resort provides camping and boat launching for a fee.

There is a shallow, weedy area at the north end, out from the resort. It extends out as much as 200 yards before dropping off to deeper water. The resort has a float out in this area.

There are snags scattered randomly along the shorelines, some of which are large. Most are found on the east and west sides of the lake, and some break the surface well out from shore.

Visible bottom areas are silt, and the shallowest areas have a covering of aquatic weed.

The water is clear.

DIRECTIONS TO:

Take Interstate 90 to exit 12 at Coeur d'Alene, Idaho. At exit 12, turn north onto Highway 95.

Take Highway 95 north for about 36 miles to mile 465.6, where East Dufort Road will be reached, on the right.

Turn onto East Dufort Road, which becomes gravel, and go 3.7 miles to a "T" intersection. The intersection is signed "Mirror Lake" to the right.

Turn right onto Talache Road, which is paved, and go 1.6 miles to Mirror Lake Resort Road, on the left. The end of the road is signed "Mirror Lake Resort".

Turn down Mirror Lake Resort Road, and take it 0.5 miles to the resort area.

An **ALTERNATE ROUTE** to Mirror Lake that is all on paved road exists, and is a good route if you are southbound on Highway 95 from Sandpoint.

Take Highway 95 to the town of Sagle, where at mile 468.2 Sagle Road will be found on the east side of the highway.

Turn onto Sagle Road, and go east for 1.2 miles to Talache Road, on the right.

Turn right, onto Talache Road, and go south for 4.2 miles to Mirror Lake Resort Road, on the left. The end of the road is signed "Mirror Lake Resort".

Turn down Mirror Lake Resort Road, and take it 0.5 miles to the resort area.

FISHING TIPS:

Spinners and flies, both cast and trolled, are very effective for both the Rainbow and Eastern Brook in the lake.

Flies were most effective worked over the shallows at the northwest corner of the lake. The best area for trolled spinners was along the middle stretch of the west side. Cast spinners were effective in all areas.

As of 2006, the lake has special regulations, including "electric motors only". See the current regulations before fishing.

MISCELLANEOUS NOTES:

Mirror Lake was the lake used in the filming of the movie "Dante's Peak" in 1996. The resort office was also used.

As of 2006, the fee for day access to launch a boat and fish is $5.00, day use is $1.00 per person, and camping is $12.00 per night. Boat rentals are also available, at $5.00 per hour or $15.00 per day, and electric motors are available for an additional fee.

MAP REFERENCES:

*Idaho Atlas & Gazetteer, Page 62.
*USGS Topographic Map, Idaho (48116-B5-TF-024-00)
  Sagle Quadrangle, 7.5 Minute Series.
*USGS Topographic Map, Idaho (48116-B4-TF-024-00)
  Talache Quadrangle, 7.5 Minute Series.
*USGS Topographic Map, Idaho-Montana (48116-A1-TM-100-00)
  Sandpoint Quadrangle, 30x60 Minute Series.

## 60  MOOSE LAKE
Also known as: Bull Moose Lake

June 18, 2006; Moose Lake, looking northeast.

SIZE: 1.5 Acres (estimated)
ELEVATION: 2,625 Feet (estimated)
MAXIMUM DEPTH: Unknown
COUNTY: Bonner, Idaho
COORDINATES: T62N R4W Sec 26D

       Longitude: 116d 49m 30s to 116d 49m 37s West
       Latitude: 48d 42m 2s to 48d 42m 4s North


SPECIES, CONFIRMED:
 Rainbow Trout

SPECIES, REPORTED:

CHARACTERISTICS:
  The lake is a small, reportedly man-made pond, lying in an area of timbered hills. On my visit in 2006, the higher hill to the east was being helicopter logged.

The area around the lake is heavily timbered, and has several large cottonwoods close to the lake.

The lake has a very irregular shape, and runs primarily east to west.

There is a small, open water bay at the west end of the lake. It is bordered by the access road that reaches it, and a dirt and gravel berm.

The north shore has a berm of dirt and gravel running about three to four feet above the water, and extending about a hundred yards down the shoreline. It provides excellent bank fishing access.

A trail continues from the end of the north shore berm to completely circle the lake. The areas on the east and southeast sides of the lake can be wet and tough to cross without getting your feet wet. Water exits the lake at some low areas on the south side, making them some of the more difficult places to cross.

The east end and south side have brush to the waters edge. Openings in the brush provide isolated access points for bank fishing.

A small island sets out from the south side, about half way up the lake. It is about 75 feet from shore. It forms a brush covered and snag lined mound in the center of the lake.

There are many snags in the lake, but most don't pose any problem for fishing. There are a couple of large ones at the southeast corner.

The bottom of the lake is silt.

The water has a light brown tinge.

DIRECTIONS TO:

Take Highway 2 to mile 5.9, at a stoplight in the middle of the town of Priest River, where Highway 57 / West Side Road will be found on the north side of the highway.

Turn onto Highway 57, and follow it north for 22.5 miles to Dickensheet Road, on the right. The continuation of Highway 57 is signed for Nordman. Dickensheet Road provides access to the south end and east side of Priest Lake.

Turn right onto Dickensheet Road and go 5.2 miles to the town of Coolin, where an intersection is reached. The road to the right provides access to the east side of Priest Lake, and the road you are on goes to the left to reach the south end of the lake. The road to the right is signed for "Priest Lake State Park, Indian Creek Unit, Lionhead Unit".

Turn right, onto East Shore Road, and take it 19.1 miles to the access road for Moose Lake, on the right. The road is reached 8.0 miles past the Indian Creek Unit of the State Park, and 0.5 miles past Sandy Shores Road. The end of the road is signed for "Moose Lake".

Turn onto the short access road, and go less than 0.1 mile to the small parking area. If you have a large vehicle, it's best to park out along the main road. There are several signs at the parking area. They are for "Moose Lake Fishing Pond", "No Motorized Vehicles Beyond This Point", "Day Use Only – No Camping", and a large one with the fishing regulations that apply to the lake.

From the parking area, take the trail a little over a hundred yards to where it intercepts an old road bed.

At the road bed, go to the right, and you will reach the west end of the lake in about another hundred yards.

Moose Lake is reached a total of 46.8 miles from Highway 2 in Priest River.

FISHING TIPS:

The planted Rainbow are easily caught using any traditional trout baits or lures. Flies are extremely effective.

MISCELLANEOUS NOTES:

The lake is listed in the Idaho fishing regulations as a "Family Fishing Water" under the name Bull Moose Lake.

MAP REFERENCES:

*Idaho Atlas & Gazetteer, Page 62 (lake not shown).

*USGS Topographic Map, Idaho (48116-F7-TF-024-00)
  Priest Lake NE Quadrangle, 7.5 Minute Series (lake not shown).

*USGS Topographic Map, Idaho (48116-E1-TM-100-00)
  Bonners Ferry Quadrangle, 30x60 Minute Series (lake not shown).

## 61  MUSKEGON LAKE
Also known as: Moss Keg Lake

June 23, 2004; Muskegon Lake, looking northwest.

SIZE: 7.5 Acres
ELEVATION: 3,441 Feet
MAXIMUM DEPTH: Unknown
COUNTY: Pend Oreille, Washington
COORDINATES: T38N R45E Sec13BG

Longitude: 117d 2m 9s to 117d 2m 18s West
Latitude: 48d 47m 49s to 48d 47m 55s North

SPECIES, CONFIRMED:
 Cutthroat Trout, West Slope
 Rainbow Trout

SPECIES, REPORTED:

CHARACTERISTICS:
 The lake lies about 1,300 feet west of the Washington-Idaho state line in
a timbered area.
 It is nearly oval, but with a slightly irregular shape.

Low, timber covered hills are visible in the distance to the west and north, and lower rises surround the lake.

The shorelines have timber and brush to the waters edge in almost all areas. The northeast corner has a small opening in the cover, beyond which is a small, very shallow, weed choked pond.

There are a large number of snags along many shoreline areas. Large concentrations are found at the northwest corner and the east side, and lesser concentrations in other areas. Some of the snags are very large.

The bottom is rock, gravel and silt, and has snags randomly scattered across it. There is little aquatic vegetation. The lack of vegetation in the lake makes the floating algae encountered during the summer months unexpected.

The depth of the water drops off gradually as you move away from the shore, with the deepest water found at the center of the lake.

The trail to the lake reaches it at a small open section of shore at the southeast corner.

The water is very clear.

## DIRECTIONS TO:

Although the lake is in Washington State, the primary access is from the state of Idaho.

Take Highway 2 to mile 5.9, at a stoplight in the middle of the town of Priest River, where Highway 57 / West Side Road will be found on the north side of the highway.

Turn onto Highway 57, and follow it north for 51.3 miles to the Muskegon Lake access area. You will enter the state of Washington at 43.4 miles, pass Huff Lake at 46.9 miles, pass the end of Road 302 (FS 22 from Metaline) at 50.1 miles, and pass the end of Road 656 at 51.0 miles.

The area is reached 0.3 miles past the end of Road 656, and 0.2 miles before the Idaho state line.

A good sized camp area will be seen on the right, and the small trailhead parking area is on the left just past it. The trailhead is marked with a small sign on a tree at the end of the trail.

The trail to Muskegon Lake is signed as 1/4 mile, but is actually only a couple of hundred yards long.

From the trailhead at roadside, the trail drops slightly to a wooden footbridge across a small creek, then angles to the left to a switchback.

The switchback cuts back to the right, and then the trail climbs to a low crest. From the crest it drops to the edge of the lake.

The trail is very good, but as of 2005 had some blowdown debris on the short section just above the lake.

An **ALTERNATE ROUTE** to Muskegon Lake is from Washington State. This route crosses a logging road pass at high elevation, so is not an option for much of the year when snow or road conditions make it impassable.

Take Highway 20 to mile 390.4, about 47 miles north of the town of Newport, where the junction with Highway 31 is reached.

Take Highway 31 north for about 3 miles to mile 3.0, where the south end of Sullivan Lake Road enters on the right.

Turn right, onto Sullivan Lake Road, cross the Pend Oreille River, run up the west side of Sullivan Lake, and at 18.0 miles from Highway 31 you will reach an intersection, where Forest Service Road 22 is found on the right. The end of the road is signed for "Salmo Mountain 21, Priest Lake 40, East Sullivan Campground 1/4".

Turn onto Road 22, and stay on the main road for 5.8 miles, to where you will reach an intersection at a small bridge. The left fork, Road #2220, is signed for "Salmo Mountain". The right fork is signed for "Priest Lake", and is the continuation of Road 22. The road is also signed "Narrow road, not suited to trailer traffic".

Take the right fork. At 13.3 miles from the start of Road 22 the road will crest at Pass Creek Pass, elevation just over 5,400 feet, and begin to loose elevation.

Stay on the main road to reach a major intersection at 20.4 miles from the start of Road 22. The road you reach is a wide gravel road, and is signed "Upper Priest Lake 6 Miles" to the left.

Turn left, and go 1.2 miles to the access area for Muskegon Lake. The area is reached 0.3 miles past the end of Road 656, and 0.2 miles before the Idaho state line.

A good sized camp area will be seen on the right, and the small trailhead parking area is on the left just past it.

FISHING TIPS:

Flies and spinners are both very effective. The only Rainbow I caught were during the low light periods just before dark and just after daylight.

While the Cutthroat are very nice fish, very large Rainbow are occasionally caught. My best Rainbow was 4.8 pounds.

## MISCELLANEOUS NOTES:

The lake has special regulations. Check the current regulations before fishing. As of 2006, the lake is open from the last Saturday in April until the end of October, has a two trout limit, and selective gear rules apply.

The lake produced a state record West Slope Cutthroat of 1.99 pounds (length 17 inches) for me on June 24, 2004. I caught the fish on the first cast at 0430 in the morning.

## MAP REFERENCES:

*USGS Topographic Map, Washington (48117-G1-TF-024-00)
  Helmer Mountain Quadrangle, 7.5 Minute Series.
*USGS Topographic Map, Washington (48117-E1-TM-100-00)
  Colville Quadrangle, 30x60 Minute Series.
*Washington Atlas & Gazetteer, Page 119 (name not indicated).

## 62  MYSTIC LAKE

July 14, 1999; Mystic Lake, looking northeast.

SIZE: 16.8 Acres
ELEVATION: 2,967 Feet
MAXIMUM DEPTH: 22 Feet
COUNTY: Pend Oreille, Washington
COORDINATES: T33N R45E Sec29LP

Longitude: 117d 8m 25s to 117d 8m 42s West
Latitude: 48d 19m 34s to 48d 19m 48s North

SPECIES, CONFIRMED:
 Cutthroat Trout, West Slope

SPECIES, REPORTED:
 Rainbow Trout

## CHARACTERISTICS:

The lake is almost rectangular, running from southwest to northeast.

The east side has low, densely timbered hills. The only areas with a break in the timber are at the northeast corner, where there is a little bit of rock and brush showing through.

The west side also has timbered hills.

An access and camp area are located above the south end of the lake. This end has low brush and smaller trees. Timber covers the hillside, but not as densely as other areas. The hill is low and open at the top from a clearcut on the far side of the ridge, which is only about 150 feet above the lake.

The shores of the west side are all completely passable and easily walked. The slopes are moderately steep, mostly of broken rock. A few small areas of hard rock are at the water's edge, but are easily negotiated.

The shores of the east side are a lot brushier, but a short section at the south end can be walked. A trail passes above the brushier areas and drops back to the water at various places along the east shore. On the east shore, a grassy point extends a short distance into the lake about 3/4 of the way down the lake. The north half of the east shore has broken rock slopes that can be walked.

A lot of snags are scattered along the shores. A couple found out from the west shore rise from the bottom to break the surface.

The bottom is small broken rock and gravel, with some silt. There is very little aquatic vegetation around the lake. It is found only in small pockets on the immediate shorelines. Most of the vegetation around the shores is not aquatic, but grasses at the water's edge and out into the lake. In most places, the shores drop off quickly to deep water.

The water has a light greenish tinge, but is fairly clear.

The camp area at the south end is undeveloped. Parking and camp areas are under heavy timber where there is no underbrush. The area is dirt and would tend to muddy up during rains. The road in through the camp area is rough.

## DIRECTIONS TO:

From the north, take Highway 20 to the town of Newport, where it will end at mile 436.8 at an intersection with Highway 2.

At the stop sign in Newport, turn left onto Highway 2. Take Highway 2 into Idaho and the bridge over the Pend Oreille River.

*As soon as you cross the river, you will need to be in the left lane to turn onto the first road as you leave the bridge. This is LeClerc Creek Road, and enters from the north at Idaho Highway 2 mile 0.5.

Turn left onto LeClerc Creek Road.

**Take LeClerk Creek Road north for 2.7 miles to Marshall Lake Road, which enters on the right. Some maps show this to be Bead Lake Road.

Follow Marshall Lake / Bead Lake Road 6.9 miles to a "Y" intersection. At the intersection, Bead Lake Road continues on the left, becoming gravel, and Bead Lake Drive is on the right. En route to the intersection, you will pass the end of Bench Lake Road at 0.9 miles, the end of Marshall Lake Road at 2.4 miles, and Bead Lake Drive (signed for "Bead Lake Trailhead 1/2 Mile") at 6.0 miles.

***At the "Y" intersection, turn to the left. At 0.2 miles the end of a gravel road on the right will be passed. It is the second road on the right, and the end of the road is signed for "No Name Lake".

Continue on Bead Lake Road, and at 1.4 miles from the "Y" intersection, and just after passing through a slate mining area, you will reach another intersection. Keep to the left here.

At 2.1 miles, and the next intersection, go to the right.

At 2.3 miles, you go to the right again.

At 3.9 miles, you will reach a major intersection. The road to the left is number 5015, and signed as "Cooks Lake Road". The road to the right is marked "Bear Paw Ridge".

Turn right onto Bear Paw Ridge Road, and go 0.3 miles to the access area for Mystic Lake, on the left. As of 1999, the last quarter mile of road leading to the access road is quite rough. It has washouts running down the center of the road that are as much as a foot and a half deep. They can be straddled to drive the road.

Signs mark the entrance to the access and camp area. The start of the access road has a short branch to the left that goes to a camp area at the top of the hill. The main road passes through open timber campsites to the south end of Mystic Lake, arriving above it after a quarter mile.

A short walk of about a hundred yards down a steep hill is required to reach the water.

An **ALTERNATE ROUTE** to Mystic Lake is from the south on Highway 2.

Take Highway 2 north about 47 miles from Interstate 90 Exit 281 in Spokane to the town of Newport.

Take Highway 2 into Idaho and the bridge over the Pend Oreille River.

From here follow the directions provided above from the point marked with an asterisk(*).

A **SECOND ALTERNATE ROUTE** is from the east on Highway 2.

Take Highway 2 west about 28 miles from Highway 95 in the town of Sandpoint to LeClerc Creek Road, which will be on the right at Highway 2 mile 0.5.

At mile 0.5, just before you reach the bridge over the Pend Oreille River, turn right onto LeClerc Creek Road.

From here follow the directions provided above from the point marked with a double asterisk(**).

**NOTE:** In 1997, the Pend Oreille River reached elevations that flooded LeClerc Creek Road. When LeClerc Creek Road is not available, there is another route that can be used for access.

East of Newport at Idaho Highway 2 mile 2.3 is the Albeni Falls Machine Shop on the north side of the road. Freeman Lake Road, a gravel road, heads north next to the shop.

Take this road to access Marshall Lake Road, which will be reached after 6.2 miles. Freeman Lake Road becomes Bench Road before you reach the end.

Turn right, and take Marshall Lake Road 6.0 miles to a "Y" intersection.

From here follow the directions above from the point marked with a triple asterisk(***).

FISHING TIPS:

If any fish are rising, flies cast to them will occasionally get one. Don't expect to catch a lot.

MAP REFERENCES:

 *USGS Topographic Map, Washington (48117-C2-TF-024-00)
   Skookum Creek Quadrangle, 7.5 Minute Series.
 *USGS Topographic Map, Washington (48117-A1-TM-100-00)
   Chewelah Quadrangle, 30x60 Minute Series.
 *Washington Atlas & Gazetteer, Page 105.

## 63  NILE LAKE
Also known as: Porters Lake

August 22, 2002; Nile Lake, looking southeast.

SIZE: 22.8 Acres
ELEVATION: 3,181 Feet
MAXIMUM DEPTH: 28 Feet
COUNTY: Pend Oreille, Washington
COORDINATES: T37N R42E Sec35N

Longitude: 117d 28m 8s to 117d 28m 27s West
Latitude: 48d 39m 19s to 48d 39m 32s North

SPECIES, CONFIRMED:
Eastern Brook Trout
Pumpkinseed Sunfish
Rainbow Trout

SPECIES, REPORTED:
Cutthroat Trout

CHARACTERISTICS:
The surrounding area is timbered to the south, east and west. The north side of the lake has a field area dotted with scrub trees, and timber a short distance away. The area is flat, with a slight hill on the south side.

The shorelines are grassy and soft. Small trees dot the area.

The edges of the lake are shallow. Lilypads are found in some areas, and other aquatic weeds are also present.

The access area at the north side is a large, grassy flat. It offers some very limited access for bank fishing.

A small inlet stream enters next to the access area, and an outlet exits at the northeast corner.

The bottom is mud. The water is clear.

## DIRECTIONS TO:

Take Highway 20 to mile 384.4, east of the town of Colville, where a gravel road will be found on the left. This road runs 0.3 miles to the shores of Nile Lake.

## FISHING TIPS:

Bait fishermen using powerbait and worms get their share of fish from the area around and south of the boat launch. Flies and small lures worked around the edges of the lake also get fish.

Pumpkinseed Sunfish are caught in the shallows at the edges of the shoreline weeds.

## MISCELLANEOUS NOTES:

One September, on a return trip home from Montana, I pulled into the camp area at Nile Lake just after dark and spent the night. Two other groups were camped in the area. In the middle of the night everyone was waken up by a commotion at a small motor home parked up on the hill. A bear had tried to get in.

## MAP REFERENCES:

*USGS Topographic Map, Washington (48117-F4-TF-024-00)
   Ione Quadrangle, 7.5 Minute Series.
*USGS Topographic Map, Washington (48117-E1-TM-100-00)
   Colville Quadrangle, 30x60 Minute Series.
*Washington Atlas & Gazetteer, Page 119.

## 64  NO NAME LAKE

September 10, 1997; No Name Lake, looking northwest.

SIZE: 17.6 Acres
ELEVATION: 2,801 Feet
MAXIMUM DEPTH: 30 Feet
COUNTY: Pend Oreille, Washington
COORDINATES: T32N R45E Sec8A

Longitude: 117d 7m 56s to 117d 8m 18s West
Latitude: 48d 17m 44s to 48d 17m 54s North

SPECIES, CONFIRMED:
 Cutthroat Trout, West Slope

SPECIES, REPORTED:
 Rainbow Trout

CHARACTERISTICS:
 There are low timbered hills all around the lake. The immediate shorelines
are mostly timbered, but there is a large clear area on the hill on the north
side, to the right of the access.

Trails run in both directions around the lake from where the trail reaches the water. The trails offer a lot of access to the water for fishing, although it leaves the waters edge in some places.

The end of the lake reached by the trail from the parking area is mostly brushy, while most of the other shorelines are steeper and have timber.

A lot of snags and logs are found on the shorelines, particularly at the south side. There are also many snags on the bottom. There are small amounts of weed growth in shallow pockets along shore, but most of the aquatic vegetation is sparse.

The visible bottom is gravel with a lot of organic material, mostly wood and bark, lying on it.

Deepest water is found at the center of the lake. The water is very clear.

The camp area located about 150 yards east of the lake has a few camp-sites and a day use parking area, but no facilities.

DIRECTIONS TO:

From the north, take Highway 20 to the town of Newport, where it will end at mile 436.8 at an intersection with Highway 2.

At the stop sign in Newport, turn left onto Highway 2. Take Highway 2 into Idaho and the bridge over the Pend Oreille River.

*As soon as you cross the river, you will need to be in the left lane to turn onto the first road as you leave the bridge. This is LeClerc Creek Road, and enters from the north at Idaho Highway 2 mile 0.5.

Turn left onto LeClerc Creek Road.

**Take LeClerk Creek Road north for 2.7 miles to Marshall Lake Road, which enters on the right. Some maps show this to be Bead Lake Road.

Follow Marshall Lake / Bead Lake Road 6.9 miles to a "Y" intersection. At the intersection, Bead Lake Road continues on the left, becoming gravel, and Bead Lake Drive is on the right. En route to the intersection, you will pass the end of Bench Lake Road at 0.9 miles, the end of Marshall Lake Road at 2.4 miles, and Bead Lake Drive (signed for "Bead Lake Trailhead 1/2 Mile") at 6.0 miles.

***At the "Y" intersection, turn to the left and go 0.2 miles to the end of a gravel road on the right. The end of the road is signed for "No Name Lake".

Turn right onto the gravel road and take it 0.1 miles to the camp area for No Name Lake. The road is narrow and a bit rough.

Once the road reaches the camp area it forms a loop through the parking and camp areas. A trail to the lake leaves the road at the far side of the loop at the side of a small gully.

The trail leads about 150 yards to the water.

If you continue past the entrance to the gravel access road to the camp area, another 0.4 miles will bring you to a small parking area on the right side of the road. The lake will be visible below through the trees. The No Name Lake Portage Trail drops down to the lake from this location.

An **ALTERNATE ROUTE** to No Name Lake is from the south on Highway 2.

Take Highway 2 north about 47 miles from Interstate 90 Exit 281 in Spokane to the town of Newport.

Take Highway 2 into Idaho and the bridge over the Pend Oreille River.

From here follow the directions provided above from the point marked with an asterisk(*).

A **SECOND ALTERNATE ROUTE** is from the east on Highway 2.

Take Highway 2 west about 28 miles from Highway 95 in the town of Sandpoint to LeClerc Creek Road, which will be on the right at Highway 2 mile 0.5.

At mile 0.5, just before you reach the bridge over the Pend Oreille River, turn right onto LeClerc Creek Road.

From here follow the directions provided above from the point marked with a double asterisk(**).

**NOTE:** In 1997, the Pend Oreille River reached elevations that flooded LeClerc Creek Road. When LeClerc Creek Road is not available, there is another route that can be used for access.

East of Newport at Idaho Highway 2 mile 2.3 is the Albeni Falls Machine Shop on the north side of the road. Freeman Lake Road, a gravel road, heads north next to the shop.

Take this road to access Marshall Lake Road, which will be reached after 6.2 miles. Freeman Lake Road becomes Bench Road before you reach the end.

Turn right, and take Marshall Lake Road 6.0 miles to a "Y" intersection.

From here follow the directions above from the point marked with a triple asterisk(***).

FISHING TIPS:
 Flies cast from shore will get fish.

MAP REFERENCES:
 *USGS Topographic Map, Washington (48117-C2-TF-024-00)
   Skookum Creek Quadrangle, 7.5 Minute Series.
 *USGS Topographic Map, Washington (48117-A1-TM-100-00)
   Chewelah Quadrangle, 30x60 Minute Series.
 *Washington Atlas & Gazetteer, Page 105.

# 65  NORTH MUSKEGON LAKE

June 6, 2005; North Muskegon Lake, looking north.

SIZE: 3.7 Acres
ELEVATION: 3,450 Feet
MAXIMUM DEPTH: Unknown
COUNTY: Pend Oreille, Washington
COORDINATES: T38N R45E Sec13AB

    Longitude: 117d 2m 7s <u>to</u> 117d 2m 15s West
    Latitude: 48d 47m 57s <u>to</u> 48d 48m 1s North

SPECIES, CONFIRMED:

SPECIES, REPORTED:

CHARACTERISTICS:
  The lake lies about 1,300 feet west of the Washington-Idaho state line in a timbered area.
  The lake is ringed by dense timber, with timber and brush to the waters edge all around. The north end and the north half of the west side have low brush and boggy areas between the timber and water.

The northeast corner has grassy shores that are wet and boggy.

The lake has a lot of snags present. They are most heavily concentrated at the south end and along the east shore. Some of the snags are very large.

A few beds of lilypads are found on the east side of the lake, and they are also found scattered sparsely around other parts of the lake. Even the most heavily covered areas have only sparse beds.

The lake has a rough pear shape, narrowest at the north end and spreading out at the south end.

The center of the lake is fairly deep. The lake is shallowest at the southwest corner, where the heaviest growths of lilypads are found.

The lake drains at its southwest corner, flowing to Muskegon Lake.

The water is very clear.

DIRECTIONS TO:

Although the lake is in Washington State, the primary access is from the state of Idaho.

Take Highway 2 to mile 5.9, at a stoplight in the middle of the town of Priest River, where Highway 57 / West Side Road will be found on the north side of the highway.

Turn onto Highway 57, and follow it north for 51.3 miles to the Muskegon Lake access area. You will enter the state of Washington at 43.4 miles, pass Huff Lake at 46.9 miles, pass the end of Road 302 (FS 22 from Metaline) at 50.1 miles, and pass the end of Road 656 at 51.0 miles.

The area is reached 0.3 miles past the end of Road 656, and 0.2 miles before the Idaho state line.

A good sized camp area will be seen on the right, and the small trailhead parking area is on the left just past it. The trailhead is marked with a small sign on a tree at the end of the trail.

The trail to Muskegon Lake is signed as 1/4 mile, but is actually only a couple of hundred yards long.

From the trailhead at roadside, the trail drops slightly to a wooden footbridge across a small creek, then angles to the left to a switchback.

The switchback cuts back to the right, and then the trail climbs to a low crest. From the crest it drops to the edge of the lake.

The trail is very good, but as of 2005 had some blowdown debris on the short section just above the lake.

At Muskegon Lake, you need to get to the far side, either by going around through the brush of the shorelines or by beaching on the point across the lake.

From the far side, there is no trail to the north lake. Pick a route to the top of the rise to the north, then down the other side to reach the lake. It's a short distance, but some areas are brushy, especially on the other side of the rise.

An **ALTERNATE ROUTE** to Muskegon Lake is from Washington State. This route crosses a logging road pass at high elevation, so is not an option for much of the year when snow or road conditions make it impassable.

Take Highway 20 to mile 390.4, about 47 miles north of the town of Newport, where the junction with Highway 31 is reached.

Take Highway 31 north for about 3 miles to mile 3.0, where the south end of Sullivan Lake Road enters on the right.

Turn right, onto Sullivan Lake Road, cross the Pend Oreille River, run up the west side of Sullivan Lake, and at 18.0 miles from Highway 31 you will reach an intersection, where Forest Service Road 22 is found on the right. The end of the road is signed for "Salmo Mountain 21, Priest Lake 40, East Sullivan Campground 1/4".

Turn onto Road 22, and stay on the main road for 5.8 miles, to where you will reach an intersection at a small bridge. The left fork, Road #2220, is signed for "Salmo Mountain". The right fork is signed for "Priest Lake", and is the continuation of Road 22. The road is also signed "Narrow road, not suited to trailer traffic".

Take the right fork. At 13.3 miles from the start of Road 22 the road will crest at Pass Creek Pass, elevation just over 5,400 feet, and begin to loose elevation.

Stay on the main road to reach a major intersection at 20.4 miles from the start of Road 22. The road you reach is a wide gravel road, and is signed "Upper Priest Lake 6 Miles" to the left.

Turn left, and go 1.2 miles to the access area for Muskegon Lake. The area is reached 0.3 miles past the end of Road 656, and 0.2 miles before the Idaho state line.

A good sized camp area will be seen on the right, and the small trailhead parking area is on the left just past it.

FISHING TIPS:

I did not attempt to fish this lake. On my one visit there was no sign of fish present.

MAP REFERENCES:
*USGS Topographic Map, Washington (48117-G1-TF-024-00)
 Helmer Mountain Quadrangle, 7.5 Minute Series.
*USGS Topographic Map, Washington (48117-E1-TM-100-00)
 Colville Quadrangle, 30x60 Minute Series.
*Washington Atlas & Gazetteer, Page 119 (name not indicated).

# 66  NORTH SKOOKUM LAKE

September 17, 2000; North Skookum Lake,
looking northeast from the access area.

SIZE: 38.5 Acres
ELEVATION: 3,577 Feet
MAXIMUM DEPTH: 20 Feet
COUNTY: Pend Oreille, Washington
COORDINATES: T33N R44E Sec36AH

Longitude: 117d 10m 25s <u>to</u> 117d 10m 55s West
Latitude: 48d 24m 8s <u>to</u> 48d 24m 32s North

SPECIES, CONFIRMED:
  Eastern Brook Trout
  Rainbow Trout

SPECIES, REPORTED:

<u>CHARACTERISTICS</u>:
  The lake lies in an area of low hills. The highest visible are to the north
and northeast. There appears to be a lookout on the one to the northeast.
The hills are timbered, and those to the north show signs of old clearcuts.
There are some sparse areas on the higher hill to the northeast.

The areas around the lake are heavily timbered, with trees and brush to the waters edge.

A point extends into the lake from the north. It is timbered, but has cover more sparse than the other areas around the lake. The point has a slight rise at its center. The shorelines of the point are lined with brush.

A shallow bay reaches to the northeast along the point. The shorelines around the bay are marshy with heavy growths of lilypads lining them. The bay is shallow, with only five to ten feet of water in the deepest places.

There are lilypads in the central area of the east shore, and also at the south end. Smaller beds can be found in other areas along the north end.

The shorelines along the west side and the bay to the northwest drop off quickly to deep water, with the area directly out from the boat launch northward being the deepest. The boat launch is about a third of the way up the west side.

The shores in the southern section of the lake drop off much more slowly.

A private campground is located on the west side under the timber south of the boat launch. Trails run from the boat launch area to the campground.

Snags extend out into the lake in several places.

A gravel road passes above the shores at the southeast corner.

The bottom is primarily silt, but has some gravel areas.

The water is clear.

DIRECTIONS TO:

Take Highway 20 to mile 421.0, about 16 miles north of the town of Newport, where Kings Lake Road will be found on the east side of the highway.

Turn onto Kings Lake Road, and go east through the town of Usk. You will cross a bridge over the Pend Oreille River, and at 1.0 miles from Highway 20 reach a sign that indicates "Skookum Lake 8 Miles", "Browns Lake 11 Miles".

At 5.0 miles, the pavement ends.

At 7.2 miles, you will reach an intersection with Road 5030, on the left. Road 5030 goes to Half Moon Lake and Browns Lake. If you continue straight ahead, the road goes to Skookum Lakes and Kings Lake.

Continue on Kings Lake Road for another 1.5 miles to an intersection. Road 5032, on the right, goes to South Skookum Lake. The end of the road is signed as Kings Mountain Road, and "South Skookum Lake 1/2 Mile, Kings Mountain 2 Miles". The end of the road is at 8.7 miles from Highway 20.

Continue past Kings Mountain Road, keeping to the left, and go 0.4 miles to a road on the left. The end of this road is marked "Public Launch". The road you are on continues to the right and is marked for "campground".

Turn left, and go 0.3 miles to the boat launch access area, on the right. It has a fairly large parking area just above a very rough, heavily rutted gravel boat ramp.

If you go past the road to the public launch, you will come to another road on the left in just another 0.1 mile. This is the entrance to the private campground located on the southwest corner of the lake.

FISHING TIPS:
Flies cast from shore in the area of the boat launch were effective for small fish on my one brief visit to this lake.

MAP REFERENCES:
*USGS Topographic Map, Washington (48117-D2-TF-024-00)
   Browns Lake Quadrangle, 7.5 Minute Series.
*USGS Topographic Map, Washington (48117-A1-TM-100-00)
   Chewelah Quadrangle, 30x60 Minute Series.
*Washington Atlas & Gazetteer, Page 105.

## 67  PARKER LAKE

September 6, 2001; Parker Lake,
looking south from near the outlet creek.

SIZE: 10 Acres (estimated)
ELEVATION: 6,318 Feet
MAXIMUM DEPTH: Unknown
COUNTY: Boundary, Idaho
COORDINATES: T64N R2W Sec28Q,33B

Longitude: 116d 35m 53s to 116d 35m 59s West
Latitude: 48d 51m 43s to 48d 51m 49s North

SPECIES, CONFIRMED:
 Arctic Grayling
 Golden Trout

SPECIES, REPORTED:

## CHARACTERISTICS:

A mountain of mostly bare rock rises steeply over the south end of the lake. The mountain to the east has much exposed rock and a lot of small trees, plus a forest of snags that would indicate the hillside has burned off in the past. Over the west side is a low hill, mostly timbered, with rock showing through.

The ring of hills is open to the north and northeast, where an outlet creek exits at the northernmost point of the lake.

The trail to the lake reaches it at the center of the east side at an area covered with a heavy growth of timber and brush.

The area immediately around the lake is very heavily timbered with mostly fir trees. The only exception is the south end where timber cover is sparse due to the large amount of rock in the area.

The shorelines have low brush to the waters edge in most places. Much of the shoreline is open enough to be able to get to the water to fish, although some areas are dense enough to make passage very awkward.

There are a lot of snags. They line the shores almost all around the lake. The heaviest concentration is at the mouth of the outlet creek. Of those along the shores, many extend well out into the lake. There are also a lot lying on the bottom.

The bottom is deep silt. A few places have rocks rising through the silt in the shallows.

The areas along the shores are all shallow for quite a distance out. The water doesn't begin to deepen appreciably until far out from shore. The largest shallow flat is out from the outlet creek at the north end.

The water is very clear.

Campsites are found in the trees at the northeast corner, and in a small brushy area at the northwest corner. Both are primitive.

On a circuit of the lake in the fall of 2001, moose tracks were found along the shores at the south end and southwest corner of the lake.

## DIRECTIONS TO:

Take Interstate 90 to exit 12, at the town of Coeur d'Alene.

From exit 12, take Highway 95 north for about 77 miles to mile 507.5, at the town of Bonners Ferry, where Riverside Road will be found on the west side of the highway just south of the bridge over the Kootenai River. The end of the road is signed for "Kootenai Wildlife Refuge 6 Miles".

Turn onto Riverside, and head west out of Bonners Ferry, keeping to the right as the road follows the banks of the river.

At 5.0 miles from Highway 95 the road will reach the base of the foothills, and a "Y" intersection. Keep to the right, and the road will begin running to the north. Past the "Y" about a quarter mile, you will pass the Kootenai Wildlife Refuge headquarters. The pavement ends in another 6.5 miles.

At 14.9 miles from Highway 95 you will reach the end of Forest Service Road 634, also shown on some maps as Trout Creek Road. The end of the road is signed "Junction Trail 6 Miles, Trail 12 7 Miles, Trail 13 9 Miles".

*Turn onto Road 634, and follow it 8.8 miles to a parking area, on the left, for the trailhead, which is on the right. The road ends in another 0.2 miles at a horse facility and camp area.

On the 8.8 mile run to the trailhead, you will reach an intersection at 4.5 miles, where you keep to the left.

You will pass the Fisher Peak trailhead, on the right, at 5.2 miles.

You will pass the Russell Peak Trail #12 parking area, on the left, at 6.1 miles. There are signs here for the trailhead that indicate "Russell Peak 2 1/2 Miles", and for the continuation of the road to the right indicating "Junction Trail #92 3 Miles".

The trailhead provides access to several lakes in the area, found off various branches of the trail system. The lakes include Pyramid, Upper Ball, Lower Ball, Trout, Big Fisher, Long Mountain, and Parker.

To reach Parker Lake, take the trail about 0.5 miles (elevation gain approximately 450 feet) to a fork. Take the right fork.

Go about 0.75 miles (gain about 150 feet) to the next fork. This fork is reached at a wooden footbridge, to the right of which is a sign indicating that the trail to the right is to Trout Lake and Big Fisher Lake, and providing distances. The trail to the left is unmarked. Take the trail to the left.

Go about 1.0 mile to a saddle on the ridgeline to the west (gain about 450 feet).

From the saddle, the trail drops about 250 feet over a distance of about 0.5 miles before reaching the next fork in the trail. The main trail continues straight, and is signed with distance to a forest road on Long Canyon Creek. The trail you need branches off to the right, and is unmarked. Take the right.

The trail now becomes steeper and rougher than what you've been on so far. It climbs about 600 feet over a distance of about 0.75 miles to the top of the ridge. Once the ridge top is gained, the trail becomes better and runs along it for about 0.25 miles to the branch that drops to Long Mountain Lake.

The trail to Long Mountain Lake is marked with signs propped on top of a boulder just before you reach it. Two signs are placed back to back, giving approximate distances in both directions.

Take the branch to the right and the trail will become narrow and steeper again as it drops about 300 feet over about 0.5 miles to Long Mountain Lake.

For Parker Lake, continue on the ridge top past the trail to Long Mountain Lake. The sign indicates Parker Lake is another 4 miles.

The trail runs along the ridge top, with a lot of up and down. The trail occasionally cuts around the highest ground of the many small "peaks" on their left sides, but is near the top in almost all places.

The high point of the trail is 7,400 feet, reached about 2.5 miles from the trail to Long Mountain Lake, and after climbing the south side to reach a short flat just below the 7,445 foot peak. The trail passes through this flat to the west of the peak, and then begins a series of short switchbacks that drop around large rock on the ridgeline before coming back to the ridge top. From the peak, the trail will run along the ridge top, reaching a low point of 6,995 feet, angling away to the east for about another 1.5 miles to reach a fork that goes to Parker Lake.

The fork that drops to Parker Lake is reached after the trail switchbacks down the south side of a 7,091 foot "peak", regains the ridge top just past the peak, and begins to climb again. The trail is signed, indicating the distance to Parker Lake on the trail to the left as 0.5 miles. The sign is wrong, it's farther.

Take the left fork, and the trail will run about 0.25 miles north along the ridge with very little drop in elevation. It will reach a couple of switchbacks and finally begin to drop to the lake, visible below. The trail drops a total of about 600 feet in about 0.75 miles to the lake.

The lower sections of the trail become steeper and travel through an area of much heavier growth. A fork in the trail will be reached a couple hundred yards from the lake. Take the right fork to reach the center of the east side of the lake. This part of the trail down is the roughest and steepest.

From where the trail reaches the lake, the first campsite is found to the right in about 50 feet. Another campsite can be reached at the northwest corner of the lake by continuing past the first campsite and going around the north end of the lake across the outlet creek. The trail isn't good, with a lot of brush and some blowdowns.

An **ALTERNATE ROUTE** to the Trout Creek trail system would be to take Highway 95 to mile 523.0, north of the town of Bonners Ferry, where Highway 1 will be found on the left.

Turn onto Highway 1, and continue north for 1.1 miles to a road on the left at the town of Copeland. The end of the road is signed for "Sportsman's Access" and "National Forest Entrance".

Turn left onto the road, and head west. At 1.6 miles you will reach a bridge over the Kootenai River. At 3.4 miles from Highway 1 you will reach a "T" intersection with West Side Road. There is a sign opposite the end of the road you are on that indicates "Maravia 20 Miles" to the left, and "Smith Creek Road and Boundary Creek Road 9 Miles" to the right.

At West Side Road, turn left and go south for 2.9 miles to a 90-degree corner. The paved road turns to the left, and a gravel road leaves the pavement straight ahead. Contrary to appearances, the gravel road is the continuation of West Side Road.

Take the gravel road, and after 1.8 miles you will reach the end of Forest Service Road 634, also shown on some maps as Trout Creek Road, on the right. The end of the road is signed "Junction Trail 6 Miles, Trail 12 7 Miles, Trail 13 9 Miles".

From here, follow the directions provided above from the point marked with an asterisk(*).

FISHING TIPS:

Flies cast from shore are effective. Where the trail reaches the lake is not only the easiest place to fish, but also one of the most productive. The south end is also good. The shallows of the north end out from the outlet creek were the least productive area of the lake.

As of 2001, it appeared that only fish planted after the bad winters of 1996 and 1997 were still present. The Grayling caught were all 10 to 10.75 inches long, indicating they were from the same planting (1999), and the Golden Trout were 4.75 to 5 inches long (2000 plants).

MAP REFERENCES:
*Idaho Atlas & Gazetteer, Page 48 (lake not shown).
*USGS Topographic Map, Idaho (48116-G5-TF-024-00)
   Pyramid Peak Quadrangle, 7.5 Minute Series.
*USGS Topographic Map, Idaho (48116-E1-TM-100-00)
   Bonners Ferry Quadrangle, 30x60 Minute Series.

# 68  PARKER LAKE

June 19, 2006; Parker Lake, looking north.

SIZE: 22.1 Acres
ELEVATION: 2,450 Feet
MAXIMUM DEPTH: 8 Feet
COUNTY: Pend Oreille, Washington
COORDINATES: T34N R43E Sec3CF

Longitude: 117d 21m 29s to 117d 21m 43s West
Latitude: 48d 28m 35s to 48d 28m 2s North

SPECIES, CONFIRMED:
 Rainbow Trout

SPECIES, REPORTED:
 Eastern Brook Trout

CHARACTERISTICS:
 The lake lies in an area of low, densely timbered hills. The high point visible to the north has some sparsely timbered areas on the west side.
 Immediately around the lake trees and brush reach to the lakeshores, although most areas have an extensive lining of cattails and other aquatic vegetation separating any open water from the shoreline brush.

A gravel road runs up the length of the west side of the lake, but is well away from the water and offers only glimpses through the trees. Its closest approach to the lake is at the southwest corner next to the outlet creek, where a short, rough road runs about 50 yards to a camp area at that corner.

Just past the access road is a wide, gravel turnout on the right. From the turnout some short trails run to some additional campsites along the lake.

The lake size has reportedly reduced from 60 acres in 1930 to its current size. Based on the shallow conditions and the encroaching marshlands, the lake is in its later stages, and will soon cease to exist as a lake at all, becoming just a marsh.

The reported maximum depth of 18 feet isn't even close. The deepest water of the lake is found at the south end near the outlet creek, and is just a fraction of that.

The lake has massive beds of lilypads that severely restrict the access to open water in the upper section of the lake. The upper areas look promising from a distance, but the open water covers a very shallow bottom of deep silt with aquatic weed rising to the surface in many spots. There are a lot of boggy hummocks with cattail growths on them dotting the areas around the open water, as well as scattered through the weed growths that cover most of the old lake bed.

A couple of beaver houses are located on the west side of the lake in the upper end.

The bottom is also deep mud and silt in all other areas, with some submerged snags found scattered randomly.

The shorelines have some visible snags. Some large snags are found along the timbered areas, which don't border open water. One good-sized snag extends out into the pool at the southwest corner camp area.

Cusick Creek flows into the lake at the north end, and out at the south end. The mouth of the outlet is spanned by small segments of beaver dam between high spots of boggy ground. The entire area has a very heavy growth of cattails and aquatic weeds.

The water has a light brown stain.

DIRECTIONS TO:

Take Highway 20 to mile 411.4, about 25 miles north of the town of Newport, where Cusick Creek Road will be found on the west side of the highway.

Turn onto Cusick Creek Road, and take it 4.0 miles to a rough access road, on the right. The road is only about 50 yards long, and reaches the southwest corner of Parker Lake at a primitive camp area.

FISHING TIPS:

Flies cast at the pool at the outlet end of the lake will get some small fish. I saw no sign of fish present in the other portions of the lake.

MAP REFERENCES:

*USGS Topographic Map, Washington (48117-D3-TF-024-00) Jared Quadrangle, 7.5 Minute Series.

*USGS Topographic Map, Washington (48117-A1-TM-100-00) Chewelah Quadrangle, 30x60 Minute Series.

*Washington Atlas & Gazetteer, Page 105.

## 69  LAKE PEND OREILLE

May 22, 1995; Lake Pend Oreille, looking southwest from Highway 200.

SIZE: 80,000 Acres
ELEVATION: 2,062 Feet
MAXIMUM DEPTH: 1,152 Feet
COUNTY: Bonner/Kootenai, Idaho
COORDINATES: T53-57N R2E-2W

Longitude: 116d 14m 11s to 116d 36m 32s West
Latitude: 47d 56m 55s to 48d 19m 2s North

SPECIES, CONFIRMED:

SPECIES, REPORTED:
 Black Crappie
 Bluegill
 Bullhead Catfish
 Channel Catfish
 Cutthroat Trout
 Dolly Varden (Bull) Trout
 Eastern Brook Trout
 German Brown Trout

Kokanee
Lake Whitefish
Largemouth Bass
Mackinaw
Mountain Whitefish
Northern Pike
Northern Squawfish
Pumpkinseed Sunfish
Pygmy Whitefish
Rainbow Trout, Kamloops
Smallmouth Bass
Sucker
Tiger Muskie
Yellow Perch

## CHARACTERISTICS:

The lake is 43 miles long, six and a half miles wide, and has 111 miles of shoreline. It has the shape of a large, irregular comma, wrapped around a large peninsula on the west side.

The large peninsula has a very irregular shoreline beginning at its northernmost reach, Contest Point, located east of the town of Sandpoint.

Between Contest Point and Anderson Point, which forms the northeast corner of the peninsula, lays Bottle Bay. Bottle Bay is the largest bay on the peninsula.

South of Anderson Point is small Martin Bay, than Picard Point, which is the easternmost reach of the peninsula. Between Picard Point and Mineral Point, at the southeast corner, lies Camp Bay.

West from Mineral Point is Long Point, and then Garfield Bay is reached at the western corner where the shoreline turns to the south. Garfield Bay is an almost rectangular body of water, about a mile long and half a mile wide that extends north from the corner. At its north end is Garfield Bay Campground.

South of Garfield Bay is Grouse Mountain Point, which lies below Grouse Mountain, a 4,239 foot rise to the west.

South from Grouse Mountain Point the lakeshores are more regular until you reach Cape Horn, near the southwest corner of the lake, where the lake makes a broad hook to the west.

Blackwell Point, where Farragut State Park is located, divides this western hook into two bays. Scenic Bay and the town of Bayview are to the north of Blackwell Point, and Idlewilde Bay is to the south. Idlewilde Bay is the westernmost point of the lake itself, but the latitude reference provided above is at the narrows at the town of Dover, Pend Oreille River mile 114.0, where the water is still more of a lake than a river. Idlewilde Bay has a point called Steamboat Rock at its east end, and Echo bay lies beyond the point to the east.

Opposite Blackwell Point, on the east shore of the lake, is Graham Point, south of the town of Lakeview and the mouth of Gold Creek.

About half way up the southern half of the east shore is Whiskey Rock Bay, a small bay only about a quarter of a mile wide. The community of Granite lies near the mouth of Granite Creek, about two miles north of Whiskey Rock Bay and one mile south of Granite Point.

At Granite Point the east shore of the lake begins to make a turn to the east, rounding Windy Point and Indian Point, and then reaching small Deadman Point, where the shoreline runs east to west. East of Deadman Point the shores angle to the northeast to reach the two mile wide delta where the Clark Fork River enters. The mouth of the Clark Fork River is the easternmost point of the lake.

Northwest of the Clark Fork delta is a small (about four square miles) peninsula, pinched at its northeast side by Denton Slough to the southeast and Ellisport Bay to the northwest. Sheepherder Point is the southernmost point of this peninsula, and Hope Point is at the northwest corner. Owens Bay forms a mile and a half wide depression in the west side of the peninsula.

A string of islands runs from the mouth of Ellisport Bay to the south end of Owens Bay. The largest is Warren Island, at the north end of the string. Directly south of Warren Island are Cottage Island and Pearl Island. Memaloose Island is just offshore at Owens Bay.

The north end of the lake has three large bays. The easternmost of the three is crossed by a railway on a bed of fill. There is an opening in the fill near the east end of the bay to allow access between the end of the bay and the lake. It is crossed by a trestle.

Sunnyside Mountain rises on the large, almost rectangular peninsula between the eastern bay and Odin Bay, to the west. Several small islands are found on the west side of the peninsula, including Fishermans Island, off the southwest corner.

Kootenai Point extends southward between Odin Bay to the east and Kootenai Bay to the west. Beyond the small point on the west side of Kootenai Bay the shoreline rounds fairly smoothly to drop southward to the town of Sandpoint.

At Sandpoint a large slough separates a narrow finger of land from the mainland. Sand Creek enters the north end of the long slough.

Two bridges cross the lake at Sandpoint. Highway 95 runs southward, while a railroad bridge angles to the southeast.

West of the Highway 95 bridge the lake remains one to two miles wide for about three miles, where it reaches a point southeast of the town of Dover. At this point, the Pend Oreille River exits Lake Pend Oreille, draining to the west.

Springy Point Campground, at Springy Point, and Murphy Bay are located on the south shore west of the Highway 95 bridge.

There are many inlet creeks entering all around the lake. In addition, the Pack River enters at the north end of the lake, at the head of the bay with the railway crossing.

Timbered mountains rise around all but the southwest tip of the lake.

With the exception of the Sandpoint area and the Bayview / Farragut State Park area, development around the lake is spotty. There are small communities along Highway 200 at the north end of the lake. There are long stretches of shoreline with timber to the waters edge. Much of the shoreline has moderately steep shores.

The water is usually pretty clear, but can become colored by heavy runoff from the Clark Fork River. The runoff affects the eastern portion of the lake the most. High water can also carry large amounts of floating debris into the lake.

DIRECTIONS TO:

The lake has many access areas. They can be reached from two main highways, Highway 95 to the west, and Highway 200 to the north.

Take Interstate 90 to exit 12 at Coeur d'Alene, Idaho. At exit 12, turn north onto Highway 95. Highway 95 crosses Interstate 90 at approximately Highway 95 mile 433.

Take Highway 95 north to the listed mileposts, and follow the directions to the access points.

**From Highway 95:**

*At mile 455.6: Bayview Road at the town of Athol. Go east about 7 miles to the town of Bayview and Blackwell Point.

*At mile 465.6: East Dufort Road at the town of Dufort. Go 3.7 miles to a "T" intersection. The intersection is signed "Mirror Lake" to the right.

Turn right onto Talache Road, which is paved, and go about 4 more miles to Talache Landing. You will pass Mirror Lake on the way.

*At mile 468.2: Sagle Road, at the town of Sagle. This road actually provides access to several locations on Lake Pend Oreille. From Highway 95, you will reach the following:

#At 8.2 miles: Garfield Bay Road, on the right. The road runs about a mile to a campground at Garfield Bay.

#At 10.0 miles: Bottle Bay Road, on the left. The road runs north to Bottle Bay, and continues around Contest Point before coming back to Highway 95 at mile 471.0.

#At 10.4 miles: Camp Bay Road, on the right. The road runs about 3 miles to Camp Bay.

#At 12.5 miles: Martin Bay Road, on the left. The road runs about 0.75 miles to Martin Bay.

#At 12.5 miles: Glengary Road, on the right. The road runs about a mile to Glengary. It passes Gamble Lake and the BLM Gamblin Lake Recreation Area on the way.

*At mile 471.0: Bottle Bay Road, about 3/4 mile before the south end of the Highway 95 bridge. Go east along the Contest Point shoreline.

*At mile 471.6: Smokehouse Road, at the south end of the Highway 95 bridge. Go west along the shoreline to the Springy Point Campground. The end of the road is signed "Springy Point Recreation Area 3 Miles".

Highway 95 will wind through the middle of the town of Sandpoint, Idaho before reaching a stop lighted intersection at a distance of about 44 miles from Interstate 90.

The left fork of this intersection is the continuation north of the combined Highway 95 and Highway 2. The right fork is Highway 200, which runs around the north end of Lake Pend Oreille to reach the Montana border after about 24 miles.

Take the right fork here and go east on Highway 200 to the listed mileposts.

**From Highway 200:**

*At mile 40.6: A roadside turnout. There is an area suitable for launching of small car top boats.

*At mile 42.4: The Trestle Creek Recreation Area, and resorts. Because of the resort facilities found here, full services are available.

*At mile 45.2: The Lake Pend Oreille Public Boat Launch. The area has a good boat launch at a small cove on the north side of the highway. The lake is reached by passing back under the Highway 200 bridge.

FISHING TIPS:
  Dead Man Point and Indian Point are reportedly best for Rainbow, then Camp Bay and Mineral Point.
  For Mackinaw, best fishing is reportedly on calm days on the flats on north end of lake. Look for rock piles, pinnacles and sandy flats.

MISCELLANEOUS NOTES:
  Lake Pend Oreille has produced the following State records:
  Kamloops Rainbow of 37 pounds, in 1947.
  Cutthroat/Rainbow Hybrid of 24 pounds (35 1/2 inches long), in 1991.
  Northern Squawfish of:
    4 pounds 6 ounces (23 inches long), in 1995.
    6 pounds 7 ounces (25 1/2 inches long), in 1996.
  Bull Trout (Dolly Varden) of 32 pounds, in 1949.
  Lake Whitefish of 3 pounds 8 ounces (22 inches long), on May 3, 2006.

MAP REFERENCES:
  *Idaho Atlas & Gazetteer; Page 32, 60, 62.
  *USGS Topographic Map, Idaho (47116-H5-TF-024-00)
    Bayview Quadrangle, 7.5 Minute Series.
  *USGS Orthophotoquad Map, Idaho (48116-B2-OQ-024-00)
    Clark Fork Quadrangle, 7.5 Minute Series.
  *USGS Topographic Map, Idaho (48116-A5-TF-024-00)
    Cocolalla Quadrangle, 7.5 Minute Series.
  *USGS Orhtophotoquad Map, Idaho (48116-B3-OQ-024-00)
    Hope Quadrangle, 7.5 Minute Series.
  *USGS Topographic Map, Idaho (47116-H4-TF-024-00)
    Lakeview Quadrangle, 7.5 Minute Series.
  *USGS Orthophotoquad Map, Idaho (48116-A4-OQ-024-00)
    Minerva Peak Quadrangle, 7.5 Minute Series.
  *USGS Orthophotoquad Map, Idaho (48116-C4-OQ-024-00)
    Oden Bay Quadrangle, 7.5 Minute Series.
  *USGS Topographic Map, Idaho (48116-B5-TF-024-00)
    Sagle Quadrangle, 7.5 Minute Series.
  *USGS Topographic Map, Idaho (48116-C5-TF-024-00)
    Sandpoint Quadrangle, 7.5 Minute Series.

*USGS Orthophotoquad Map, Idaho (48116-B4-OQ-024-00)
   Talache Quadrangle, 7.5 Minute Series.
*USGS Orthophotoquad Map, Idaho (48116-C3-OQ-024-00)
   Trout Peak Quadrangle, 7.5 Minute Series.
*USGS Topographic Map, Idaho (47116-E1-TM-100-00)
   Coeur d'Alene Quadrangle, 30x60 Minute Series.
*USGS Topographic Map, Idaho (48116-A1-TM-100-00)
   Sandpoint Quadrangle, 30x60 Minute Series.

## 70   PETIT LAKE

June 6, 2005; Petit Lake, looking southwest from the boat launch area.

SIZE: 10.6 Acres
ELEVATION: 3,911 Feet
MAXIMUM DEPTH: Unknown
COUNTY: Pend Oreille, Washington
COORDINATES: T36N R45E Sec10AH

Longitude: 117d 5m 1s to 117d 5m 19s West
Latitude: 48d 38m 10s to 48d 38m 26s North

SPECIES, CONFIRMED:
Cutthroat Trout, West Slope

SPECIES, REPORTED:
Eastern Brook Trout

CHARACTERISTICS:
The lake lies on the northwest side of Diamond Peak. With the exception of Diamond Peak, rising over the southeast side of the lake, the hills around the lake are low. All are densely covered with timber. An old road, Road 657, cuts the slopes about half way up and is visible from the lake. The end

of Road 657 can be accessed 0.3 miles from Road 311C to Petit Lake. The end of the road is gated, but it can be walked to the vantage point above.

Timber extends to the waters edge or near it all around the lake, but most shorelines have either strips of aquatic weed growth or marshy areas. The weeds and marshy shores severely limit bank access.

There is an undeveloped campground with a few sites on the west side of the lake. The sites are crude, with little level ground and no facilities. At the center of the west side is a rough boat launch area, where a dirt road reaches the water. It is suitable for launching small boats and floating devices, but not trailered boats.

A large snag extends straight out from shore near the northwest corner, in the area of the last campsite, providing some "bank" access to the water.

The north end of the lake holds two small, grass covered islands. The northernmost is the smallest and lowest, and has a small beaver house on it. It has shallow water all around.

The southernmost island is the larger of the two. In addition to grass cover it also has a couple of small shrubs on it. The southwest corner of the island has remnant sticks of an old beaver house extending from an overhanging bog shore. The north and east sides have shallow water, while the west, and especially the southwest corner, border deeper water.

Several large snags are found around the lake, but they are scattered randomly, with no large concentrations.

The bottom is silt.

Aquatic vegetation is found everywhere in the lake. It is comprised of a fairly heavy growth of bottom hugging cover, and a very sparse scattering of taller weeds.

The water is extremely clear. The clarity of the water makes the depth deceptive. The lake looks very shallow from shore, but even the shallow areas are deeper than they look. The center of the lake is deep.

DIRECTIONS TO:

Petit Lake can be accessed from either Washington or Idaho. Both options are presented below. Access from each route is from a single major road, but in the case of the Washington route, that road can be accessed at multiple points.

## FROM WASHINGTON:

Take Highway 20 to mile 421.0, about 16 miles north of the town of Newport, where Kings Lake Road will be reached, on the east side of the highway.

Turn onto Kings Lake Road, and go east through the town of Usk. You will cross a bridge over the Pend Oreille River, and reach an intersection where LeClerk Road and Kings Lake Road cross.

Turn left onto LeClerk Road, and go north for 15.6 miles to LeClerk Creek Road, which will be on the right just before LeClerk Road makes a fairly sharp turn to the left.

*Turn onto LeClerk Creek Road.

Go north for 1.1 miles to an intersection. Here, West Branch LeClerk Creek Road goes to the left, and East Branch LeClerk Creek Road continues on the right. East Branch LeClerk Creek Road is signed "Monumental Mountain" and "Priest Lake". Keep to the right.

The pavement ends 0.1 mile up East Branch LeClerk Creek Road.

At 4.7 miles from LeClerk Road you will cross a cattleguard.

At 4.9 miles, 0.2 miles past the cattleguard, a major intersection will be reached. Here, Middle Branch LeClerk Creek Road (Forest Service Road 1935) goes to the left, and Kalispell-LeClerk Road (Forest Service Road 308) goes to the right. The roads are signed. Keep to the right.

At 9.1 miles you will cross a small bridge.

At 9.5 miles is a "Y" intersection. The road to the left is gated, and Road 308 continues to the right. Keep right.

At 9.7 miles is another "Y". Here a road climbs on the right, and Road 308 goes to the left. Keep left.

At 12.0 miles the road crests, and begins losing elevation.

At 13.1 miles is an intersection. Take the right, staying on Road 308.

At 14.4 miles is the intersection you are looking for. It is a triangular intersection, with a sign indicating you are on "Kalispell LeClerk", and that "State Highway 57 9 Miles" is straight ahead. It also indicates "Pend Oreille River 19 Miles" in the direction from which you have come. Road 311 goes to the left here.

Turn left, onto Road 311, and take it 0.6 miles to Road 311C, on the right. The end of Road 311C is signed for Petit Lake.

Turn onto Road 311C, and the first campsite at Petit Lake will be reached in just 0.1 mile. The boat launch area is reached at 0.2 miles, and the end of the drivable road will be reached at 0.3 miles, at the last and largest campsite.

The launch area of Petit Lake is reached a total of 15.2 miles from LeClerk Road.

An **ALTERNATE** <u>**WASHINGTON**</u> **ROUTE** to Petit Lake, from the north, is to take Highway 20 to mile 390.4, where it makes a 90-degree turn to the south about 47 miles north of Newport. At this intersection, Highway 31 goes to the north.

Turn north onto Highway 31, and take it north for 3 miles to mile 3.0, where the south end of Sullivan Lake Road enters on the right.

Turn onto Sullivan Lake Road, and go east for 0.5 miles to the north end of LeClerk Road, on the right.

Turn onto LeClerk Road, and take it south for 15.7 miles to the end of LeClerk Creek Road, on the left

From this point, follow the directions provided above at the point marked with an asterisk(*).

**NOTE**: LeClerk Road runs up the east side of the Pend Oreille River, all the way from Highway 2 (east of Newport) to Sullivan Lake Road (east of Ione). LeClerk Road can be accessed at Highway 2, and driven about 29 miles north to the end of LeClerk Creek Road.

## FROM IDAHO:

Take Highway 2 to mile 5.9, at a stoplight in the middle of the town of Priest River, where Highway 57 / West Side Road will be found on the north side of the highway.

Turn onto Highway 57, and follow it north for about 34 miles to Highway 57 mile 34.0, where the end of Kalispell Creek Road, Forest Service Road 308, will be found, on the left.

Turn onto Kalispell Creek Road, and take it 9.3 miles to the intersection with Road 311, on the right.

At 1.9 miles you will reach an intersection. Road 1351 goes to the left, and Road 308, which is signed, continues straight ahead. A sign here indicates that if you stay on Road 308, its: "Nordman 7 Miles" and "Indian Mountain Road 1362 1/2 Mile". Stay on Road 308.

At 2.2 miles you will cross a small bridge over Kalispell Creek. Just past the bridge is Road 1362, on the right. It is signed for "Nordman 6 Miles" and "Road 302 13 Miles". Stay on Road 308, which is signed for "Petit Lake 7 Miles".

At 9.3 miles is the intersection with Road 311. It is a triangular intersection, with a sign indicating you are on "Kalispell LeClerk" and "Pend Oreille River 19 Miles" straight ahead. It also indicates "State Highway 57

9 Miles" in the direction from which you have come. Road 311 goes to the right here.

Turn right, onto Road 311, and take it 0.6 miles to Road 311C, on the right. Road 311C is signed for Petit Lake.

Turn onto Road 311C, and the first campsite at Petit Lake will be reached in just 0.1 mile. The boat launch area is reached at 0.2 miles, and the end of the derivable road will be reached at 0.3 miles, at the last and largest campsite.

The launch area of Petit Lake is reached a total of 10.1 miles from Idaho State Highway 57.

The map shows an **ALTERNATE IDAHO ROUTE** to Petit Lake, also from Highway 57, but from the north on Forest Service Road 311.

The end of Road 311 is reached 41.5 miles north from the town of Priest River, and is signed "Indian Mountain Road 1362" and "Kalispell Creek Road 13".

As of 2005, this is not a viable option. Road 311 is gated 0.4 miles from the end of Road 311C.

**NOTE:** Regardless of whether you access the lake from Washington or Idaho, you will pass many small side roads that branch from Road 308. Many are gated, but some aren't. Most are obviously secondary roads. It is important to stay on Road 308, the main road. The directions provided detail the major intersections where errors would most likely be made.

Also, almost every road from the Washington side contains the word "LeClerk", making the directions a lot more confusing than they would otherwise be.

FISHING TIPS:
Flies are extremely effective, both trolled and cast to either cover or rising fish.

The area along the southwest side of the larger island, where overhanging bog provides cover, consistently produced larger fish.

MISCELLANEOUS NOTES:
The lake lies in a bear area, with reports of grizzlies.

MAP REFERENCES:
*USGS Topographic Map, Washington (48117-F1-TF-024-00)
 Orwig Hump Quadrangle, 7.5 Minute Series.

*USGS Topographic Map, Washington (48117-E1-TM-100-00)
   Colville Quadrangle, 30x60 Minute Series.
*Washington Atlas & Gazetteer; Page 119.

# 71  PIERRE LAKE

May 11, 2005; Pierre Lake, north half,
looking northeast from the boat launch.

SIZE: 105.6 Acres
ELEVATION: 2,005 Feet
MAXIMUM DEPTH: 75 Feet
COUNTY: Stevens, Washington
COORDINATES: T39N R37E Sec5GKQ,8BG

Longitude: 118d 8m 4s <u>to</u> 118d 8m 25s West
Latitude: 48d 53m 50s <u>to</u> 48d 54m 44s North

SPECIES, CONFIRMED:
 Cutthroat Trout, West Slope

SPECIES, REPORTED:
 Black Crappie
 Brown Bullhead Catfish
 Eastern Brook Trout
 Kokanee
 Largemouth Bass
 Rainbow Trout

## CHARACTERISTICS:

The lake lies in an area of rocky, timbered hills. The hills are lowest to the north, where they are visible in the distance. The lake is long and narrow, running from north to south.

The lake has a Forest Service campground and boat launch located at the center of the west side of the lake. The campground is a fee area. The boat launch area is gravel, with a small parking area just above it.

The hills above the lake are rockiest along the north half of the east side, where a large rocky knob rises over the northeast corner.

The north end of the lake has low, flat shorelines. Grass fields with a few small trees are found up from shore. Houses are visible above the north end, setting behind some trees that run above the fields.

The southern half of the lake has the deepest water.

With the exception of the north end, trees and brush run to the waters edge around most of the lake. Some places on the east shore have a few small open areas.

A cove at the center of the west side holds the boat launch area. A small point out from the south side of the cove has a shallow, weed covered reef extending northward from its end.

A smaller cove is found on the east shore, opposite the one where the boat launch is located. This cove has shorelines lined with a strip of aquatic weed, and a good-sized snag rising above the surface of the lake out from it.

Several beds of aquatic weed are found around the lake, with some of the heaviest concentrations at the boat launch cove and at the north and south ends of the lake. Weeds also line most of the north half of the west shore.

Visible bottom areas are primarily silt.

The water is very clear.

## DIRECTIONS TO:

Pierre Lake can be reached from two major routes, both of which have Highway 20 as a starting point. They are from the west from Highway 395, and from the east from Highway 25. The route from the east is only of use if you are in the Northport area to start with.

### **FROM THE WEST:**

Many roads branch off of Highway 395 and can be taken to Pierre Lake. I have only detailed the most northerly route here.

Take Highway 20 to the junction with Highway 395 on west end of the bridge over the Columbia River at Kettle Falls. The junction is at Highway 395 mile 241.9.

From the junction, go north on Highway 395 for 22 miles to Rock Cut Road, on right at mile 263.8. Rock Cut Road is reached 3.6 miles past Main Street of the town of Orient. On the opposite side of the road from the end of Rock Cut Road is Little Boulder Road. The end of Rock Cut Road is signed for Pierre Lake.

Turn onto Rock Cut Road, and take it northeast. It will pass through a single lane railroad underpass, then cross the Kettle River before climbing. At 0.4 miles from Highway 395, the road you are on becomes Sand Creek Road, and Rock Cut Road turns to the left.

Stay on Sand Creek Road until, at 3.9 miles from Highway 395, it reaches an intersection at a 90-degree corner and pavement starts. Here Sand Creek Road becomes Pierre Lake Road and turns to the south. At this intersection, the gravel road on the left is Churchill Mine Road.

Continue south on Pierre Lake Road for 1.3 miles to the main entrance to the Pierre Lake Campground, on the left. The northern entrance to the area will be passed at 1.0 miles.

Via this route, Pierre Lake is reached a total of 5.2 miles from Highway 395, and 27.2 miles from where you left Highway 20.

An **ALTERNATE ROUTE** to the lake is found at Highway 395 mile 259.9 at the town of Orient, where Main Street is signed for Pierre Lake.

From here, Orient Cut-Off Road runs east for about 2.5 miles to Pierre Lake Road, where you would turn north and go about 2.3 miles to the lake.

### FROM THE EAST:

Take combined Highway 20 / Highway 395 to mile 239.1, where the intersection with Highway 25 will be reached. The intersection is on the east side of the Columbia River, and at the western side of the town of Kettle Falls.

Turn onto Highway 25 North, and take it 33.6 miles, through the town of Northport and over the Columbia River, to Sheep Creek Road, on the left at mile 114.7.

This intersection is a double intersection, with paved Flat Creek Road to the hard left, and unpaved Sheep Creek Road to the left. The intersection is signed for "Sheep Creek Campground".

Turn left, onto Sheep Creek Road, and follow it west.

At 0.5 miles you will pass a dirt race track, on the left.

At 3.0 miles you will pass a well used road, on the left.

At 4.2 miles you will pass Sheep Creek Campground, on the right.

At 4.3 miles you will pass a Placer Mining historical marker, on the right.

At 8.4 miles you will reach a major intersection. As of 2005, the number "9" was painted on the trees here. Keep to the left.

At 8.5 miles is a marker identifying the road as Forest Service Road 15.

At 9.8 miles, just past a cattleguard, is milepost 14.

At 9.9 miles is a road to the right, keep left.

At 10.6 miles is a marker saying you are entering the Colville National Forest.

At 10.7 miles is milepost 13.

At 11.1 miles is another cattleguard.

At 11.2 miles is a large cross intersection. The road to the right is marked as FS 670. The road to the left is unmarked. Continue straight ahead.

At 11.3 miles is an unnamed lake, to the right.

At 12.1 miles is another cattleguard.

At 12.3 miles is a road on the left, the end of which is signed for Elbow Lake.

At 13.6 miles is milepost 10.

At 13.9 miles is another intersection. Here the road you are on is identified as FS 15 and signed "Elbow Lake" and "Northport". Keep to the left.

At 14.0 miles is an intersection with two roads on the left. Keep right, remaining on the main road.

At 14.6 miles is milepost 9.

At 14.9 miles you will cross a cattleguard.

At 18.5 miles is milepost 5.

At 22.0 miles is a large four-way intersection. Straight ahead is unmarked. The road to the left is signed "Sheep Creek 12", "Northport 22". The road you are on is signed "Sheep Creek 14", Northport 24", "Forest Service Road 15". Turn right, and you will be on Churchill Mine Road.

At 23.3 miles you will reach an intersection with a paved road. Pierre Lake Road goes to the left, and Sand Creek Road goes to the right. Immediately before the paved road is a gravel road on the right. This is Box Canyon Road, and the end is signed for "Summit Lake, 3 Miles".

Turn left onto Pierre Lake Road, and take it south for 1.3 miles to the main entrance to the Pierre Lake Campground, on the left. The northern entrance to the area will be passed at 1.0 miles.

Pierre Lake is reached a total of 24.6 miles from Highway 25, and 58.6 miles from where you left Highway 20.

## FISHING TIPS:

Flies cast to rising fish are very effective for Cutthroat.

Bass are reportedly found at the north end and at a beaver lodge about half way up lake from launch area.

Crappie are reportedly found at the south end where logs provide cover.

## MAP REFERENCES:

\*USGS Topographic Map, Washington (48118-H2-TF-024-00)
  Laurier Quadrangle, 7.5 Minute Series.
\*USGS Topographic Map, Washington (48118-E1-TM-100-00)
  Republic Quadrangle, 30x60 Minute Series.
\*Washington Atlas & Gazetteer, Page 117.

## 72  POTTERS POND

Also known as: Pond Number 1

May 17, 1997; Potters Pond, looking southeast.

SIZE: 1.3 to 24.0 Acres (varies with water level)
ELEVATION: 2,400 Feet
MAXIMUM DEPTH: Unknown
COUNTY: Stevens, Washington
COORDINATES: T34N R41E Sec20KQ

Longitude: 117d 39m 37s to 117d 39m 48s West
Latitude: 48d 25m 33s to 48d 25m 43s North

SPECIES, CONFIRMED:
Rainbow Trout

SPECIES, REPORTED:
Eastern Brook Trout

CHARACTERISTICS:
The lake lies in a small flat with low hills to all but the south side, where
the steeper hills above Bayley Lake are visible.

A gravel road runs down the west side and across the south side. The south side of the lake is diked, and the road passes below it en route to Bayley Lake.

A large, nearly flat grassy area is found at the west side and the southwest corner. This corner also provides boat access to the water, and has a camp area and pit toilets. The grassy area is also pretty well covered with goose crap.

The south side has a nice fishing dock at its center. The dock has high rails with drilled in pole holders, plus benches for sitting.

The shorelines along the dike are grass lined, similar to other areas of the lake, but the grass strip is narrower and some bank fishing access is available.

The northwest corner of the lake is shallow and marshy, with a great deal of aquatic grass and weed present. The north and east shores have similar conditions, but on a smaller scale.

Small trees dot the area around the lake, with a heavy concentration on the northeast side.

The water out from the dike and at the fishing dock is deepest, shallowing up as you approach the north and west sides of the lake.

The bottom in the dike area is rocky, and is silt in all other areas. The water is clear.

DIRECTIONS TO:

Take Highway 20 to mile 363.6, east of the town of Colville, where Kitt-Narcisse Road will be reached.

Turn onto Kitt-Narcisse Road and go south for 1.4 miles to Narcisse Creek Road, on the left.

Turn onto Narcisse Creek Road and go southeast for 1.7 miles to the next intersection. You will pass a sign marking the entrance to the Little Pend Oreille Wildlife Refuge 0.4 miles before the intersection.

At the intersection, turn right and go 1.0 mile to the next one.

*At this intersection, turn left. You will pass the refuge headquarters buildings after 0.7 miles, and Cliff Ridge Road, on the right, after 4.1 miles. Stay on the main road, and at 4.5 miles from the last turn you will come to a four way intersection.

Take the road to the right. It will reach the access area for Potters Pond after 0.9 miles, and the end of the road at the Bayley Lake access at 1.2 miles.

The Bayley Lake access is a total of 9.8 miles from Highway 20.

An **ALTERNATE ROUTE** is to take Highway 20 to mile 364.9, where Starvation Lake Road is reached, on the left.

Turn onto Starvation Lake Road and go south. At 0.9 miles a gravel road on the right enters the public access area for Starvation Lake. Continue on Starvation Lake Road, and at 1.3 miles you will reach an intersection.

Go to the right. After 0.4 miles you will reach another intersection.

Stay to the right. After another 0.7 miles you will reach the next intersection. This one is signed for McDowell Lake to the left.

Turn to the right, and you will come to a large four way intersection after only 0.1 mile.

At this intersection turn to the left. Go 1.0 mile to the next intersection.

From here, follow the directions above from the point marked with an asterisk(*).

FISHING TIPS:

Flies worked over the shallow areas of the west and north sides of the lake will get fish.

MAP REFERENCES:

*USGS Topographic Map, Washington (48117-D6-TF-024-00)
  Cliff Ridge Quadrangle, 7.5 Minute Series.
*USGS Topographic Map, Washington (48117-A1-TM-100-00)
  Chewelah Quadrangle, 30x60 Minute Series.
*Washington Atlas & Gazetteer, Page 104 (name not indicated).

# 73   PRIEST LAKE

August 22, 2002; Priest Lake, looking north from Coolin.

SIZE: 23,700 Acres
ELEVATION: 2,438 Feet
MAXIMUM DEPTH: 300+ Feet
COUNTY: Bonner, Idaho
COORDINATES: T59-62N R4-5W

Longitude: 116d 49m 15s to 116d 55m 43s West
Latitude: 48d 28m 27s to 48d 44m 42s North

SPECIES, CONFIRMED:

SPECIES, REPORTED:
 Cutthroat Trout
 Dolly Varden (Bull) Trout
 Kokanee
 Largemouth Bass
 Mackinaw
 Rainbow Trout
 Whitefish
 Yellow Perch

## CHARACTERISTICS:

The lake is very large, much longer than it is wide, and runs about 24 miles from north to south.

The large, main body of the lake stretches for about 19 miles in the southern half, and is about two miles wide. The north half is narrower, but still quite wide.

The area the lake lies in is mountainous. Most of the hills around the lake are heavily timbered.

There are three large islands in the south half. They include: Bartoo Island, the southernmost of the three, located at the center of the lake; Kalispell Island, located northwest of Bartoo Island and close to the west shore; and Eightmile Island, located northeast of Bartoo Island, and very close to the east shore. Kalispell Island has two campgrounds, North Cove Campground at the north end and Schneider Campground at the south end.

A smaller island, Fourmile Island, is located south of Bartoo Island.

A large peninsula is found at the center of the east side, extending to the southwest. Cape Horn is located on the west side of the peninsula.

A second large peninsula is found at the southeast corner of the lake. Cavanaugh Bay is located on the east side of this peninsula.

The other main bays in the southern section of the lake include: Kalispell Bay, west of Kalispell Island; Luby Bay, west of Bartoo Island; Shoshone Bay, west of Fourmile Island and barely recognizable as a bay; Reader Bay, on the west shore at the center of the lake between the large south section and the narrowest part of the lake.

Indian Creek Bay is found at the northeast corner of the southern section of the lake. It has a good-sized spit of land extending southward from the large peninsula.

There are two bays on opposite sides of the lake about half way up the north section of the lake. They are Distillery Bay on the west side, and Huckleberry Bay on the east side. Squaw Bay is located at the northeast corner.

There is a small east to west expansion in width at the north end of the lake, bracketed by Tripod Point on the west side and Canoe Point on the east side.

Much of the area around the lake is undeveloped forest. Development is scattered along the shores, and very concentrated in some areas. Roads, some good and some poor, are found all around the lake. Many are along or close to the shores.

State parks are found at the northeast corner (Lionhead Unit) and the center of the east side (Indian Creek Unit).

Because of its very large size, the lake has many inlet streams. They include an inlet from Upper Priest Lake at the northwest corner. Major creeks on the west side include Beaver Creek, Tango Creek, Granite Creek, Kalispell Creek, and Lamb Creek. Those on the east side include Lion Creek, Squaw Creek, Two Mouth Creek, Bear Creek, Indian Creek, Horton Creek, Cougar Creek and Soldier Creek.

The Priest River drains the lake at Outlet Bay, near the southwest corner of the lake. The community of Outlet Bay is found there.

The town of Coolin is located at the southern tip of the lake.

Visible bottom areas are rocky.

The water is clear.

DIRECTIONS TO:

Take Highway 2 to mile 5.9, at a stoplight in the middle of the town of Priest River, where Highway 57 / West Side Road will be found on the north side of the highway.

Turn onto Highway 57, and follow it north for 22.5 miles to Dickensheet Road, on the right. The continuation of Highway 57 is signed for Nordman. Dickensheet Road provides access to the south end and east side of Priest Lake.

Turn right onto Dickensheet Road and go 5.2 miles to the town of Coolin, where an intersection is reached. The road to the right, East Shore Road, provides access to the east side of the lake, and the road you are on goes to the left to reach the south end. The road to the right is signed for "Priest Lake State Park, Indian Creek Unit, Lionhead Unit".

Keep to the left at the intersection, and continue another 0.4 miles to Bishop's Marina, on the left. In addition to the full service marina facilities available here, there is a public boat launch. The end of the concrete ramp is signed as "Public Access" provided by Bonner County Waterways Commission. The sign is posted on a pole next to the ramp. Portable toilets are on the other side of the ramp.

In addition to the access information provided above, there are many others available. They are found on both the east and west sides of the lake, with the majority on the west side. Most of the marinas that provide access charge fees for the service. Because these conditions are subject to frequent change, I won't even try to detail them here.

## ON THE EAST SIDE OF PRIEST LAKE:

Priest Lake State Park has two units on the east side of the lake. They are reached via East Shore Road from the town of Coolin.

From the end of the road in Coolin, you will reach the following on the east side of the lake:

*At 4.4 miles: Cavanaugh Bay Road, on the left. The end of the road is signed for "Cavanaugh Bay Marina 0.5 Miles", and "Blue Diamond Marina 2 Miles".

*At 6.5 miles: A roadside turnout on the shore of the lake.

*At 10.5 miles: State Park Marina Road, on the left. This is part of the Indian Creek Unit of the state park.

*At 11.8 miles: Indian Creek Unit of Priest Lake State Park, on the left. The unit offers 93 campsites (some with RV hookups), a beach, swimming area, boat ramp, docks, picnic area, showers and a park store. All is for a fee, and because they are subject to change I won't list them here. Be advised though that as of 2006, the fee for just entering any Idaho State Park is $4.00 per day.

*At about 23 miles: Lionhead Unit of Priest Lake State Park. The park entrance, which is reached first, provides access to the boat ramp. There is a separate exit from the park reached further up east Shore Road. The unit offers 47 tent campsites, pit toilets, boat launch, and a sand beach.

## ON THE WEST SIDE OF PRIEST LAKE:

Highway 57 continues up the west side of the lake, but gradually gets further from the lake as it goes north. Side roads run from Highway 57 to the west side of the lake at several locations. The main roads are to the community of Outlet Bay, and from the town of Nordman. The other roads are Forest Service roads.

From Highway 57, the following are reached on the west side of the lake:

*At Mile 26.0: Outlet Bay Road, on the right. The end of the road is signed for "Outlet Bay Campground 1 Mile". Outlet Bay has two Forest Service campgrounds, Outlet Campground and Osprey Campground. Both are fee areas. Neither has a boat ramp, although Outlet has a swimming area.

*At Mile 28.6: Luby Bay Road, on the right. This area has a Forest Service campground, which is also a fee area. It also has Hill's Resort, which offers all amenities, including boat launching.

*At Mile 29.3: Kalispell Bay Road, on the right. There is a Forest Service access area that has a boat launch, picnic area and toilets, but no camping. North of the Forest Service access is Priest Lake Marina, which offers most amenities.

*At Mile 36.7: Reeder Bay Road, on the right. The end of the road is signed for "Priest Lake, Reeder Bay Campground 2 Miles", and is reached just north of the town of Nordman. The area has Kaniksu Resort, Grandview Resort and Elkins Resort. The amenities they offer vary, but all have a boat launch. In addition to the resorts, the Forest Service also has Reeder Bay Campground and Ledgewood Picnic Area in the area. Both have swimming areas, but neither has a boat launch.

From Reeder Bay, Forest Service Road 2412 runs north along the lake to reach Beaver Creek Campground, at the extreme northwest corner of Priest Lake, and at the mouth of the "thorofare" between Priest Lake and Upper Priest Lake. This campground has a boat launch area.

FISHING TIPS:
I have not attempted to fish this lake.

MISCELLANEOUS NOTES:
A state record Mackinaw of 57 1/2 pounds (49 inches long) was caught in 1971.
A state record Kokanee of 6 pounds 9 1/2 ounces (24 1/2 inches long) was caught in 1975.

MAP REFERENCES:
*Idaho Atlas & Gazetteer, Page 62.
*USGS Topographic Map, Idaho (48116-D7-TF-024-00)
   Coolin Quadrangle, 7.5 Minute Series.
*USGS Topographic Map, Idaho (48116-D8-TF-024-00)
   Outlet Bay Quadrangle, 7.5 Minute Series.
*USGS Topographic Map, Idaho (48116-F7-TF-024-00)
   Priest Lake NE Quadrangle, 7.5 Minute Series.
*USGS Topographic Map, Idaho (48116-F8-TF-024-00)
   Priest Lake NW Quadrangle, 7.5 Minute Series.
*USGS Topographic Map, Idaho (48116-E7-TF-024-00)
   Priest Lake SE Quadrangle, 7.5 Minute Series.
*USGS Topographic Map, Idaho (48116-E8-TF-024-00)
   Priest Lake SW Quadrangle, 7.5 Minute Series.

*USGS Topographic Map, Idaho (48116-E1-TM-100-00)
  Bonners Ferry Quadrangle, 30x60 Minute Series.
*USGS Topographic Map, Idaho (48116-A1-TM-100-00)
  Sandpoint Quadrangle, 30x60 Minute Series.

## 74   PYRAMID LAKE

September 9, 2000; Pyramid Lake,
looking northeast from the Ball Lakes trail.

SIZE: 20 Acres (estimated)
ELEVATION: 6,050 Feet
MAXIMUM DEPTH: Unknown
COUNTY: Boundary, Idaho
COORDINATES: T63N R2W Sec20H,21E

Longitude: 116d 36m 40s to 116d 36m 54s West
Latitude: 48d 47m 54s to 48d 48m 3s North

SPECIES, CONFIRMED:
Cutthroat Trout, West Slope

SPECIES, REPORTED:
Rainbow Trout

## CHARACTERISTICS:

Pyramid Lake is at the headwaters of Trout Creek, which exits at the northeast corner.

A steep ridgeline rises south of the lake, and wraps partially around the east and west sides. To the south is mostly vertical rock. The lower portions of the slope are steep broken rock, some of which is quite large. Tree cover is very sparse.

The shoreline on the south side has large broken rock and almost no trees.

The lake runs from southwest to northeast, where it drains. Once away from the rocky south end the area is heavily timbered with small to medium sized trees.

The shorelines in the timbered areas have only low brush and are relatively open.

The center of the lake narrows from both sides to form an hourglass shape, resulting in two very different sections of lake. The southwest end is deep while the northeast end is shallow. The neck between the sections is very shallow with a silt bottom studded with good sized rocks. Many of the rocks break the surface.

The shorelines in the southwest section have a lot of rock, even in the timbered areas. The bottom of the southwest section is rocky with some silted spots.

The bottom of the shallow northeast section is mostly silt. Snags and thin growths of aquatic vegetation line the shores.

On all but the south end, shorelines are very low and mostly level, sloping gently to the higher ground around the lake.

Camp areas are located at the north corner before the trail crosses the outlet creek. The trail runs along the east side of the lake after crossing the creek, entering timber before switching back to the right and beginning the climb up the steep, open slopes to the south. There are some great views of Pyramid Lake from the higher portion of the trail.

The mouth of the outlet creek is over a shallow, mud bottomed flat. The flat has rocks rising up through the silt, and a few scattered snags. The heaviest growths of aquatic weed growing within the wetted perimeter of the lake are at the mouth of the outlet creek.

The water is extremely clear.

## DIRECTIONS TO:

Take Interstate 90 to exit 12, at the town of Coeur d'Alene.

From exit 12, take Highway 95 north for about 77 miles to mile 507.5, at the town of Bonners Ferry, where Riverside Road will be found on the west side of the highway just south of the bridge over the Kootenai River. The end of the road is signed for "Kootenai Wildlife Refuge 6 Miles".

Turn onto Riverside, and head west out of Bonners Ferry, keeping to the right as the road follows the banks of the river.

At 5.0 miles from Highway 95 the road will reach the base of the foothills, and a "Y" intersection. Keep to the right, and the road will begin running to the north. Past the "Y" about a quarter mile, you will pass the Kootenai Wildlife Refuge headquarters. The pavement ends in another 6.5 miles.

At 14.9 miles from Highway 95 you will reach the end of Forest Service Road 634, also shown on some maps as Trout Creek Road. The end of the road is signed "Junction Trail 6 Miles, Trail 12 7 Miles, Trail 13 9 Miles".

*Turn onto Road 634, and follow it 8.8 miles to a parking area, on the left, for the trailhead, which is on the right. The road ends in another 0.2 miles at a horse facility and camp area.

On the 8.8 mile run to the trailhead, you will reach an intersection at 4.5 miles, where you keep to the left.

You will pass the Fisher Peak trailhead, on the right, at 5.2 miles.

You will pass the Russell Peak Trail #12 parking area, on the left, at 6.1 miles. There are signs here for the trailhead that indicate "Russell Peak 2 1/2 Miles", and for the continuation of the road to the right indicating "Junction Trail #92 3 Miles".

The trailhead provides access to several lakes in the area, found off various branches of the trail system. The lakes include Pyramid, Upper Ball, Lower Ball, Trout, Big Fisher, Long Mountain, and Parker.

To reach Pyramid Lake, take the trail about 0.5 miles (elevation gain approximately 450 feet) to a fork. Take the left fork.

Go south about 0.3 miles (gain about 150 feet) to reach the northeast end of the lake.

An **ALTERNATE ROUTE** to the Trout Creek trail system would be to take Highway 95 to mile 523.0, north of the town of Bonners Ferry, where Highway 1 will be found on the left.

Turn onto Highway 1, and continue north for 1.1 miles to a road on the left at the town of Copeland. The end of the road is signed for "Sportsman's Access" and "National Forest Entrance".

Turn left onto the road, and head west. At 1.6 miles you will reach a bridge over the Kootenai River. At 3.4 miles from Highway 1 you will reach a "T" intersection with West Side Road. There is a sign opposite the end of the road you are on that indicates "Maravia 20 Miles" to the left, and "Smith Creek Road and Boundary Creek Road 9 Miles" to the right.

At West Side Road, turn left and go south for 2.9 miles to a 90-degree corner. The paved road turns to the left, and a gravel road leaves the pavement straight ahead. Contrary to appearances, the gravel road is the continuation of West Side Road.

Take the gravel road, and after 1.8 miles you will reach the end of Forest Service Road 634, also shown on some maps as Trout Creek Road, on the right. The end of the road is signed "Junction Trail 6 Miles, Trail 12 7 Miles, Trail 13 9 Miles".

From here, follow the directions provided above from the point marked with an asterisk(*).

## FISHING TIPS:

Flies cast from shore around the neck at the center of the lake and along shore in the deep half of the lake will get fish.

## MISCELLANEOUS NOTES:

Planting records indicate that the lake received plants of Hayspur Triploid Rainbow Trout on September 14, 2000 (1,175) and September 16, 2000 (420). It also received plants of West Slope Cutthroat Trout on August 6 and 7, 1998.

## MAP REFERENCES:

*Idaho Atlas & Gazetteer, Page 48 (lake not shown).
*USGS Topographic Map, Idaho (48116-G5-TF-024-00)
   Pyramid Peak Quadrangle, 7.5 Minute Series.
*USGS Topographic Map, Idaho (48116-E1-TM-100-00)
   Bonners Ferry Quadrangle, 30x60 Minute Series.

# 75  ROSE LAKE

June 29, 1996; Rose Lake, looking northeast.

SIZE: 300 Acres
ELEVATION: 2,122 Feet
MAXIMUM DEPTH: Unknown
COUNTY: Kootenai, Idaho
COORDINATES: T49N R1W Sec33

> Longitude: 116d 27m 28s to 116d 28m 38s West
> Latitude: 47d 32m 42s to 47d 33m 36s North

SPECIES, CONFIRMED:
 Black Crappie
 Bluegill
 Largemouth Bass
 Pumpkinseed Sunfish
 Yellow Perch

SPECIES, REPORTED:
 Bullhead Catfish

## CHARACTERISTICS:

There are wooded hills all around the lake, with open skyline to the south.

Two public access areas are found at the northeast corner. The southern-most has a boat ramp and a large fishing dock, as well as a camp area. The second, found just a couple of hundred yards to the north, also has a large dock, but no boat ramp or camping.

Homes, many with docks, are found along much of the south half of the east shore. All other shoreline areas are shallow and marshy with cattails, lilypads, dollar pads and other aquatic vegetation.

The bottom at the access area is gravel, and mud in all other areas.

The water has a greenish tinge.

## DIRECTIONS TO:

Take Interstate 90 to exit 34 east of Coeur d'Alene, Idaho. At exit 34, turn south onto Highway 3.

Take Highway 3 south for 1.8 miles to mile 117.7, where a gravel road enters on the right. The end of the road is signed for Rose Lake Sports-man's Access.

Take the gravel road 0.3 miles to the lake. The main public access area has a gravel boat launch area with a nice fishing dock, an area for camping, and pit toilets.

There is also a second access area to the north. This second access has limited parking, no camping or boat launch, a pit toilet, and a nice fishing dock. To reach it, take a right when you reach the main access area.

Go 0.2 miles to a "T" intersection.

Turn left, and go 0.3 miles to the second access area, on the left. The toilets are on the right side of the road.

## FISHING TIPS:

Spinners fished along the weed beds will get bass and crappie. Small jigs are also effective, and will also get bluegill.

Casting jigs along the weeds at the docks and shoreline areas at the access areas will also get a variety of fish.

## MAP REFERENCES:

*Idaho Atlas & Gazetteer, Page 60.

*USGS Topographic Map, Idaho (47116-E4-TF-024-00)
  Rose Lake Quadrangle, 7.5 Minute Series.

*USGS Topographic Map, Idaho (47116-E1-TM-100-00)
  Coeur d'Alene Quadrangle, 30x60 Minute Series.

# 76  ROUND LAKE

June 17, 2006; Round Lake, looking southwest.

SIZE: 58 Acres
ELEVATION: 2,122 Feet
MAXIMUM DEPTH: 37 Feet
COUNTY: Bonner, Idaho
COORDINATES: T56N R3W Sec36(northeast 1/4)

Longitude: 116d 38m 2s to 116d 38m 26s West
Latitude: 48d 9m 35s to 48d 9m 51s North

SPECIES, CONFIRMED:
 Black Crappie
 Pumpkinseed Sunfish
 Rainbow Trout
 Yellow Perch

SPECIES, REPORTED:
 Cutthroat Trout, West Slope
 Eastern Brook Trout
 Largemouth Bass

## CHARACTERISTICS:

The lake is named round, but is actually almost square, but with rounded corners. The surrounding area has low, mostly timbered hills, with some rocky areas showing through the timber cover.

The area immediately around the lake is heavily timbered. Timber and brush reach to the waters edge all around the lake, with the only open areas at the access and a small gravel bar at the mouth of the inlet creek.

An inlet creek enters at the center of the east side, and the lake drains at a small cove near the southwest corner. A small channel lined with lilypads leads into the shallow, timber lined cove.

The deepest water is reportedly near the center of the lake.

The State Park access area is at the center of the north side of the lake. It has a gravel boat launching area, and two long fishing docks with a swimming area between them. There is a limited amount of parking available for boat trailers. A picnic and camping area, with restrooms, is located above the boat launch / swimming area.

With the exception of a small section of the south shore, most shorelines have beds of lilypads or dollar pads along them. In addition to the visible weeds, the bottom has a heavy covering of aquatic growth. In the shallower areas that weed growth rises to near the surface, and in many cases reaches it.

There are several snags along the shorelines. Most are small, but there are a few good-sized ones.

The bottom is silt.

The water has a murky green color.

## DIRECTIONS TO:

Take Interstate 90 to exit 12 at Coeur d'Alene, Idaho. At exit 12, turn north onto Highway 95.

Take Highway 95 north for about 36 miles to mile 465.6, where Dufort Road will be reached, on the left.

Turn onto Dufort Road, and go 1.7 miles to the entrance of Round Lake State Park, on the left.

From Dufort Road, the boat launch area at the lake is 0.3 miles.

## FISHING TIPS:

Round Lake offers excellent fishing for multiple species. The Rainbow are hatchery plants, but the panfish are both plentiful and of decent size.

For Rainbow Trout, trolled or cast spinners are very effective.

For panfish, micro jigs are very effective. I had my best luck near the southwest corner at the mouth of the outlet creek.

MISCELLANEOUS NOTES:

Round Lake State Park offers access. It has swimming, picnicking and camping areas, as well as water and a boat launch. It is a fee area, with entrance costing $4.00 as of 2006.

MAP REFERENCES:
 *Idaho Atlas & Gazetteer, Page 62.
 *USGS Topographic Map, Idaho (48116-B6-TF-024-00)
  Morton Quadrangle, 7.5 Minute Series.
 *USGS Topographic Map, Idaho-Montana (48116-A1-TM-100-00)
  Sandpoint Quadrangle, 30x60 Minute Series.

## 77  SACHEEN LAKE

May 22, 1995; Sacheen Lake, east end,
looking west from the public access.

SIZE: 282.2 Acres
ELEVATION: 2,236 Feet
MAXIMUM DEPTH: 70 Feet
COUNTY: Pend Oreille, Washington
COORDINATES: T31N R43E Sec24,25,26,36
        T31N R44E Sec30

        Longitude: 117d 18m 3s to 117d 20m 6s West
        Latitude: 48d 8m 44s to 48d 9m 53s North

SPECIES, CONFIRMED:

SPECIES, REPORTED:
  Eastern Brook Trout
  Green Sunfish
  Rainbow Trout
  Tiger Trout

## CHARACTERISTICS:

The lake has an extremely irregular shape. There are numerous small bays and points.

The areas around the lake are very developed, and homes are found almost everywhere. Even with the houses, the shorelines are still well wooded.

Much of the shoreline is rocky and fairly steep. More gentle slopes are found in some of the bays.

The bottom is rock and silt. There is a lot of aquatic vegetation in the shallows.

The water is stained light brown.

## DIRECTIONS TO:

Take Highway 2 north from Spokane to mile 321.2, where Highway 211 comes in on the left. This junction is at Highway 211 mile 0.0.

Turn left onto Highway 211 and go north to mile 4.2, where the end of Terrace Drive is reached, on the left.

Turn onto Terrace Drive, and the public access for Sacheen Lake will be reached on the left after just 0.3 miles.

The public access has a large gravel parking area, pit toilets and a boat ramp. The area is posted for no overnight parking.

## FISHING TIPS:

I'm unable to offer any tips due to a lack of success in this lake. I it fished only once, very briefly, from shore.

## MAP REFERENCES:

*USGS Topographic Map, Washington (48117-B3-TF-024-00)
  Sacheen Lake Quadrangle, 7.5 Minute Series.
*USGS Topographic Map, Washington (48117-A1-TM-100-00)
  Chewelah Quadrangle, 30x60 Minute Series.
*Washington Atlas & Gazetteer, Page 105.

## 78   SHEPHERD LAKE

June 16, 2006; Shepherd Lake, looking southwest
from the public access on the east side of the lake.

SIZE: 120 Acres
ELEVATION: 2,280 Feet
MAXIMUM DEPTH: Unknown
COUNTY: Bonner, Idaho
COORDINATES: T56N R2W Sec23(east 1/3),24DE

>   Longitude: 116d 31m 22s to 116d 31m 53s West
>   Latitude: 48d 10m 47s to 48d 11m 31s North

SPECIES, CONFIRMED:
 Bluegill
 Largemouth Bass
 Pumpkinseed Sunfish

SPECIES, REPORTED:
 Black Crappie
 Tiger Muskie
 Yellow Perch

## CHARACTERISTICS:

The lake lies in an area with low, timbered hills to the north, south and east. The skyline is low to the west. Higher hills are visible in the distance to the northwest.

The area around the lake is mostly heavily timbered. A major exception is a developed area at the south end of the lake. There are only a couple of homes visible, but large lawn areas that stretch to the shoreline are present. The lawn areas are dotted with trees.

There are also some homes visible in the trees on the hillsides to the north.

The shorelines have trees and very low brush to the waters edge in most places. The north end of the lake has a large marshy area lining the shores. The west side shorelines are fairly open, with some randomly scattered snags and aquatic weed.

The east side of the lake has a lot of snags close along the mostly shallow shores. Out from the snags, as well as interspersed among them, are beds of dollar pads that extend out fifty yards or more. These conditions exist for the full length of the east shore.

The rough shorelines limit bank fishing to the dock at the boat launch area on the east side of the lake.

Public accesses exist on both the east and west sides of the lake, but as of 2006, the access on the west side has been closed. The public access area on the center of the east side provides camping and picnic areas, as well as a concrete boat launch with a dock, a large gravel parking area, and a pit toilet. A sign indicates a camping limit of three days.

The bottom is mud, but almost everywhere is covered by a heavy growth of aquatic weeds.

The water is clear, but has a slight brownish tinge.

## DIRECTIONS TO:

Take Interstate 90 to exit 12 at Coeur d'Alene, Idaho. At exit 12, turn north onto Highway 95.

Take Highway 95 north for about 39 miles to mile 468.2, where Sagle Road will be found on the east side of the highway.

Turn onto Sagle Road, and go east for 1.2 miles to Talache Road, on the right.

Turn right, onto Talache Road, and go south for 1.4 miles to the public access area for Shepherd Lake, on the right. The end of the road is signed "Sportsman's Access".

The access road runs 0.1 mile to the boat launch area.

**NOTE:** At 1.0 mile from Sagle Road you will pass the end of the access road for the west side public access area for Shepherd Lake, on the right. As of 2006, this area is closed and gated at Talache Road.

An **ALTERNATE ROUTE** to Shepherd Lake is to take Highway 95 north for about 36 miles to mile 465.6, where East Dufort Road will be reached, on the right.

Turn onto East Dufort Road, which becomes gravel, and go 3.7 miles to a "T" intersection.

Turn left onto Talache Road, which is paved, and go north for 1.1 miles to the public access area for Shepherd Lake, on the left. The end of the road is signed "Sportsman's Access".

The access road runs 0.1 mile to the boat launch area.

FISHING TIPS:

Bluegill and Pumpkinseed are readily caught on small jigs and baits from the dock at the access area. Bass are also occasionally caught on the same tackle.

The lake is most effectively fished from a boat.

As of 2006, the lake has special regulations, including "electric motors only". See the current regulations before fishing.

MAP REFERENCES:

*Idaho Atlas & Gazetteer, Page 62.

*USGS Topographic Map, Idaho (48116-B5-TF-024-00)
  Sagle Quadrangle, 7.5 Minute Series.

*USGS Topographic Map, Idaho-Montana (48116-A1-TM-100-00)
  Sandpoint Quadrangle, 30x60 Minute Series.

## 79  LAKE SHERRY

August 22, 2002; Lake Sherry, looking south.

SIZE: 26.1 Acres
ELEVATION: 3,147 Feet
MAXIMUM DEPTH: 85 Feet
COUNTY: Stevens, Washington
COORDINATES: T36N R42E Sec20E

      Longitude: 117d 32m 25s to 117d 32m 40s West
      Latitude: 48d 36m 24s to 48d 36m 42s North

SPECIES, CONFIRMED:
  Cutthroat Trout, West Slope
  Pumpkinseed Sunfish
  Yellow Perch

SPECIES, REPORTED:
  Eastern Brook Trout
  Rainbow Trout
  Tiger Trout

CHARACTERISTICS:

The lake lies in an area of low, timbered hills.

Although the lake is timbered all around, it is also developed all around. The only exception is a small section of shoreline at the southwest corner. The shorelines are occupied by homes, many with manicured lawns to the waters edge. Many also have docks. All around the lake is private property.

Buoys are set in the lake for water skiing.

The lake is located about 250 feet south of Lake Gillette, and connected to Lake Gillette by a navigable channel of the Little Pend Oreille River. A bridge carrying the road to the access area crosses the channel. The section of the channel under the bridge has been enclosed with vertical walls of wooden beams with fill behind them supporting the road approach, and wing-walls at either end. The bottom in the channel area is cobbled rock with sparse aquatic vegetation.

The river exits at the south end of the lake.

A small bed of lilypads is found at the northeast corner, alongside of and out from the inlet stream. Smaller beds of aquatic vegetation are found elsewhere around the lake.

The bottom is mostly silt, with some gravel and rock.

The water is clear, but has a slight brownish color at times.

DIRECTIONS TO:

Take Highway 20 to mile 379.2, east of the town of Colville, where Lake Pend Oreille Road will be found on the south side of the highway.

Turn onto Lake Pend Oreille Road and follow it 0.5 miles to the public access area for Lake Gillette, on the left. The area has a campground, boat ramp, picnic area and beach.

Launch on Lake Gillette, and go to the left to reach the channel between Lakes Gillette and Sherry. The land around Lake Sherry is all privately owned, and access is by water only.

FISHING TIPS:

Flies worked around the weed beds are very effective, especially at the mouth of the channel to Lake Gillette.

MISCELLANEOUS NOTES:

As of 2004, there is a "parking fee" of $3.00 per day to use the access area at Lake Gillette.

MAP REFERENCES:
*USGS Topographic Map, Washington (48117-E5-TF-024-00)
  Lake Gillette Quadrangle, 7.5 Minute Series.
*USGS Topographic Map, Washington (48117-E1-TM-100-00)
  Colville Quadrangle, 30x60 Minute Series.
*Washington Atlas & Gazetteer, Page 118.

## 80  SMITH LAKE

September 8, 2000; Smith Lake, looking southeast from the access area.

SIZE: 30 Acres
ELEVATION: 2,981 Feet
MAXIMUM DEPTH: 40 Feet
COUNTY: Boundary, Idaho
COORDINATES: T63N R2W Sec30MN,31D

> Longitude: 116d 15m 32s <u>to</u> 116d 15m 43s West
> Latitude: 48d 46m 28s <u>to</u> 48d 46m 51s North

SPECIES, CONFIRMED:
 Rainbow Trout

SPECIES, REPORTED:
 Arctic Grayling
 Bluegill
 Brown Bullhead Catfish
 Channel Catfish
 Cutthroat Trout, West Slope
 Eastern Brook Trout
 Kokanee

Largemouth Bass
Pumpkinseed Sunfish

## CHARACTERISTICS:

The lake is long and fairly narrow, running north to south.

The lake is wooded all around, with the exception of the north end, where there is an open, grassy area with few trees.

Mountains are visible in the distance to the north.

There are trees and brush to the waters edge in almost all areas to the east, west and south.

Some shallow water can be found along the edges of the lake, but most of the lake is deep water. Small snags lie in the shallows.

Small beds of lily pads are scattered around the lake in the shallow pockets.

The bottom is silt. The water has a slight brownish tinge.

The public access area is located near the northwest corner of the lake. It has a concrete strip boat ramp, fishing dock, pit toilet and gravel parking area. The access area also has seven campsites, located above the lake.

The site is very popular and heavily used.

## DIRECTIONS TO:

Take Interstate 90 to exit 12, at the town of Coeur d'Alene.

From exit 12, take Highway 95 north for about 82 miles to mile 512.5, about five miles north of the town of Bonners Ferry, where Smith Lake Road will be reached, on the right. The end of Smith Lake Road is signed for "Sportsman's Access, Smith Lake".

Turn onto Smith Lake Road, and follow it 1.4 miles to an intersection. At the intersection, go to the right. As of the fall of 2000, there was a handwritten sign for "Smith Lake" at the fork.

Go another 1.1 miles to the next intersection. At this one, the right goes to the Smith Lake campground and the left goes to the boat launch area and the lake itself.

Take the left, and the parking area and boat launch will be reached after 0.1 miles. The lake is a total of 2.6 miles from Highway 95.

Smith Lake Road is gravel.

## FISHING TIPS:

Bait fishermen soaking Berkley Power Bait from the fishing dock take the planted trout.

Out on the lake, trolled flies are effective. If fish are rising, drifting and casting flies to the active fish is best.

MISCELLANEOUS NOTES:
  Planting records indicate that the lake received:
  Eastern Brook Trout, 1,000 on May 16, 1997;
  Arctic Grayling, 3,250 fry in 2000, and another 750 in 2001;
  Channel Catfish, 5,340 three to six-inch fish in 1999, and 500 six-inch
plus fish in both 2000 and 2003.

MAP REFERENCES:
 *Idaho Atlas & Gazetteer, Page 62 (name not indicated).
 *USGS Topographic Map, Idaho (48116-G3-TF-024-00)
  Ritz Quadrangle, 7.5 Minute Series.
 *USGS Topographic Map, Idaho (48116-E1-TM-100-00)
  Bonners Ferry Quadrangle, 30x60 Minute Series.

## 81   SOUTH SKOOKUM LAKE

September 17, 2000; South Skookum Lake,
looking northeast from the access area.

SIZE: 31.8 Acres
ELEVATION: 3,529 Feet
MAXIMUM DEPTH: 15 Feet
COUNTY: Pend Oreille, Washington
COORDINATES: T33N R44E Sec1(northeast 1/4)

Longitude: 117d 10m 38s to 117d 10m 58s West
Latitude: 48d 23m 25s to 48d 23m 42s North

SPECIES, CONFIRMED:

SPECIES, REPORTED:
 Eastern Brook Trout
 Rainbow Trout

CHARACTERISTICS:
 The lake lies in an area of low, timber covered hills. The highest hills visible are to the northwest and northeast. Kings Mountain rises to the southwest. Timber cover is sparse in some places.

The area immediately around the lake is also timbered, but the east side has some spots where rock shows through, as well as some areas where cover is thin.

The north end has a large area covered by growths of aquatic weed and shoreline weeds. The other shores are somewhat steeper, with trees and brush to or nearly to the waters edge.

The east and west sides in the southern 3/4 of the lake drop off to deep water fairly quickly. The deepest water is found at the center of the lake, and the shallowest areas of any size are at the shallow bays of the north end.

The campground, which provides access to the lake, is located on the west shore. The boat launch is at the center of the west shore. The campground is not very impressive. It has brushy sites located away from the water.

The water is clear.

DIRECTIONS TO:

Take Highway 20 to mile 421.0, where Kings Lake Road will be found on the east side of the highway. The end of Kings Lake Road is about 16 miles north of the town of Newport.

Turn onto Kings Lake Road, and go east through the town of Usk. You will cross a bridge over the Pend Oreille River, and at 1.0 miles from Highway 20 reach a sign that indicates "Skookum Lake 8 Miles", "Browns Lake 11 Miles".

At 5.0 miles, the pavement ends.

At 7.2 miles, you will reach an intersection with Road 5030, on the left. Road 5030 goes to Half Moon Lake and Browns Lake. If you continue straight ahead, the road goes to Skookum Lakes and Kings Lake.

Continue on Kings Lake Road for another 1.5 miles to an intersection. Road 5032, on the right, goes to South Skookum Lake. The end of the road is signed as Kings Mountain Road, and "South Skookum Lake 1/2 Mile, Kings Mountain 2 Miles". The end of the road is at 8.7 miles from Highway 20.

Turn right onto Kings Mountain Road, and go 0.2 miles to the entrance to the South Skookum Lake campground. The end of the access road is signed Colville National Forest Skookum Lake Camp, and another sign indicates it is a fee area, with even a day use fee of $3.00 as of the fall of 2000. It costs even more to camp at this piss poor excuse for a campground.

Turn left into the camp area, and go 0.2 miles to a parking area for the boat launch. The road to the boat launch is opposite the parking area, on the right. It runs about a hundred yards to a gravel launch in an area with no parking available.

The road in the camp area forms about a 1/2 mile loop, coming back out near the entrance.

FISHING TIPS:
  I did not attempt to fish this lake.

MAP REFERENCES:
 *USGS Topographic Map, Washington (48117-D2-TF-024-00)
    Browns Lake Quadrangle, 7.5 Minute Series.
 *USGS Topographic Map, Washington (48117-A1-TM-100-00)
    Chewelah Quadrangle, 30x60 Minute Series.
  *Washington Atlas & Gazetteer, Page 105.

## 82  SPIRIT LAKE

June 25, 2004; Spirit Lake, east end,
looking south from the public access area.

SIZE: 1,300 Acres
ELEVATION: 2,441 Feet
MAXIMUM DEPTH: Unknown
COUNTY: Kootenai, Idaho
COORDINATES: T53N R4W Sec6-8,17,18
       T53N R5W Sec13,14,22-24

     Longitude: 116d 51m 38s to 116d 56m 17s West
     Latitude: 47d 55m 49s to 47d 57m 56s North

SPECIES, CONFIRMED:

SPECIES, REPORTED:
 Black Crappie
 Bullhead Catfish
 Cutthroat Trout
 Eastern Brook Trout
 German Brown Trout
 Kokanee

Largemouth Bass
Pumpkinseed Sunfish
Rainbow Trout
Yellow Perch

CHARACTERISTICS:
The lake lies in an area of mostly rolling hills. They are heavily timbered in many places, and show signs of active logging.

The area around the lake is also timbered, but is also very developed.

A highway cuts off a small segment of the lake at its northernmost point, at the northeast corner. It isolates what is actually a good-sized segment of lake to the north, connected to the main body of the lake by a navigable channel under a bridge.

The segment to the north has trees and mostly low, dense brush to the waters edge in all but the developed areas.

The public access area for the lake is located on the main body of the lake at the northeast corner. Fireside Resort is located across the road from the public access, but is situated on the northern segment of the lake.

The access area has two side by side boat ramps, a pair of docks, a public swimming area and a large parking area. It is very heavily used by non-fishermen during warm weather, especially on weekends.

The main body of the lake is surrounded by private property with no shore access. Most of the shores are fairly steep.

The main body of the lake is developed all around, although sparsely in some areas. Even the most heavily developed areas have a lot of trees. Many of the houses around the lake have docks out from them.

The water is clear.

DIRECTIONS TO:
Take Interstate 90 to exit 7, just east of Post Falls, Idaho, where Highway 41 enters from the north.

Take Highway 41 north for 19 miles to mile 19.0, where Main Street will be reached in the town of Spirit Lake. The intersection is signed for "Spirit Lake Recreation Area, 3/4 Miles", to the left.

Turn left onto Main Street, and go 0.6 miles to the public access area for Spirit Lake, on the left.

An **ALTERNATE ROUTE** to Spirit is to leave Interstate 90 at exit 12 at Coeur d'Alene.

From exit 12, turn left and go north for 8.2 miles to mile 438.9, where Highway 53 will be found on the left.

Turn onto Highway 53 and go west about four miles to an intersection with Highway 41, reached at Highway 41 mile 7.7.

Turn right, and go north on Highway 41 for about 11 miles to Highway 41 mile 19.0, where Main Street will be reached in the town of Spirit Lake. The intersection is signed for "Spirit Lake Recreation Area, 3/4 Miles", to the left.

Turn left onto Main Street, and go 0.6 miles to the public access area for Spirit Lake, on the left.

A **SECOND ALTERNATE ROUTE** is to take Highway 2 to the town of Newport, Washington / Old Town, Idaho, located on the state line. The junction of Highway 2 and Highway 41 is stoplighted.

At the junction of Highways 2 and 41, turn south onto Highway 41. Go south on Highway 41 for 20 miles to mile 19.0, at the intersection with Main Street in the town of Spirit Lake.

Turn right onto Main Street, and go 0.6 miles to the public access area for Spirit Lake, on the left.

FISHING TIPS:
I did not attempt to fish this lake.

MAP REFERENCES:
*Idaho Atlas & Gazetteer, Page 12, 60.
*USGS Topographic Map, Idaho (47116-H7-TF-024-00)
  Spirit Lake East Quadrangle, 7.5 Minute Series.
*USGS Topographic Map, Idaho (47116-H8-TF-024-00)
  Spirit Lake West Quadrangle, 7.5 Minute Series.
*USGS Topographic Map, Idaho (47116-E1-TM-100-00)
  Coeur d'Alene Quadrangle, 30x60 Minute Series.

## 83  SPORTSMAN POND
Also known as: Tacoma Sportsman Pond

June 19, 2006; Sportsman Pond, looking northwest.

SIZE: 4.4 Acres
ELEVATION: 2,420 Feet (estimated)
MAXIMUM DEPTH: Unknown
COUNTY: Pend Oreille, Washington
COORDINATES: T34N R43E Sec22M

Longitude: 117d 21m 50s to 117d 21m 59s West
Latitude: 48d 25m 50s to 48d 25m 57s North

SPECIES, CONFIRMED:

SPECIES, REPORTED:

CHARACTERISTICS:
  The lake is nearly circular. It lies in an area of low hills in an active timber harvest area.
  The east and west sides of the lake have timber and brush to the waters edge.
  The north end has marshy grass lining the shores. An extensive weed bed extends from the north end to about half way down the lake.

The lake drains at the south end at a small concrete spillway, and then flows under the logging road that passes that end of the lake. The south end of the lake has mostly open water, but sparse patches of aquatic weeds are scattered over the area.

The access area is at the southwest corner. It provides parking only, and has no facilities.

A rough trail runs up the west side of the lake, offering access for a short distance. Because of the brush, access here is still very poor. Where the trail ends at the trees, a couple of large snags extend out into the lake.

Shoreline brush makes access almost impossible at all but the southwest corner access area.

The bottom is silt.

The water has a light brownish tinge.

## DIRECTIONS TO:

Take Highway 20 to mile 415.0, about 21 miles north of the town of Newport, where Tacoma Creek Road will be found on the west side of the highway. The end of the road is signed for "USAF Survival School".

Turn onto Tacoma Creek Road, and take it 4.2 miles to Sportsman Pond, on the right.

## FISHING TIPS:

I did not attempt to fish this lake. Forest Service reports are that no fish are present, and on my one visit to this lake I saw no reason to doubt the report.

## MISCELLANEOUS NOTES:

During my limited time in the area of this lake I saw moose.

## MAP REFERENCES:

*USGS Topographic Map, Washington (48117-D3-TF-024-00)
  Jared Quadrangle, 7.5 Minute Series.
*USGS Topographic Map, Washington (48117-A1-TM-100-00)
  Chewelah Quadrangle, 30x60 Minute Series.
*Washington Atlas & Gazetteer, Page 105.

## 84  SPRUCE LAKE
Also known as: Big Twin Lake
Upper Twin Lake
Little Twin "Lakes"

May 18, 1996; Spruce Lake, looking northeast.

SIZE: 26.8 Acres
ELEVATION: 3,719 Feet
MAXIMUM DEPTH: 27 Feet
COUNTY: Stevens, Washington
COORDINATES: T35N R41E Sec4B

Longitude: 117d 38m 24s to 117d 38m 39s West
Latitude: 48d 34m 11s to 48d 34m 31s North

SPECIES, CONFIRMED:
Cutthroat Trout, Coastal
Cutthroat Trout, West Slope
Rainbow Trout

SPECIES, REPORTED:

### CHARACTERISTICS:

The lake is located in a high plateau area, with only low, rolling hills around it.

The area around the lake is all wooded, except for the strip between Cedar and Spruce lakes at the middle of the south end. This is the strip that high water covers to combine the two lakes. This high water condition appears to be the normal condition for these lakes.

There are rocky areas at either side of the flooded strip.

The shorelines are brushy with many snags in the shallows bordering shore. There is some floating bog, but not as much as is found in Cedar Lake.

The access area is found at the northwest corner, and has a camp area, concrete strip boat ramp and dock. Campsites are found along most of the west side, but most don't offer bank access.

The southern portion of the west shore has some grassy, open areas that offer good access to open water not too far from campsites.

Cattails and lilypads are found in the corners and along much of the shoreline. Much of the shallow areas out from them hold weed beds.

The water is clear.

### DIRECTIONS TO:

Take Highway 20 to mile 366.7, east of the town of Colville, where Little Twin Lakes Road will be found on the north side of the highway.

Turn onto Little Twin Lakes Road, and take it 4.8 miles to a road on the left.

Turn onto the road to the left, which runs up the west side of the lakes, and take it to the Spruce Lake camp and access area.

**NOTE:** If you continue 0.1 mile past the road to the Spruce Lake access, you will reach the Cedar Lake camp and access area, on the left.

An **ALTERNATE ROUTE** to Little Twin Lakes is to take Highway 20 to the end of Black Lake-Squaw Creek Road at mile 372.5, on the north side of the highway.

Turn onto Black Lake-Squaw Creek Road, and take it north about 100 yards to a tee intersection, where you will go to the left.

Continue 1.7 miles, and a road on the left that is signed for public fishing will be passed. This is the Black Lake access road. Keep to the right and continue northward.

The road will run up the east side of Black Lake, and around the north end. At the northwest corner, an intersection will be reached. The left fork runs down the west side of Black Lake, and the right fork continues on to Cedar and Spruce (Little Twin Lakes).

Keep to the right, and another intersection will be reached at 1.9 miles past the Black Lake access road (3.6 miles from Highway 2). The right fork goes up the east side of Spruce Lake, and the left goes to the access areas.

Turn left, and go 0.4 miles to the access area at the south end of Cedar Lake, on the right. If you continue past the Cedar access, an intersection will be reached in 0.1 miles. The right fork runs up the west side of the lakes to the Spruce Lake access at its northwest corner.

Because neither route is fully maintained during the winter, one or both may be impassable due to downed trees, washouts or snow until late spring.

FISHING TIPS:

Spinners and flies worked around the strip between the lakes, around any bogs areas, and along shore cover at the north end and east side are productive.

MAP REFERENCES:

*USGS Topographic Map, Washington (48117-E6-TF-024-00)
   Park Rapids Quadrangle, 7.5 Minute Series.
*USGS Topographic Map, Washington (48117-E1-TM-100-00)
   Colville Quadrangle, 30x60 Minute Series.
*Washington Atlas & Gazetteer, Page 118.

# 85  STARVATION LAKE

May 21, 1996; Starvation Lake, looking southwest.

SIZE: 28.4 Acres
ELEVATION: 2,375 Feet
MAXIMUM DEPTH: 12 Feet
COUNTY: Stevens, Washington
COORDINATES: T36N R40E Sec36K

> Longitude: 117d 42m 26s to 117d 42m 47s West
> Latitude: 48d 29m 23s to 48d 29m 36s North

SPECIES, CONFIRMED:
 Rainbow Trout

SPECIES, REPORTED:
 Eastern Brook Trout

CHARACTERISTICS:
 The hills around the lake are grassy, sparsely treed pastureland. Homes are found on the south shore.
 The public access is found at the center of the north shore, and has a dock extending into the lake.

There are large beds of lilypads around most of the shoreline. In some areas, the water drops off quickly at the outer edge of the lilypads. The remaining shoreline areas are mostly brushy.

A large marshy area is found at the east end of the lake. A stand of birch trees is on the west side of the access area.

The water is clear.

## DIRECTIONS TO:

Take Highway 20 to mile 364.9, east of the town of Kettle Falls, where Starvation Lake Road is reached, on the south side of the highway.

Turn onto Starvation Lake Road and go south for 0.9 miles to a gravel road on the right. This gravel road enters the public access area, and a parking area is reached in 0.2 miles. The access has a gravel boat ramp, fishing dock, picnic tables and pit toilets.

## FISHING TIPS:

Spinners and flies worked along the edges of the lilypad beds will get fish. Many people fish worms or Berkley Power Bait from the dock.

## MAP REFERENCES:

*USGS Topographic Map, Washington (48117-D6-TF-024-00)
   Cliff Ridge Quadrangle, 7.5 Minute Series.
*USGS Topographic Map, Washington (48117-A1-TM-100-00)
   Chewelah Quadrangle, 30x60 Minute Series.
*Washington Atlas & Gazetteer, Page 104.

## 86  SULLIVAN LAKE

June 23, 2004; Sullivan Lake,
looking south from the bridge at the north end.

SIZE: 1,290.7 Acres
ELEVATION: 2,583 Feet
MAXIMUM DEPTH: 332 Feet
COUNTY: Pend Oreille, Washington
COORDINATES: T38N R44E Sec6,7,18
        T39N R44E Sec31-32

        Longitude: 117d 16m 27s to 117d 18m 1s West
        Latitude: 48d 47m 21s to 48d 50m 22s North

SPECIES, CONFIRMED:

SPECIES, REPORTED:
 Burbot
 Cutthroat Trout, West Slope
 Eastern Brook Trout
 German Brown Trout
 Kokanee
 Rainbow Trout
 Sucker

## CHARACTERISTICS:

The lake is surrounded by heavily timbered hills. There are some areas of bare rock and meadow visible.

The shorelines are almost all steep and inaccessible. The lake shores have trees and brush at or nearly to the waters edge almost everywhere. The areas without brush are very steep rock.

Sullivan Lake Road, a paved, two-lane road, runs the length of the west side. The road is close to the lake in some places, but at the top of a steep bank, and offers no access to the water.

The north end has a large Forest Service campground and a good boat access. The access area has a concrete boat ramp with launching dock, parking area and pit toilet. The main camp area is west of the boat launch. A picnic area is on the low rise to the east.

The south end also has a large Forest Service campground and boat launch at Noisy Creek, which enters the lake in the area.

An old single lane, wooden bridge on Sullivan Lake Road crosses a creek at the southwest corner of the lake. A more modern bridge crosses a creek at the northwest corner. Both offer good views of the lake.

The lake is almost entirely deep water. Most shores drop off to deep water quickly.

The bottom is silt and gravel with some rock in the shallows along shore. The water is very clear.

## DIRECTIONS TO:

Take Highway 20 about 47 miles north from the town of Newport, to where it makes a 90-degree turn to the left at mile 390.4 and runs west toward the town of Colville. At this corner is the junction with Highway 31, which goes to the north.

Take Highway 31 north for about 3 miles to mile 3.0, where the south end of Sullivan Lake Road enters on the right.

Turn right, onto Sullivan Lake Road, cross the Pend Oreille River, and at 13.4 miles from Highway 31 you will reach the Noisy Creek Campground access area at the south end of Sullivan Lake, on the right.

Turn into the access area, and then keep to the left to reach the boat launch area in 0.3 miles.

Sullivan Lake Road continues up the west side of the lake. It reaches the ranger station at the north end in 4.2 miles.

Another 0.4 miles brings you to an intersection. Straight ahead takes you to the town of Metaline. The road to the right, Forest Service Road 22, goes to the East Sullivan and Sullivan Lake Group Camp access areas at the north end. The access area is on the right after 0.4 miles.

The north access is reached at a distance of 18.4 miles from Highway 31 mile 3.0.

An **ALERNATE ROUTE** to Sullivan Lake is **from the north**:

The north end of the lake is easily reached from Highway 31 near the town of Metaline Falls. The north end of Sullivan Lake Road is at Highway 31 mile 16.4, northeast of Metaline Falls.

Take Sullivan Lake Road 4.8 miles southeast to an intersection. If you continue straight, you will go down the road on the west side of the lake. This road is signed for "Ione 14 Miles", and is the southern route to Sullivan Lake.

The end of the road to the left, Forest Service Road 22, is signed "Salmo Mountain 21, Priest Lake 40, East Sullivan Campground 1/4".

Turn left and go 0.4 miles to the end of the access road to the camp areas and north end boat launch, on the right. There is a trailer dump station at the end of the access road. The side roads that branch off of the access road are well signed for the various camp areas and the boat launch.

The boat launch is reached at 0.4 miles from the road to Priest Lake, 0.8 miles from Sullivan Lake Road, and 5.6 miles from Highway 31 mile 16.4.

FISHING TIPS:

I did not attempt to fish this lake.

MISCELLANEOUS NOTES:

Sullivan Lake produced a state record German Brown of 22 pounds on May 22, 1965.

It also produced a state record West Slope Cutthroat of 2.41 pounds on August 28, 2005, breaking a record I had held with a fish from Muskegon Lake.

The Forest Service access areas are "Fee Areas", charging parking fees for use of the boat launch facilities.

MAP REFERENCES:

*USGS Topographic Map, Washington (48117-G3-TF-024-00)
  Metaline Falls Quadrangle, 7.5 Minute Series.
*USGS Topographic Map, Washington (48117-E1-TM-100-00)
  Colville Quadrangle, 30x60 Minute Series.
*Washington Atlas & Gazetteer, Page 119.

## 87  SULLIVAN MILL POND
Also known as: Sullivan Reservoir

September 18, 2000; Sullivan Mill Pond, looking southeast.

SIZE: 62.8 Acres (86.1 acres at high water)
ELEVATION: 2,514 Feet
MAXIMUM DEPTH: Unknown
COUNTY: Pend Oreille, Washington
COORDINATES: T39N R43E Sec25A
            T39N R44E Sec30CD

            Longitude: 117d 17m 27s to 117d 18m 14s West
            Latitude: 48d 51m 15s to 48d 51m 32s North

SPECIES, CONFIRMED:

SPECIES, REPORTED:
 Cutthroat Trout, West Slope
 German Brown Trout
 Kokanee
 Rainbow Trout

CHARACTERISTICS:

The lake lies in an area of low, rolling, heavily timbered hills. Hills are visible all around.

A large earthen dam built in 1910 lines the west end. The dam has a spillway at the northwest corner. A trail runs along the top of the dam.

A floating log barricade crosses the mouth of a narrow bay that approaches the spillway where Sullivan Creek exits at the northwest corner. The spillway is open, with the creek flowing over the top and dropping a considerable distance to the creek bed below.

There are shallows and gently sloped ground at the east end, where Sullivan Creek enters. The east end has some gravel bars and brush with timber set back from them.

The southwest corner has a shallow flat covered with stumps and an abundance of snags. Snags also line the shores in almost all other areas around the lake. They are very concentrated in some places, especially on the south shore. Snags also rise from the bottom and break the surface in places out in the lake.

The shorelines are steep and brushy on the south side. They are steep with grass and loose rock along the dam, and more gently sloped but still quite brushy along the north side.

A lot of aquatic vegetation grows along the shorelines. Tall plants rise up from a heavy mat of shorter material that covers most of the bottom.

A park-like access area is located on the west half of the north shore. It has hiking trails running from it, including one that crosses the dam. There are some very interesting historical markers and information boards both in the park area and along the trails.

The water is very clear.

DIRECTIONS TO:

Take Highway 20 about 47 miles north from the town of Newport, to where it makes a 90-degree turn to the left at mile 390.4 and runs west toward the town of Colville. At this corner is the junction with Highway 31, which goes to the north.

Take Highway 31 north for 16.4 miles to mile 16.4, where the north end of Sullivan Lake Road will be found, on the right, northeast of the town of Metaline Falls.

Turn onto Sullivan Lake Road, and take it 3.3 miles southeast to the entrance to the Mill Pond Historic Site, on the right. The area is posted as day use only, with hours of 0600-2200. Parking is reached after 0.1 mile, and the lake in 0.2 miles.

The access area has a picnic area, pit toilet, gravel parking area and hiking trails with historical markers.

To reach the Mill Pond Campground, stay on Sullivan Lake Road for another 0.5 miles (3.8 miles from Highway 31), to where the end of the campground access road will be found on the right. The campground is a Forest Service fee area. As of the fall of 2000, a sign reached at the fee station 0.2 miles down the road indicates fees of $10.00 per day are charged through the end of September.

FISHING TIPS:
 I did not attempt to fish this lake.

MAP REFERENCES:
 *USGS Topographic Map, Washington (48117-G3-TF-024-00)
  Metaline Falls Quadrangle, 7.5 Minute Series.
 *USGS Topographic Map, Washington (48117-E1-TM-100-00)
  Colville Quadrangle, 30x60 Minute Series.
 *Washington Atlas & Gazetteer, Page 119.

## 88  SUMMIT LAKE

May 11, 2005; Summit Lake, looking north.

SIZE: 6.9 Acres
ELEVATION: 2,540 Feet (estimated)
MAXIMUM DEPTH: Unknown
COUNTY: Stevens, Washington
COORDINATES: T40N R37E Sec16N,17R,20A,21D

> Longitude: 118d 7m 30s to 118d 7m 39s West
> Latitude: 48d 57m 26s to 48d 57m 40s North

SPECIES, CONFIRMED:
 Rainbow Trout

SPECIES, REPORTED:
 Eastern Brook Trout

CHARACTERISTICS:
 The lake lies in a timber covered area. A heavily timbered hill rises to the east, and a rocky, timbered hill rises high over the west side. The hill to the west has a large vertical rock knob at its peak, and is the high ground that dominates the features around the lake.

The skyline is open to the north and south, with timber lining it, but no hills.

The lake is small and roughly circular, with a small bay extending to the southwest at that corner. A second, smaller bay is found at the northeast corner.

The shorelines have cattail growths in a lot of areas, especially along the north end and at the extreme southwest corner. There are many snags, several of which are very large, lining the shores in almost all areas. A lot are on the surface, and many more are submerged.

The water is shallow all along the shores and out for a distance of 30 to 50 feet in a ring around the deep center of the lake.

The lake has a campground at its south end. The area has a few crude sites and a pit toilet. It has a gravel boat launch area and a small parking area.

The lake can reportedly cover as much as 10.3 acres during high water periods.

An outlet stream exits at a small channel at the north end of the lake.

The bottom is primarily silt, with heavy growths of aquatic vegetation in almost all areas.

The water is very clear.

DIRECTIONS TO:

Summit Lake can be reached from two major routes, both of which have Highway 20 as a starting point. They are from the west from Highway 395, and from the east from Highway 25. The route from the east is only of use if you are in the Northport area to start with.

**FROM THE WEST:**

Many roads branch off of Highway 395 and can be taken to reach Box Canyon Road. I have only detailed the most northerly, and most direct, route here.

Take Highway 20 to the junction with Highway 395 on west end of the bridge over the Columbia River at Kettle Falls. The junction is at Highway 395 mile 241.9.

From the junction, go north on Highway 395 for 22 miles to Rock Cut Road, on right at mile 263.8. Rock Cut Road is reached 3.6 miles past Main Street of the town of Orient. On the opposite side of the road from the end of Rock Cut Road is Little Boulder Road. The end of Rock Cut Road is signed for Pierre Lake.

Turn onto Rock Cut Road, and take it northeast. It will pass through a single lane railroad underpass, then cross the Kettle River before climbing. At 0.4 miles from Highway 395, the road you are on becomes Sand Creek Road, and Rock Cut Road turns to the left.

Stay on Sand Creek Road until, at 3.9 miles from Highway 395, it reaches an intersection at a 90-degree corner and pavement starts. Here Sand Creek Road becomes Pierre Lake Road and turns to the south. At this intersection, the gravel road on the left is Churchill Mine Road.

Turn onto Churchill Mine Road, and you will immediately see the end of Box Canyon Road, on the left. The end of Box Canyon Road is signed for "Summit Lake, 3 Miles".

Turn onto Box Canyon Road, and take it north for 2.5 miles to a road on the left. The end of the road is signed for Summit Lake. It enters the campground and access area for the lake.

Summit Lake is reached a total of 6.4 miles from Highway 395, and 28.4 miles from where you left Highway 20.

### FROM THE EAST:

Take combined Highway 20 / Highway 395 to mile 239.1, where the intersection with Highway 25 will be reached. The intersection is on the east side of the Columbia River, and at the western side of the town of Kettle Falls.

Turn onto Highway 25 North, and take it 33.6 miles, through the town of Northport, and over the Columbia River, to Sheep Creek Road, on the left at mile 114.7.

This intersection is a double intersection, with paved Flat Creek Road to the hard left, and unpaved Sheep Creek Road to the left. The intersection is signed for "Sheep Creek Campground".

Turn left, onto Sheep Creek Road, and follow it west.

At 0.5 miles you will pass a dirt race track, on the left.

At 3.0 miles you will pass a well used road, on the left.

At 4.2 miles you will pass Sheep Creek Campground, on the right.

At 4.3 miles you will pass a Placer Mining historical marker, on the right.

At 8.4 miles you will reach a major intersection. As of 2005, the number "9" was painted on the trees here. Keep to the left.

At 8.5 miles is a marker identifying the road as Forest Service Road 15.

At 9.8 miles, just past a cattleguard, is milepost 14.

At 9.9 miles is a road to the right, keep left.

At 10.6 miles is a marker saying you are entering the Colville National Forest.

At 10.7 miles is milepost 13.

At 11.1 miles is another cattleguard.

At 11.2 miles is a large cross intersection. The road to the right is marked as FS 670. The road to the left is unmarked. Continue straight ahead.

At 11.3 miles is an unnamed lake, to the right.

At 12.1 miles is another cattleguard.

At 12.3 miles is a road on the left, the end of which is signed for Elbow Lake.

At 13.6 miles is milepost 10.

At 13.9 miles is another intersection. Here the road you are on is identified as FS 15 and signed "Elbow Lake" and "Northport". Keep to the left.

At 14.0 miles is an intersection with two roads on the left. Keep right, remaining on the main road.

At 14.6 miles is milepost 9.

At 14.9 miles you will cross a cattleguard.

At 18.5 miles is milepost 5.

At 22.0 miles is a large four-way intersection. Straight ahead is unmarked. The road to the left is signed "Sheep Creek 12", "Northport 22". The road you are on is signed "Sheep Creek 14", Northport 24", "Forest Service Road 15". Turn right, and you will be on Churchill Mine Road.

At 23.3 miles you will reach an intersection with a paved road. Pierre Lake Road goes to the left, and Sand Creek Road goes to the right. Immediately before the paved road is a gravel road on the right. This is Box Canyon Road, and the end is signed for "Summit Lake, 3 Miles".

Turn onto Box Canyon Road, and take it north for 2.5 miles to a road on the left. The end of the road is signed for Summit Lake. It enters the campground and access area for the lake.

Summit Lake is reached a total of 25.8 miles from Highway 25, and 59.8 miles from where you left Highway 20.

FISHING TIPS:

Flies worked along shoreline cover are effective. Bait fishermen using Berkley Power Bait also catch fish.

MAP REFERENCES:

*USGS Topographic Map, Washington (48118-H2-TF-024-00)
    Laurier Quadrangle, 7.5 Minute Series.
*USGS Topographic Map, Washington (48118-E1-TM-100-00)
    Republic Quadrangle, 30x60 Minute Series.
*Washington Atlas & Gazetteer, Page 117.

## 89  LAKE THOMAS

August 22, 2002; Lake Thomas, looking northeast
from the channel between Lake Gillette and Lake Thomas.

SIZE: 162.6 Acres
ELEVATION: 3,162 Feet
MAXIMUM DEPTH: 55 Feet
COUNTY: Stevens, Washington
COORDINATES: T36N R42E Sec8N,17(northwest 1/4)

Longitude: 117d 31m 51s to 117d 32m 40s West
Latitude: 48d 37m 7s to 48d 37m 51s North

SPECIES, CONFIRMED:
 Cutthroat Trout, West Slope
 Pumpkinseed Sunfish
 Yellow Perch

SPECIES, REPORTED:
 Eastern Brook Trout
 Rainbow Trout
 Tiger Trout

CHARACTERISTICS:

The lake is about 4,700 feet long from inlet to outlet, and lies in an area of low, timbered hills.

The area around the lake is heavily developed, but still timbered around its perimeter. Houses are found set back into the timber as well as right on shore. Many of the homes on the lake have docks.

A campground is located at the center of the east side of the lake, and covers most of the northeast shore. With the exception of the inlet area at the northeast corner, it is the only section of the lake not dotted with homes.

The inlet stream, the Little Pend Oreille River, enters from Lake Heritage at the northeast corner, and a narrow channel forms the outlet to Lake Gillette at the southwest corner.

The channel to Lake Heritage is undeveloped, with brushy, boggy shores, and timber back from the brush. Large beds of lilypads fill the shallows that surround the deeper main channel.

The outlet channel is navigable, and passes through a narrows where a bridge used to be located. The gravel embankments of the old bridge approach are still visible. Beds of aquatic weeds line the shallows where the shores open up into Lake Thomas.

Good-sized bays are found at the northeast corner where the inlet is found, and also at the northwest corner. The shallows of the bays hold lilypads. The bay at the northeast corner is spanned by power lines, and has some homes in the timber above the east side.

The bottom is gravelly sand, with some silt deposits and small rock.

The water is clear, but has a slight brownish color.

DIRECTIONS TO:

Take Highway 20 to mile 379.2, east of the town of Colville, where Lake Pend Oreille Road will be found on the south side of the highway.

Turn onto Lake Pend Oreille Road and follow it 0.5 miles to the public access area for Lake Gillette, on the left. The area has a campground, boat ramp, picnic area and beach.

Launch on Lake Gillette, and go to the right to reach the channel between Gillette and Thomas. With the exception of a campground at the center of the east side, the land around Lake Thomas is all privately owned. Access is either by water from Lake Gillette or from the Lake Thomas Campground.

To reach the Lake Thomas Campground, continue on Lake Pend Oreille Road. The entrance to the campground will be found on the left at 1.2

miles from Highway 20. The campground has 16 campsites, and pit toilets. Most of the sites have picnic tables, fire pits and tent pads. The sites on the lake side of the road have trails that lead to the lake, and a wide trail runs parallel to and close to shore for access from the others. Water access is limited, and there is no boat launch. As of 2002, the camping fee is $8 per night.

## FISHING TIPS:

Flies worked around the weed beds are very effective, especially at the channel area between Lakes Gillette and Thomas.

## MISCELLANEOUS NOTES:

As of 2004, there is a "parking fee" of $3.00 per day to use the access area at Lake Gillette.

## MAP REFERENCES:

*USGS Topographic Map, Washington (48117-E5-TF-024-00)
  Lake Gillette Quadrangle, 7.5 Minute Series.
*USGS Topographic Map, Washington (48117-F5-TF-024-00)
  Aladdin Mountain Quadrangle, 7.5 Minute Series.
*USGS Topographic Map, Washington (48117-E1-TM-100-00)
  Colville Quadrangle, 30x60 Minute Series.
*Washington Atlas & Gazetteer, Page 118.

## 90  THOMPSON LAKE

June 21, 1997; Thompson Lake, looking southwest.

SIZE: 200 Acres
ELEVATION: 2,130 Feet
MAXIMUM DEPTH: Unknown
COUNTY: Kootenai, Idaho
COORDINATES: T48N R3W Sec20,21,28-30

      Longitude: 116d 42m 54s to 116d 46m 2s West
      Latitude: 47d 28m 0s to 47d 29m 38s North

SPECIES, CONFIRMED:

SPECIES, REPORTED:
 Bullhead Catfish
 Crappie
 Largemouth Bass
 Northern Pike
 Pumpkinseed Sunfish
 Yellow Perch

CHARACTERISTICS:

The north side of the lake has sparsely timbered hills with a gravel road, Thompson Lake Road, running its length. The road is well away from the water except at the east end, where it is posted as private property. The only access from Thompson Lake Road is at the Three Cedars Campground area.

The south side has a paved road, Blue Lake Road, running up a fairly narrow strip of land between the lake and the Coeur d'Alene River. Low timbered hills can be seen to the south across the river.

The east end also has timbered hills, with a shallow valley running to the east. There is a small farm at the east end, and some development scattered along the north side as well.

The west end has a narrow strip with a dike on which Highway 97 runs. On the west side of the dike is Coeur d'Alene Lake.

The western section is a very heavily weeded marshy area with a lot of lilypads. While the lake is all shallow, the west end is extremely so in most places, and has little open water.

The eastern third of the lake begins to spread out to the north and has more open water. The east end has large, boggy, island-like areas covering much of it. Heavily weeded channels are found between and around the bogs. The marshy islands have a few duck blinds scattered through their tall grasses and small trees. The west end also has small islands, but they are just grass covered and have very few small trees.

The shallow areas of the lake, which is most places, have dollar pads, lilypads and aquatic grasses growing in them.

The bottom is all silt and heavy aquatic vegetation. The water has a light brown stain.

A channel drains to the Coeur d'Alene River about 2/3 of the way up the south side. The public access is found at this channel.

DIRECTIONS TO:

Take Interstate 90 to exit 34 east of Coeur d'Alene, Idaho. At exit 34, turn south onto Highway 3.

Take Highway 3 south for about 21.6 miles to mile 95.9, where Highway 97 will be reached.

Turn right and go 0.1 mile to a stop sign. This marks the actual intersection with Highway 97, at Highway 97 mile 60.8. A sign indicates "Harrison 7 Miles, Coeur d'Alene 36 Miles".

Turn right onto Highway 97, and take it north, through the town of Harrison, for about nine miles to mile 69.6, where Blue Lake Road will be reached, on the right.

Turn onto Blue Lake Road and go east for 2.4 miles to a public access area at a channel from Thompson Lake to the Coeur d'Alene River. The access area has a parking area, boat ramp and portable toilet. From the boat ramp, go up the channel to the right to reach the lake.

If you continue past the access area, the road becomes gravel in another 0.5 miles, and will reach an intersection with Thompson Lake Road after 0.7 miles.

If you turn onto Thompson Lake Road, you will reach a crude access on the right that is signed for "Three Cedars Campground" at 1.6 miles from Blue Lake Road.

Continue west on Thompson Lake Road, and you will complete the loop by reaching Highway 97 at mile 70.1. The loop formed by Blue Lake Road and Thompson Lake Road is 4.9 miles long, not counting the 0.3 miles separating their ends on Highway 97.

An **ALTERNATE ROUTE** to Thompson Lake is to take Highway 97 south from Interstate 90. Highway 97 leaves the interstate at exit 22.

FISHING TIPS:
I did not attempt to fish this lake.

MAP REFERENCES:
*Idaho Atlas & Gazetteer; Page 60.
*USGS Topographic Map, Idaho (47116-D6-TF-024-00)
  Black Lake Quadrangle, 7.5 Minute Series.
*USGS Topographic Map, Idaho (47116-A1-TM-100-00)
  St. Maries Quadrangle, 30x60 Minute Series.

## 91  TROUT LAKE

August 15, 2006; Trout Lake, looking west.

SIZE: 15 Acres (estimated)
ELEVATION: 6,352 Feet
MAXIMUM DEPTH: Unknown
COUNTY: Boundary, Idaho
COORDINATES: T63N R2W Sec10N

> Longitude: 116d 35m 7s to 116d 35m 20s West
> Latitude: 48d 49m 16s to 48d 49m 21s North

SPECIES, CONFIRMED:
 Cutthroat Trout, West Slope

SPECIES, REPORTED:
 Rainbow Trout

CHARACTERISTICS:
 High, rocky cliffs rise over the west end of the lake. As you move away from the nearly barren vertical rock to both the north and south sides the slopes become sparsely dotted with trees.

Below the vertical and near vertical rock are some small meadows and slopes of broken rock. Broken rock slopes reach to the waters edge at the west end of the lake.

The north and south shores have trees and brush to the waters edge, as well as boulders dotting their shorelines.

The shorelines at the southwest corner have some open, grassy areas. Trees and brush are set back from the water a short distance.

The lake drains at the east end, where a small creek flows under a wooden footbridge that the trail crosses.

The outlet area is grassy and marshy, with many large rocks and some massive boulders between the creek mouth and the main body of the lake. The largest boulder at the east end rises about 12 feet above the water, and has small, stunted trees growing from its cracks.

Another large boulder, close to the size of the one at the east end, is found near the west end of the lake. Smaller boulders rise above the surface near the center of the north side.

There are quite a few snags along the shorelines. Many are submerged and lie on the bottom. There aren't enough to prove much of a hindrance to fishing.

The bottom is a combination of rock, gravel and silt.

The water is extremely clear.

DIRECTIONS TO:

Take Interstate 90 to exit 12, at the town of Coeur d'Alene.

From exit 12, take Highway 95 north for about 77 miles to mile 507.5, at the town of Bonners Ferry, where Riverside Road will be found on the west side of the highway just south of the 95 bridge over the Kootenai River. The end of the road is signed for "Kootenai Wildlife Refuge 6 Miles".

Turn onto Riverside, and head west out of Bonners Ferry, keeping to the right as the road follows the banks of the river.

At 5.0 miles from Highway 95 the road will reach the base of the foothills, and a "Y" intersection. Keep to the right, and the road will begin running to the north. Past the "Y" about a quarter mile, you will pass the Kootenai Wildlife Refuge headquarters. The pavement ends in another 6.5 miles.

At 14.9 miles from Highway 95 you will reach the end of Forest Service Road 634, also shown on some maps as Trout Creek Road. The end of the road is signed "Junction Trail 6 Miles, Trail 12 7 Miles, Trail 13 9 Miles".

*Turn onto Road 634, and follow it 8.8 miles to a parking area, on the left, for the trailhead, which is on the right. The road ends in another 0.2 miles at a horse facility and camp area.

On the 8.8 mile run to the trailhead, you will reach an intersection at 4.5 miles, where you keep to the left.

You will pass the Fisher Peak trailhead, on the right, at 5.2 miles.

You will pass the Russell Peak Trail #12 parking area, on the left, at 6.1 miles. There are signs here for the trailhead that indicate "Russell Peak 2 1/2 Miles", and for the continuation of the road to the right indicating "Junction Trail #92 3 Miles".

The trailhead provides access to several lakes in the area, found off various branches of the trail system. The lakes include Pyramid, Upper Ball, Lower Ball, Trout, Big Fisher, Long Mountain, and Parker.

To reach Trout Lake, take the trail about 0.5 miles (elevation gain approximately 450 feet) to a fork. Take the right fork.

Go about 0.75 miles (gain about 150 feet) to the next fork. This fork is reached at a wooden footbridge, to the right of which is a sign indicating that the trail to the right is to Trout Lake and Big Fisher Lake, and providing distances. The trail to the left is unmarked.

Take the right fork. This fork will run about 1.75 miles to the lake, gaining about 450 feet of elevation, and then dropping about 150 feet just before the lake is reached. The drop to the lake is over slab rock and through boulders, and somewhat steep.

The trail reaches the lake at a boardwalk over the outlet creek.

An **ALTERNATE ROUTE** to the Trout Creek trail system would be to take Highway 95 to mile 523.0, north of the town of Bonners Ferry, where Highway 1 will be found on the left.

Turn onto Highway 1, and continue north for 1.1 miles to a road on the left at the town of Copeland. The end of the road is signed for "Sportsman's Access" and "National Forest Entrance".

Turn left onto the road, and head west. At 1.6 miles you will reach a bridge over the Kootenai River. At 3.4 miles from Highway 1 you will reach a "T" intersection with West Side Road. There is a sign opposite the end of the road you are on that indicates "Maravia 20 Miles" to the left, and "Smith Creek Road and Boundary Creek Road 9 Miles" to the right.

At West Side Road, turn left and go south for 2.9 miles to a 90-degree corner. The paved road turns to the left, and a gravel road leaves the pavement straight ahead. Contrary to appearances, the gravel road is the continuation of West Side Road.

Take the gravel road, and after 1.8 miles you will reach the end of Forest Service Road 634, also shown on some maps as Trout Creek Road, on the right. The end of the road is signed "Junction Trail 6 Miles, Trail 12 7 Miles, Trail 13 9 Miles".

From here, follow the directions provided above from the point marked with an asterisk(*).

FISHING TIPS:
The fish can be finicky, but once you find a fly that they'll hit like they mean it, you will get them.

MISCELLANEOUS NOTES:
Planting records indicate that Hayspur Triploid Rainbow Trout (1,175) were planted in the lake on September 13, 2000.

Moose frequent the area, so be cautious. On August 15, 2006 I encountered a cow and calf on the trail at a distance of less than fifty feet.

MAP REFERENCES:
*Idaho Atlas & Gazetteer, Page 48 (lake not shown).
*USGS Topographic Map, Idaho (48116-G5-TF-024-00)
   Pyramid Peak Quadrangle, 7.5 Minute Series.
*USGS Topographic Map, Idaho (48116-E1-TM-100-00)
   Bonners Ferry Quadrangle, 30x60 Minute Series.

## 92  UPPER BALL LAKE

September 9, 2000; Upper Ball Lake, looking north.

SIZE: 12 Acres (estimated)
ELEVATION: 6,708 Feet
MAXIMUM DEPTH: Unknown
COUNTY: Boundary, Idaho
COORDINATES: T63N R2W Sec20Q

> Longitude: 116d 37m 11s to 116d 37m 20s West
> Latitude: 48d 47m 33s to 48d 47m 40s North

SPECIES, CONFIRMED:
 Cutthroat Trout, West Slope

SPECIES, REPORTED:

CHARACTERISTICS:
 Upper Ball Lake is at the headwaters of Spanish Creek, which exits at the southeast corner, flowing to Lower Ball Lake.

The trail reaches the lake at the southeast corner just north of where the outlet creek exits. A few campsites are located along this area.

The west side has large areas of hard rock, much of which is nearly vertical, as well as a lot of broken rock. There are very few trees on the west side of the lake.

The ridgeline drops from the rocky slopes of the west side. On the lower half of the slopes to the north there is timber. The timber cover continues around the east and south sides of the lake.

The shorelines all around the lake are very rocky. Most of the rock is large. Many rocks rise from the bottom to break the surface next to shore. These rocks provide some good access for fishing, especially in the areas that have timber lined shores.

There are no trees at all along the shorelines from the middle of the north end around to the west side, and down the west side to the southwest corner.

At the southeast corner, where the trail comes in, trees run to the waters edge. Most of the trees are fairly small.

The bottom is rocky, with a lot of the rock very large. There are very few snags.

The water is very clear.

DIRECTIONS TO:

Take Interstate 90 to exit 12, at the town of Coeur d'Alene.

From exit 12, take Highway 95 north for about 77 miles to mile 507.5, at the town of Bonners Ferry, where Riverside Road will be found on the west side of the highway just south of the bridge over the Kootenai River. The end of the road is signed for "Kootenai Wildlife Refuge 6 Miles".

Turn onto Riverside, and head west out of Bonners Ferry, keeping to the right as the road follows the banks of the river.

At 5.0 miles from Highway 95 the road will reach the base of the foothills, and a "Y" intersection. Keep to the right, and the road will begin running to the north. Past the "Y" about a quarter mile, you will pass the Kootenai Wildlife Refuge headquarters. The pavement ends in another 6.5 miles.

At 14.9 miles from Highway 95 you will reach the end of Forest Service Road 634, also shown on some maps as Trout Creek Road. The end of the road is signed "Junction Trail 6 Miles, Trail 12 7 Miles, Trail 13 9 Miles".

*Turn onto Road 634, and follow it 8.8 miles to a parking area, on the left, for the trailhead, which is on the right. The road ends in another 0.2 miles at a horse facility and camp area.

On the 8.8 mile run to the trailhead, you will reach an intersection at 4.5 miles, where you keep to the left.

You will pass the Fisher Peak trailhead, on the right, at 5.2 miles.

You will pass the Russell Peak Trail #12 parking area, on the left, at 6.1 miles. There are signs here for the trailhead that indicate "Russell Peak 2 1/2 Miles", and for the continuation of the road to the right indicating "Junction Trail #92 3 Miles".

The trailhead provides access to several lakes in the area, found off various branches of the trail system. The lakes include Pyramid, Upper Ball, Lower Ball, Trout, Big Fisher, Long Mountain, and Parker.

To reach Upper Ball Lake, take the trail about 0.5 miles (elevation gain approximately 450 feet) to a fork. Take the left fork.

Go south about 1.3 miles (gain about 750 feet) to the east side of the lake. Pyramid Lake will be reached after about 0.3 miles, and the trail will run along its east side. Pass Pyramid, and the trail will switchback up the steep grade to the south, providing a great look down on Pyramid, and then resume a more gradual run to the lake.

The trail forks about 50 yards before reaching Upper Ball Lake. The fork to the right makes the short run to the lake, while the fork to the left makes a gradual drop and switches back to Lower Ball Lake after about a quarter of a mile.

An **ALTERNATE ROUTE** to the Trout Creek trail system would be to take Highway 95 to mile 523.0, north of the town of Bonners Ferry, where Highway 1 will be found on the left.

Turn onto Highway 1, and continue north for 1.1 miles to a road on the left at the town of Copeland. The end of the road is signed for "Sportsman's Access" and "National Forest Entrance".

Turn left onto the road, and head west. At 1.6 miles you will reach a bridge over the Kootenai River. At 3.4 miles from Highway 1 you will reach a "T" intersection with West Side Road. There is a sign opposite the end of the road you are on that indicates "Maravia 20 Miles" to the left, and "Smith Creek Road and Boundary Creek Road 9 Miles" to the right.

At West Side Road, turn left and go south for 2.9 miles to a 90-degree corner. The paved road turns to the left, and a gravel road leaves the pavement straight ahead. Contrary to appearances, the gravel road is the continuation of West Side Road.

Take the gravel road, and after 1.8 miles you will reach the end of Forest Service Road 634, also shown on some maps as Trout Creek Road, on the right. The end of the road is signed "Junction Trail 6 Miles, Trail 12 7 Miles, Trail 13 9 Miles".

From here, follow the directions provided above from the point marked with an asterisk(*).

FISHING TIPS:
 Flies cast from shore will get fish.

MAP REFERENCES:
 *Idaho Atlas & Gazetteer, Page 48 (lake not shown).
 *USGS Topographic Map, Idaho (48116-G5-TF-024-00)
  Pyramid Peak Quadrangle, 7.5 Minute Series.
 *USGS Topographic Map, Idaho (48116-E1-TM-100-00)
  Bonners Ferry Quadrangle, 30x60 Minute Series (name not indicated).

# 93  UPPER GLIDDEN LAKE

September 16, 2001; Upper Glidden Lake, looking southwest.

SIZE: 14 Acres (estimated)
ELEVATION: 5,896 Feet
MAXIMUM DEPTH: Unknown
COUNTY: Shoshone, Idaho
COORDINATES: T48N R6E Sec7R,8N,18A

>    Longitude: 115d 42m 57s <u>to</u> 115d 43m 11s West
>    Latitude: 47d 30m 57s <u>to</u> 47d 31m 9s North

SPECIES, CONFIRMED:
 Eastern Brook Trout

SPECIES, REPORTED:
 Arctic Grayling

<u>CHARACTERISTICS</u>:
 The ridges around the lake are timbered, although some areas are sparsely
covered due to rock outcroppings. There are also some small meadow areas
above the lake. The ridge top to the east marks the border between Idaho
and Montana.

The shorelines are all steep, with the exception of the area immediately around the outlet. Some areas on the south side have vertical rock that forms an impassible barrier on the shore. Most shoreline areas are broken rock. The north end shores are mostly open and easily accessible.

A small inlet creek is found on the south side, but is seasonal, flowing from snowmelt from the slopes above. An outlet stream exits at the north end.

The bottom is rock with silt deposits and scattered snags, most of which are small. The heaviest concentration of snags is found at the mouth of the outlet creek.

The northern portion of the lake is fairly shallow, with the deepest water found at the center and south end. Shallow flats are found at the outlet area and at the northeast corner.

The water is very clear.

In the fall of 2001, the lake was down about eight feet from its normal level, exposing a lot of snags at the mouth of the outlet creek and a strip of rock around the shores that would usually be under water.

DIRECTIONS TO:

Take Interstate 90 to exit 62 at Wallace, Idaho, where Highway 4 enters from the north.

Follow Highway 4 through the many small, side of the road "towns" to the town of Burke, where it will become the Burke-Can Creek Road.

Continue east on Burke-Can Creek Road, and a power station will be reached on the left at 7.7 miles from Interstate 90.

Continue past the power station to the intersection with Road 615, on the right at 11.1 miles from the interstate.

Turn right onto Road 615. It will drop downhill and reach power lines after 0.1 mile.

At the power lines, keep to the left until you reach a small wooden bridge.

Cross the bridge and continue up the road to a wide spot on the right 0.4 miles from the start of Road 615.

Park at the wide spot, and you will find an old road up on the hill to your left.

Follow the abandoned road up the hill for about 0.5 miles to reach the lake at the outlet creek.

From where you parked on the road coming in, if you continue another 0.7 miles you will reach Lower Glidden Lake.

FISHING TIPS:

Flies worked over the cover in the shallow shoreline areas at the outlet and the northeast corner will get fish.

Planting records of the Idaho Department of Fish & Game show that the lake received an Arctic Grayling plant numbering 4,515 fish in 1975. I have seen no evidence that there are any currently present.

MAP REFERENCES:

*Idaho Atlas & Gazetteer, Page 61.

*Montana Atlas & Gazetteer, Page 80.

*USGS Topographic Map, Montana-Idaho (47115-E6-TF-024-00)
 Thompson Pass Quadrangle, 7.5 Minute Series.

*USGS Topographic Map, Montana-Idaho (47115-E1-TM-100-00)
 Thompson Falls Quadrangle, 30x60 Minute Series.

# 94   UPPER LEAD KING LAKE

May 18, 1997; Upper Lead King Lake, looking south.

SIZE: 4.2 Acres
ELEVATION: 2,575 Feet
MAXIMUM DEPTH: Unknown
COUNTY: Pend Oreille, Washington
COORDINATES: T40N R43E Sec22P

Longitude: 117d 21m 18s to 117d 21m 24s West
Latitude: 48d 56m 45s to 48d 56m 53s North

SPECIES, CONFIRMED:
Cutthroat Trout, Coastal
Pumpkinseed Sunfish
Rainbow Trout

SPECIES, REPORTED:

CHARACTERISTICS:
The area has low hills to the east and west, and is open to the north and
south.

A paved road runs up the east side and around the north end, but provides no access. Power lines cross the north end of the lake and run down the west side. The gravel road that accompanies the power lines provides limited access to the water. There are no suitable bank fishing areas, and launching of any floating device is difficult.

Small trees line much of the shoreline. All of the shorelines are very shallow and mostly brushy. Much of the shoreline area has extremely shallow flats covered with thick growths of algae. There is heavy aquatic vegetation at all edges, including beds of lilypads.

The center portion of the lake is deepest, and the only open water. The open water makes up only about a third of the total surface area.

A stream exits the south end of the lake, and flows to the lower lake. The actual outlet is lost in the heavy weed growth.

There are active beaver lodges on the lake.

The bottom is silt and algae. The water is clear.

## DIRECTIONS TO:

Take Highway 20 about 47 miles north from the town of Newport, to where it makes a 90-degree turn to the left at mile 390.4 and runs west toward the town of Colville. At this corner is the junction with Highway 31, which goes to the north.

Turn north onto Highway 31, and take it about 13 miles to the town of Metaline. At mile 13.1, Boundary Road will be found on the left.

Turn left onto Boundary Road and follow it north for 8.3 miles to a gravel road on the left. You will pass both Lower and Upper Lead King Lakes before you reach the gravel road at the north end of the lakes.

Turn left onto the gravel road. The road runs toward the trees, then turns back to the south and passes under the power lines along the west side of the lakes.

Access for the upper lake will be reached at 0.3 miles, and consists of small, little used branches of road.

Access for the lower lake is another 0.3 miles, at 0.6 miles down the gravel road, and is also by a small branch road.

## FISHING TIPS:

Flies fished along the edges of the shallow water where it drops off into the deeper water of the center of the lake will get fish. For sunfish, the same area is productive, but they can also be found further into the shallows than the trout.

MISCELLANEOUS NOTES:

For an interesting side trip while in the area, visit the Gardiner Cave at Crawford State Park. The park is just north of the lakes. As of 1997 the park opened at 0900, with guided cave tours every even hour. The tour lasts about 30 to 40 minutes, is provided by the park service, and is free of charge.

MAP REFERENCES:

*USGS Topographic Map, Washington (48117-H3-TF-024-00) Boundary Dam Quadrangle, 7.5 Minute Series.
*USGS Topographic Map, Washington (48117-E1-TM-100-00) Colville Quadrangle, 30x60 Minute Series (lake not shown).
*Washington Atlas & Gazetteer, Page 119.

## 95   UPPER PRIEST LAKE

June 24, 2004; Upper Priest Lake,
looking southeast from Navigation Campground.

SIZE: 1,300 Acres (estimated)
ELEVATION: 2,438 Feet
MAXIMUM DEPTH: Unknown
COUNTY: Bonner, Idaho
COORDINATES: T63N R4W Sec18P,19,20MNP,28N,29,30ABH,32
(northeast 1/4), 33(northwest 1/3)
        T63N R5W Sec24H

        Longitude: 116d 51m 45s to 116d 54m 55s West
        Latitude: 48d 45m 58s to 48d 48m 16s North

SPECIES, CONFIRMED:
 Yellow Perch

SPECIES, REPORTED:
 Cutthroat Trout, West Slope
 Dolly Varden (Bull) Trout

Kokanee
Largemouth Bass
Mackinaw
Rainbow Trout
Whitefish

## CHARACTERISTICS:

The lake lies in a mountainous area, with rolling hills all around. The hills are heavily timbered in most places. A few places have sparse timber cover due to rocky areas.

The area immediately around the lake is also heavily timbered.

The shorelines have timber and brush to the waters edge in most places. There are a few exceptions where rock is found on the shores.

The lake has the shape of a rough rectangle, tilted to the left so that it runs from northwest to southeast.

Navigation Campground is found near the northwest corner of the lake. It is a very crude campground, offering only a few rough tent sites. There is limited shore access in the area.

Near the northeast corner of the lake, across from Navigation Campground, is a beach with gravel shores at a small cove.

Plowboy Campground is found near the southwest corner.

Priest River enters at the center of the northwest end, and exits at the southeast end, flowing to Priest Lake. Powerboat traffic is seen on the lake, entering from the navigable channel to Priest Lake.

The bottom is rocky.

The water is very clear.

## DIRECTIONS TO:

Take Highway 2 to mile 5.9, at a stoplight in the middle of the town of Priest River, where Highway 57 / West Side Road will be found on the north side of the highway.

Turn onto Highway 57, and follow it north for 54.4 miles to an intersection. The intersection is signed for "Trail 308 7 Miles" and "Trail 28 20 Miles" to the right, and for "Hughes Meadows 3 Miles" to the left.

Take the right, and go another 1.0 mile to a road on the right, signed for "Navigation Trail 291".

On the way to the road end, you will enter the state of Washington at 43.4 miles, pass Huff Lake at 46.9 miles, pass the end of Road 302 (FS 22 from Metaline) at 50.1 miles, pass the end of Road 656 at 51.0 miles, and reenter the state of Idaho at 51.5 miles.

Turn onto the side road, and go 0.4 miles to the trailhead at its end.

The trail starts out over an abandoned roadbed. It crosses a good foot-bridge after a short distance, and then continues to another more recently used road.

Take a left at this road, and walk it. The road will cross a large bridge in a corner, and then come to a fork just past it. Keep to the right, remaining on the main roadbed.

About 30 minutes from the start of the hike, you will come to another major fork in the old road. A small sign here says "Trail" to the right.

Keep to the right, and the start of the old trail will be reached in a couple of hundred yards. The trailhead is on the left at the point where the old road becomes almost impassable.

The old trailhead is about half way from your starting point to the lake. Follow the trail to the southeast as it makes its way to Navigation Camp-ground.

The trail will drop steeply for a short distance just before leveling back out at a spot where water will become visible through the trees to the left.

You will then pass through a heavily timbered flat to a fork in the trail. The left fork runs a couple of hundred yards to the lake at Navigation Camp-ground. The fork was signed as of 2004.

An **ALTERNATE ROUTE** to Upper Priest Lake is from the south, via a trail from the northeast corner of Priest Lake.

To reach the southern access, use the following directions:

Turn left onto Highway 57, and go north 22.5 miles to Dickensheet Road, which will be on the right just south of Priest Lake.

Turn right onto Dickensheet Road and go 5.2 miles to the town of Coolin, where an intersection is reached. The road to the right provides access to the east side of Priest Lake, and the road you are on goes to the left to reach the south end of Priest Lake. The road to the right is signed for "Priest Lake State Park, Indian Creek Unit, Lionhead Unit".

Roads run the length of the east shore, reaching the north end of the lake after about 20 miles.

At the north end of Priest Lake, a trailhead will be found which runs about 1.5 miles to the south end of Upper Priest Lake.

FISHING TIPS:

My one visit to the lake was very brief. I cast flies and small spinners from shore at Navigation Campground, and caught only Perch.

MAP REFERENCES:
- *Idaho Atlas & Gazetteer, Page 48, 62.
- *USGS Topographic Map, Idaho (48116-G7-TF-024-00)
  Caribou Creek Quadrangle, 7.5 Minute Series.
- *USGS Topographic Map, Idaho (48116-G8-TF-024-00)
  Upper Priest Lake Quadrangle, 7.5 Minute Series.
- *USGS Topographic Map, Idaho (480116-E1-TM-100-00)
  Bonners Ferry Quadrangle, 7.5 Minute Series.

## 96  UPPER ROMAN NOSE LAKE

August 21, 2002; Upper Roman Nose Lake, looking south.

SIZE: 19 Acres (estimated)
ELEVATION: 6,194 Feet
MAXIMUM DEPTH: Unknown
COUNTY: Boundary, Idaho
COORDINATES: T61N R2W Sec15N,16R

> Longitude: 116d 35m 9s <u>to</u> 116d 35m 26s West
> Latitude: 48d 37m 55s <u>to</u> 48d 38m 9s North

SPECIES, CONFIRMED:
 Eastern Brook Trout

SPECIES, REPORTED:

<u>CHARACTERISTICS</u>:
 The skyline around the lake is dominated by barren rock. Over the south end the vertical rock of Roman Nose Peak, elevation 7,260 feet, frames the skyline. It gives way to a combination of broken rock and vertical cliffs. Some very sparse strips of low brush and small trees are on the slopes.

The hill to the east is rocky, and covered with a large number of standing snags on its northern slopes. The snags remain from when the area was burned in the Sundance fire of 1967.

The lower slopes over the northern half of the east side of the lake become sparsely timbered, with more dense cover as you move north toward the outlet creek.

On the west side of the lake, conditions are similar. Rocky slopes with low brush, and dotted with timber, are found over the southern half, becoming more heavily timbered as you move north.

Over the southwest corner is another rocky peak that rises to an elevation of 6,943 feet.

The shorelines are moderately steep along the south half of the lake, becoming more gentle in the northern half. The shorelines have a lot of rock along them, plus quite a bit of brush, and in some places timber to the waters edge. Most of the shores are fairly easy to walk. There are a few places with vertical rock to go around, and some areas where the brush is dense.

The shorelines of the southern half of the lake drop off to deep water very quickly.

The center of the lake is all deep water.

An outlet creek exits at the end of a narrow neck at the northeast corner, draining to Lower Roman Nose Lake. The lake is the headwaters of Caribou Creek. The neck is mostly shallow, and has many snags scattered on a bottom of silt. The bottom in the area is studded with boulders.

A small logjam spans the mouth of the outlet creek, providing easy access to the far side of the lake.

The water is extremely clear.

The trail to the lake reaches it at the northeast corner, and continues up the east side.

## DIRECTIONS TO:
### From the north:
Take Highway 95 to mile 507.5, at the town of Bonners Ferry, where Riverside Road will be found on the west side of the highway just south of the bridge over the Kootenai River. The end of the road is signed for "Kootenai Wildlife Refuge 6 Miles".

Turn onto Riverside, and head west out of Bonners Ferry, keeping to the right as the road follows the banks of the river.

At 5.0 miles from Highway 95 the road will reach the base of the foothills, and a "Y" intersection.

Turn to the left, onto the gravel road, West Side Road, which will run south.

Go approximately 2.8 miles to the end of Forest Service Road 402, on the right. A sign as you start up Road 402 indicates "Cooks Pass 13", "Little Creek 18", and "Roman Nose Lakes 20".

*Turn up Road 402, Snow Creek Road, and go 16.2 miles to Ruby Pass, staying on the main road for the distance. Some parts of the road, especially where it climbs, are badly washboarded.

At Ruby Pass, you will come to Road 2667, on the right. The end of the road is signed for "Roman Nose Lakes 2 Miles". The continuation of the road straight ahead is signed "Naples 13 Miles".

Turn right onto Road 2667, and in 0.5 miles you will come to an intersection with Road 294, on the left. The road to the right is signed "1.7 Miles to East Roman Nose Lake" and "3 Miles to Lower Roman Nose Lake".

Keep to the right, and at 1.3 miles from Ruby Pass you will reach another intersection. Keep to the right again.

At 1.8 miles is another road on the left. This one is signed for "Camp Area", and "Narrow Steep Road, No Trailers". This road runs 0.2 miles, with campsites and a pit toilet along it.

Keep to the right to reach the parking area for the trailheads for Roman Nose Lakes. This parking lot is posted "No Overnight Camping". It has a concrete pit toilet, and a signboard with a map of the trail system.

There are two trails that exit from the parking area.

From the far end of the parking lot, to the left of the pit toilet, is a board-walk that runs the entire distance to East Roman Nose Lake. The distance is about 150 yards or so.

The second trail, Trail 160, exits from the center of the parking lot, on the right. It runs to Upper Roman Nose Lake and Lower Roman Nose Lake.

Take this trail, and it will switchback to the top of the low saddle to the west.

Before reaching the top, you will come to a fork in the trail. Turn uphill to the left at this fork.

About 50 feet past the fork you will come to another. This is the "scenic loop" trail. Go to the right here.

After cresting the saddle the trail will begin to drop down the other side and run to the left, reaching another fork about a mile from the trailhead.

Take the right fork here, and the trail will drop a short distance to yet another fork.

At this fork, the left goes about 0.5 miles to Upper Roman Nose Lake, and the right goes about 0.5 miles to Lower Roman Nose Lake.

Take the left fork, and the trail will wrap around the hillside before climbing briefly to the flat holding the upper lake.

**From the south:**

Take Interstate 90 to exit 12, at the town of Coeur d'Alene.

From exit 12, take Highway 95 north for about 67 miles to mile 496.8, where a road on the left exits for the town of Naples.

Turn off of Highway 95, and go 6.3 miles to West Side Road, on the left. The end of the road is signed "Snow Creek Road 2 Miles", "Kootenai National Wildlife Refuge 5 Miles".

Turn left onto West Side Road, and go 2.0 miles to Forest Service Road 402, Snow Creek Road, on the left.

From here, follow the direction above from the point marked with an asterisk(*).

FISHING TIPS:

Flies cast from shore are very effective.

MAP REFERENCES:

*Idaho Atlas & Gazetteer, Page 62 (name not indicated).
*USGS Topographic Map, Idaho (48116-F5-TF-024-00)
  Roman Nose Quadrangle, 7.5 Minute Series.
*USGS Topographic Map, Idaho (48116-E1-TM-100-00)
  Bonners Ferry Quadrangle, 30x60 Minute Series.

## 97   UPPER TWIN LAKE

June 25, 2004; Upper Twin Lake,
looking southwest from the public access area.

SIZE: 500 Acres
ELEVATION: 2,306 Feet
MAXIMUM DEPTH: Unknown
COUNTY: Kootenai, Idaho
COORDINATES: T52N R5W Sec1,2
          T53N R5W Sec35,36

          Longitude: 116d 53m 36s to 116d 55m 44s West
          Latitude: 47d 52m 58s to 47d 53m 38s North

SPECIES, CONFIRMED:
 Pumpkinseed Sunfish

SPECIES, REPORTED:
 Bullhead Catfish
 Cutthroat Trout
 Eastern Brook Trout
 German Brown Trout
 Kokanee

Largemouth Bass
Rainbow Trout
Yellow Perch

## CHARACTERISTICS:

The lake is heavily developed on the north side and east end. It is lesser developed on the east side, but there are still houses scattered through the timber on that side of the lake.

The south side of the lake has heavily timbered, rolling hills. They show signs of past clearcutting.

The west end has low, brushy shorelines.

The public access area is located on the north side, about a third of the way up the lake. It has a paved parking area, toilets, picnic table, concrete boat ramp, and a very nice dock.

The lake drains to Lower Twin Lake at the east end, where a narrow channel runs between the two. The channel has rocky shores.

The bottom of the lake is a combination of rock and silt, with weed beds in some areas.

The water is murky during the summer months.

## DIRECTIONS TO:

Take Interstate 90 to exit 7, just east of Post Falls, Idaho, where Highway 41 enters from the north.

Take Highway 41 north for 12.5 miles to mile 12.5, where Twin Lakes Road will be reached, on the left. The intersection is signed for "Sportsman's Access".

Turn left onto Twin Lakes Road, and there is a sign for "Upper Twin 2.5 Miles" and "Lower Twin 1.5 Miles". Go 2.7 miles to the public access area for Upper Twin Lake, on the left.

You will pass the access for Lower Twin Lake at 1.6 miles, also on the left.

An **ALTERNATE ROUTE** to Twin Lakes is to leave Interstate 90 at exit 12 at Coeur d'Alene.

From exit 12, turn left and go north for 8.2 miles to mile 438.9, where Highway 53 will be found on the left.

Turn onto Highway 53 and go west for about four miles to an intersection with Highway 41, reached at Highway 41 mile 7.7.

Turn right, and go north on Highway 41 for about five miles to Highway 41 mile 12.5, where Twin Lakes Road will be reached, on the left. The intersection is signed for "Sportsman's Access".

Turn left onto Twin Lakes Road, and there is a sign for "Upper Twin 2.5 Miles" and "Lower Twin 1.5 Miles". Go 2.7 miles to the public access area for Upper Twin Lake, on the left.

You will pass the access for Lower Twin Lake at 1.6 miles, also on the left.

A **SECOND ALTERNATE ROUTE** is to take Highway 2 to the town of Newport, Washington / Old Town, Idaho, located on the state line. The junction of Highway 2 and Highway 41 is stoplighted.

At the junction of Highways 2 and 41, turn south onto Highway 41. Go south on Highway 41 for 26.5 miles to mile 12.5, where Twin Lakes Road will be reached, on the right. The intersection is signed for "Sportsman's Access".

Turn right onto Twin Lakes Road, and there is a sign for "Upper Twin 2.5 Miles" and "Lower Twin 1.5 Miles". Go 2.7 miles to the public access area for Upper Twin Lake, on the left.

You will pass the access for Lower Twin Lake at 1.6 miles, also on the left.

FISHING TIPS:

I have visited the lake only once, and fished it very briefly, so can't offer many tips.

Micro jigs cast from shore at the access area were very effective for Pumpkinseed Sunfish.

MAP REFERENCES:
*Idaho Atlas & Gazetteer, Page 60.
*USGS Topographic Map, Idaho (47116-H8-TF-024-00)
   Spirit Lake West Quadrangle, 7.5 Minute Series.
*USGS Topographic Map, Idaho (47116-E1-TM-100-00)
   Coeur d'Alene Quadrangle, 30x60 Minute Series.

## 98  WAITTS LAKE

May 23, 2002; Waitts Lake, looking northwest from the public access.

SIZE: 455.4 Acres
ELEVATION: 1,946 Feet
MAXIMUM DEPTH: 68 Feet
COUNTY: Stevens, Washington
COORDINATES: T31N R40E Sec17,20(northeast 1/4)

Longitude: 117d 46m 44s to 117d 47m 59s West
Latitude: 48d 10m 28s to 48d 11m 31s North

SPECIES, CONFIRMED:
 Rainbow Trout

SPECIES, REPORTED:
 Cutthroat Trout, Coastal
 Cutthroat Trout, West Slope
 German Brown Trout
 Largemouth Bass
 Yellow Perch

## CHARACTERISTICS:

The lake lies in an area of low, rolling, wooded hills. The higher hills rise to the west. Most of the hills around the lake are dotted with trees and homes, with those in the distance to the west heavily timbered. Close to the water to the south, the more gentle slopes are covered with fields.

The shores of the lake are heavily developed at the northeast corner and around the north end. A few homes are also found on the west side and along the south end, but the density in these areas is very low. Many of the waterfront homes have docks extending into the lake.

The public access area and a resort occupy a section of shoreline at the southeast corner.

The area north of the public access has a lot of cattails lining the shores. Beyond the cattails the heavy development starts.

The shorelines have shallows with weed beds that extend out a good distance from shore along the southeast corner. The drop off to deep water is very gradual in most places.

Visible bottom in the area of the access is gravel, while most other places are silt covered with aquatic weed growth.

Inlet creeks enter at the southwest corner and near the northwest corner. Waitts Creek exits at the center of the east side, just north of the access area.

The water is usually clear, but the lake is prone to algae blooms late in the spring that can cause a lot of suspended algae, some of which will collect into floating mats.

## DIRECTIONS TO:

Take Highway 395 to mile 202.4, south of the town of Chewelah, where Highway 231 enters from the west. The intersection is signed for "Waitts Lake 6 miles".

Turn onto Highway 231 and go south for 3.4 miles to Highway 231 mile 71.8 at the town of Valley, where a road exits to the west. The end of this road is signed for "Waitts Lake 3 miles".

Turn right and go 2.6 miles to the end of Waitts Lake South Road, on the left. The end of the road is signed for "Public Access Area".

Turn left onto Waitts Lake South Road and go 0.7 miles to the end of the public access area road, on the right. The access area has a large gravel parking area, pit toilets and concrete strip boat ramp. The area is signed for no overnight parking or camping.

FISHING TIPS:

Flatfish plugs, size F4 in a green frog finish, proved effective for catching the planted Rainbows along the outer edge of the weed beds on my one time on this lake.

Most other fishermen were trolling with gang-trolls in the deeper water out in the center of the lake.

MISCELLANEOUS NOTES:

Waitts Lake produced a state record Rainbow Trout of 22.5 pounds in 1957.

MAP REFERENCES:

*USGS Topographic Map, Washington (48117-B7-TF-024-00)
   Waitts Lake Quadrangle, 7.5 Minute Series.
*USGS Topographic Map, Washington (48117-A1-TM-100-00)
   Chewelah Quadrangle, 30x60 Minute Series.
*Washington Atlas & Gazetteer, Page 104.

## 99  WILLIAMS LAKE

May 9, 2005; Williams Lake, looking north from the campground area.

SIZE: 37.7 Acres
ELEVATION: 1,950 Feet
MAXIMUM DEPTH: Unknown
COUNTY: Stevens, Washington
COORDINATES: T38N R38E Sec36CF

> Longitude: 117d 57m 50s to 117d 58m 7s West
> Latitude: 48d 45m 9s to 48d 45m 28s North

SPECIES, CONFIRMED:

SPECIES, REPORTED:
Rainbow Trout

CHARACTERISTICS:
  The lake lies in an area of low, timbered hills. The hills to the west are heavily timbered, with timber running almost to the waters edge. The shorelines are open and grassy, with thick brush between the grass and trees.
  To the north of the lake are some small fields and a few buildings.
  Cattails are found in some shoreline areas.
  Williams Lake Road runs up the east side of the lake, but is away from the water at all but the access area. The east shore is mostly lined with a heavy growth of aquatic weeds.

The heaviest growths of aquatic weed are found at the north and south ends of the lake, where they extend far out into the lake. There are a lot of cattails at the north and south ends.

The lake can reportedly cover as much as 45 acres during high water periods.

The bottom is primarily silt, with some rock.

The water is very clear.

## DIRECTIONS TO:

Take combined Highway 20 / Highway 395 to mile 239.1, where the intersection with Highway 25 will be reached. The intersection is on the east side of the Columbia River, and at the western side of the town of Kettle Falls.

Turn onto Highway 25 North, and take it 17 miles to the north end of Williams Lake Road, on the right at mile 98.6.

Turn right, onto Williams Lake Road, and follow it southeast for 3.8 miles to the lake. An access area on the right offers limited parking and a crude gravel boat launch area.

If you continue past the access, another 0.4 miles will bring you to Brooks Road, on the right. Just after turning onto Brooks Road, the entrance to the Williams Lake Campground will be found on the right.

An **ALTERNATE ROUTE** is to take Highway 20 to just west of the town of Colville, where the south end of Williams Lake Road is reached.

Turn north, onto Williams Lake Road, and take it 13.6 miles to the lake.

## FISHING TIPS:

The lake has a winter only season. Check the current regulations before fishing.

## MAP REFERENCES:

*USGS Topographic Map, Washington (48117-G8-TF-024-00)
  China Bend Quadrangle, 7.5 Minute Series.
*USGS Topographic Map, Washington (48117-E1-TM-100-00)
  Colville Quadrangle, 30x60 Minute Series.
*Washington Atlas & Gazetteer, Page 118.

## 100  YOCUM LAKE

June 25, 2004; Yokum Lake, looking south.

SIZE: 41.7 Acres
ELEVATION: 2,950 Feet (estimated)
MAXIMUM DEPTH: 60 Feet
COUNTY: Pend Oreille, Washington
COORDINATES: T36N R43E Sec23(northeast 1/4)

Longitude: 117d 19m 39s to 117d 19m 59s West
Latitude: 48d 36m 30s to 48d 37m 5s North

SPECIES, CONFIRMED:
 Cutthroat Trout, West Slope

SPECIES, REPORTED:

CHARACTERISTICS:
 The area around the lake is heavily timbered.
 The shorelines have timber and brush to the waters edge all around the
lake. The only exceptions are where roads reach the lake.

The lake has an unimproved access area with crude campsites at the northwest corner, where an old Forest Service road reaches it. The access has no facilities. The boat launch area is steep dirt, and not suited to trailered boats. An extremely crude dock has been scabbed together at the launch area, and is used by bank fishermen.

Another branch of the road reaches a spot near the center of the west side of the lake, but this "access" is very poor.

A road reaches an open gravel area at the southeast corner of the lake. This road comes in over private property.

A small bed of lilypads and cattails is found at the south end, near where the private road reaches the lake.

The west side of the lake has a fairly straight, featureless shoreline.

The east side has a good-sized cove at its center. The cove has small beds of lilypads and many snags.

The shores are lined extremely heavily with snags, both at the surface and on the bottom. They are concentrated especially heavily on the west side. The shorelines also have small patches of cattails found in isolated spots around the lake.

The bottom is heavy silt. Many places are bare, but spotty growths of tall, leafy bottom vegetation are scattered through the shallower areas.

The water is clear.

DIRECTIONS TO:

Take Highway 20 to mile 421.0, about 16 miles north of the town of Newport, where Kings Lake Road will be found on the left.

Turn onto Kings Lake Road, and go east through the town of Usk. You will cross a bridge over the Pend Oreille River, and reach an intersection where LeClerk Road and Kings Lake Road cross.

Turn left onto LeClerk Road, and go north for 23.6 miles to an old, unmarked road on the right. The road is Forest Service Road 1900-096. The end of the road is reached 8.0 miles north of LeClerk Creek Road, which will be on the right just before the road turns to the left, and 1.3 miles north of the old "Chapel Hill General Store and Resort".

Turn onto the gravel road, and take it 1.6 miles to an intersection.

At the intersection, take a left, and go 0.2 miles to the public access area at the northwest corner of the lake.

The road up from LeClerk Road is very rough and narrow.

**NOTE:** LeClerk Road runs up the east side of the Pend Oreille River, all the way from Highway 2 (east of Newport) to Sullivan Lake Road (east of Ione). LeClerk Road can be accessed at Highway 2, and driven about 37 miles north to the end of the road to Yocum. It can also be reached from Highway 31 at Ione on Sullivan Lake Road, and driven south for about eight miles to the road.

FISHING TIPS:
  Spinners trolled along the shorelines and cast around cover were effective. Flies cast to rising fish at the north end of the lake also produced fish.
  The lake has special regulations, and as of 2004 is open from the last Saturday in April until October 31. Check the current regulations before fishing.

MAP REFERENCES:
  *USGS Topographic Map, Washington (48117-E3-TF-024-00)
    Ruby Quadrangle, 7.5 Minute Series.
  *USGS Topographic Map, Washington (48117-E1-TM-100-00)
    Colville Quadrangle, 30x60 Minute Series.
  *Washington Atlas & Gazetteer; Page 119.